Harms and Wrongs in Epistemic Practice

ROYAL INSTITUTE OF PHILOSOPHY SUPPLEMENT: 84

EDITED BY

Simon Barker, Charlie Crerar, and Trystan S. Goetze

CAMBRIDGE
UNIVERSITY PRESS

PUBLISHED BY THE PRESS SYNDICATE OF THE UNIVERSITY OF CAMBRIDGE
The Pitt Building, Trumpington Street, Cambridge, CB2 1RP,
United Kingdom

CAMBRIDGE UNIVERSITY PRESS
UPH, Shaftesbury Road, Cambridge CB2 8BS, United Kingdom
32 Avenue of the Americas, New York, NY 10013–2473, USA
477 Williamstown Road, Port Melbourne, VIC 3207, Australia
C/Orense, 4, planta 13, 28020 Madrid, Spain
Lower Ground Floor, Nautica Building, The Water Club, Beach Road,
Granger Bay, 8005 Cape Town, South Africa

Printed in the United Kingdom at Bell and Bain Ltd.
Typeset by Techset Composition Ltd, Salisbury, UK

A catalogue record for this book is available from the British Library

ISBN 9781108712637
ISSN 1358-2461

Contents

Notes on the Contributors

Alison Bailey is Professor of Philosophy and Director of the Women's and Gender Studies Program at Illinois State University. She has published extensively on issues at the intersections of feminist theory, philosophy of race, critical whiteness studies, and social epistemology.

Olivia Bailey is Assistant Professor of Philosophy at Tulane University. Her work is concerned with the moral and epistemic significance of emotion and imagination, with a particular focus on the insights of 18th century Scottish sentimentalism.

Simon Barker is a PhD Candidate in Philosophy at the University of Sheffield. His work focuses on deep disagreement and epistemic self-trust.

Heather Battaly is Professor of Philosophy at the University of Connecticut. She is the author of *Virtue* (Polity Press, 2015), and the editor of *The Routledge Handbook of Virtue Epistemology* (Routledge, 2019). She is currently writing a book on epistemic vice.

Havi Carel is Professor of Philosophy at the University of Bristol and a Wellcome Trust Senior Investigator, leading the Life of Breath project (2014–2020; <www.lifeofbreath.org>). She is the author of several books, most recently *Phenomenology of Illness* (Oxford, 2016).

Quassim Cassam is Professor of Philosophy at the University of Warwick. He has also taught at Cambridge, Oxford, and UCL. He is the author of five books, all published by Oxford University Press.

Charlie Crerar is an Assistant Research Professor in the Department of Philosophy at the University of Connecticut. He previously completed a PhD in philosophy at the University of Sheffield.

Miranda Fricker is Presidential Professor of Philosophy at The Graduate Center, CUNY. Her research is mainly in Moral Philosophy, Feminist Philosophy, and Social Epistemology. She is a Fellow of the British Academy.

doi:10.1017/S1358246118000516   © The Royal Institute of Philosophy and the contributors 2018

Notes on the Contributors

Trystan S. Goetze recently completed his PhD in Philosophy at the University of Sheffield. His thesis concerns our moral and epistemic responsibilities regarding our social and moral concepts. He is currently working on a project on epistemic culpability.

Heidi Grasswick is the George Nye and Anne Walker Boardman Professor of Mental and Moral Science in the Philosophy Department at Middlebury College. Her interests include feminist epistemology, epistemic trust relations, and the relationship between individuals and communities in responsible inquiry.

Keith Harris is a Postdoctoral Fellow at the University of Missouri. His research spans several topics in social and individual epistemology including group belief and group knowledge, the norms of assertion, and knowledge-how.

Casey Rebecca Johnson is Assistant Professor of Philosophy in the Politics and Philosophy Department at the University of Idaho. Previously, she was a Postdoctoral Fellow on the project on Humility and Conviction in Public Life at the University of Connecticut.

Ian James Kidd is Assistant Professor of Philosophy at the University of Nottingham. His interests include epistemology and the philosophies of illness and of healthcare. He is currently co-editing *Vice Epistemology* (Routledge, 2020), with Heather Battaly and Quassim Cassam.

Alessandra Tanesini is Professor of Philosophy at Cardiff University. Her current work lies at the intersection of ethics, the philosophy of language, and epistemology with a focus on epistemic vice, silencing, and ignorance.

Harms and Wrongs in Epistemic Practice

SIMON BARKER, CHARLIE CRERAR AND
TRYSTAN S. GOETZE

Abstract

This volume has its roots in two recent developments within mainstream analytic epistemology: a growing recognition over the past two or three decades of the active and social nature of our epistemic lives; and, more recently still, the increasing appreciation of the various ways in which the epistemic practices of individuals and societies can, and often do, go *wrong*. The theoretical analysis of these breakdowns in epistemic practice, along with the various harms and wrongs that follow as a consequence, constitutes an approach to epistemology that we refer to as *non-ideal epistemology*. In this introductory chapter we introduce and contextualise the ten essays that comprise this volume, situating them within four broad sub-fields: vice epistemology, epistemic injustice, inter-personal epistemic practices, and applied epistemology. We also provide a brief overview of several other important growth areas in non-ideal epistemology.

This volume has its roots in two recent developments within mainstream analytic epistemology. The first has been an increasing recognition of the active and social nature of our epistemic lives. For most of the 20th century, the impression generated by the epistemological literature was of epistemic agents as generic and isolated individuals, more or less passively inheriting beliefs from their environments. It was these beliefs, and not the epistemic agents themselves, that served as the prime focus of epistemic analysis, with the two central questions in the field focussing on when it is that beliefs count as justified, and when it is they count as knowledge. This idea of our epistemic lives as something isolated or passive is, of course, a philosophical fiction; a useful one at times, perhaps, but a fiction nonetheless. Knowing, believing, and understanding, and the practices of inquiry, deliberation, and investigation that endow us with these states, are not just things that happen to us, but are very often things that we do, that require making choices about how to act or about what steps to take. What's more, they are things that we do together, in groups, as part of larger social networks and communities, and with our own particular identities and characters.

doi:10.1017/S1358246118000528

Simon Barker *et al.*

The recognition of our epistemic lives as something active and involving interaction with other epistemic agents has become a central part of epistemological theorising in the past couple of decades, as manifested in particular by the flourishing fields of social and virtue epistemology. The second development we wish to draw attention to remains somewhat more nascent. Inspired by the work of 20th century feminist epistemologists and drawing upon insights from moral and political philosophy, a growing number of theorists have begun to place at the centre of their work the insight that, insofar as our epistemic lives involve things that we do, they involve things that we – both as individuals and as communities – can do *badly*. So, for example, whilst some people's epistemic activities are facilitated by epistemic virtues, others' are impeded by epistemic *vices*. Whilst certain groups find society geared towards their epistemic interests, others find large bodies of *ignorance* encapsulating topics that are of real significance to them. Whilst some find themselves treated fairly in their epistemic lives, others find themselves on the receiving end of distinctly epistemic *injustices*. And whilst the acquisition and sharing of knowledge is often supported by networks of trust, at other times the makeup of society and the state of social relations can leave people *unable to trust* those whom it is most in their interests to do so. When our epistemic practices break down in these ways, people are often harmed or wronged in various aspects of their lives – not just epistemically, but also socially, morally, and politically.

The increase in interest in these and other breakdowns in epistemic practice reflects a growing appreciation of the import of what we might think of as *non-ideal epistemology*.[1] This kind of epistemology focusses not on what our epistemic lives look like when everything runs as it should – on the nature of justification, the sources of knowledge, or the mechanisms of testimony and trust – but on what our epistemic lives look like when things go *wrong,* as they so often do. It thus encompasses topics like the epistemology of ignorance; disagreement; epistemic injustice; vice epistemology; the critical epistemology of race, gender, indigeneity, and disability; and various areas of applied and social epistemology. It examines what it means for our epistemic practices and activities to go wrong in these ways,

---

[1]   The distinction between ideal and non-ideal theory in political theory is typically traced to John Rawls' *A Theory of Justice* (Oxford: Clarendon Press, 1972). Charles W. Mills offers a powerful defence of the significance of non-ideal theory within political philosophy in his '"Ideal Theory" as Ideology', *Hypatia* **20** (2005), 165–184.

why they do so, the epistemic and non-epistemic harms that follow, and the extent to which these harms are wrongful. Crucially, it also explores how we might try and respond to or ameliorate these harms and wrongs.

This volume assembles a collection of essays that offer a snapshot of the kinds of issues explored within non-ideal epistemology. We do not claim that this represents a cohesive field of study, still less that it forms a singular research project. The papers presented here cover a diverse range of topics, and do so by drawing upon a wide array of different theoretical resources. Nonetheless, they are united by a shared interest in the challenges, impediments, inequities, dangers, and failures that are part and parcel of our epistemic lives. The aim behind this volume, and the 2017 *Royal Institute of Philosophy* Departmental Conference at the University of Sheffield from which it originated, is that bringing together theorists with this shared interest in the negative could highlight the extent of the recent shift in this direction within epistemological theorising. In so doing, it could also illuminate new ways in which theorists from quite different sub-fields and exploring quite different issues could learn from and work with one another.

Our main task in the remainder of this introductory chapter is to provide an overview of the papers presented in this volume. We do so by ordering them loosely according to four central themes: vice epistemology, epistemic injustice, inter-personal epistemic practices, and applied epistemology. We also end by briefly detailing several important themes that are not directly covered by this volume, but which nonetheless represent significant growth areas in non-ideal epistemology. Carving the volume, and non-ideal epistemology more generally, according to these themes helps to lend some order to proceedings, but it should not be taken to signify any hard and fast divisions. Several of the papers included touch upon two or more of these themes, and they frequently speak to one another in ways that transcend these categories.

Vice Epistemology

One of the areas in which this recent uptake of interest in the non-ideal manifests itself is in the field of character-based, or 'responsibilist', virtue epistemology. The defining feature of virtue epistemology is its focus on the evaluation of epistemic agents, and specifically the exploration of what qualities make someone an excellent or deficient epistemic agent.[2] For much of its recent history, however, virtue epistemologists have focussed more or less exclusively on the epistemic virtues themselves, traits like open-mindedness, intellectual humility, conscientiousness, and diligence.[3] It is only in the past few years that sustained attention has been turned towards the (arguably more common) intellectual *vices*, traits like arrogance, dogmatism, negligence, and intellectual rigidity.[4]

The study of the intellectual vices specifically, what Quassim Cassam has referred to as 'vice epistemology', raises questions including what is it that makes a character trait intellectually vicious, what are the nature and effects of specific vices, and how do the intellectual vices relate to the intellectual virtues.[5] Two contributions to this volume engage directly with such issues. Heather Battaly's 'Can

[2]   Heather Battaly, 'Virtue Epistemology', *Philosophy Compass* **3** (2008), 639–663; John Turri, Mark Alfano, and John Greco, 'Virtue Epistemology', *Stanford Encyclopedia of Philosophy* (Summer 2018 Edition), Edward N. Zalta (ed.), <https://plato.stanford.edu/archives/sum2018/entries/epistemology-virtue/>.

[3]   Some relatively early exceptions to virtue epistemology's focus on the positive include: Casey Swank, 'Epistemic Vice', in Guy Axtell (ed.) *Knowledge, Belief, and Character: Readings in Contemporary Virtue Epistemology* (Lanham, MD: Rowman and Littlefield, 2000), 195–204; Miranda Fricker, *Epistemic Injustice* (Oxford: Oxford University Press, 2007). For discussion of why vice has been overlooked in the virtue epistemological literature, see Charlie Crerar, 'Motivational Approaches to Intellectual Vice', *Australasian Journal of Philosophy* (Forthcoming).

[4]   A further, arguably related, non-ideal approach to virtue epistemology is represented by the *situationist* challenge, which employs psychological evidence to argue that true epistemic virtues are, in fact, vanishingly rare. See, for example, Mark Alfano, *Character as Moral Fiction* (Cambridge, Cambridge University Press, 2013); Lauren Olin and John M. Dorris, 'Vicious Minds', *Philosophical Studies* **168** (2014), 665–692; Abrol Fairweather and Mark Alfano (eds.), *Epistemic Situationism* (Oxford, Oxford University Press, 2017).

[5]   Quassim Cassam, 'Vice Epistemology', *The Monist* **99** (2016), 159–180. Other prominent works in vice epistemology include: Heather Battaly, 'Epistemic Virtue and Vice: Reliabilism, Responsibilsm, and Personalism' in Chienkuo Mi, Michael Slote, and Ernest Sosa (eds.), *Moral and Intellectual Virtues in Chinese and Western Philosophy: The Turn Towards Virtue* (New York, NY: Routledge, 2016), 99–120; Ian James Kidd, 'Charging Others with Epistemic Vice', *The Monist* **99** (2016), 181–197; Alessandra Tanesini, '"Calm Down Dear": Intellectual Arrogance, Silencing, and Ignorance', *Aristotelian Society Supplementary Volume* **90** (2016), 71–92.

Closed-Mindedness be an Intellectual Virtue?' does so by raising the intriguing possibility that closed-mindedness, seemingly a paradigmatic vice that represents a 'popular favourite' for vice epistemologists,[6] might on occasion count as an intellectual *virtue*. Building upon an account of closed-mindedness as an 'unwillingness or inability to engage seriously with relevant intellectual options',[7] Battaly identifies three different conceptions of intellectual vice: effects-vice, responsibilist-vice, and personalist-vice. Focusing specifically on effects-vices, according to which traits are vicious 'whenever they produce a preponderance of bad epistemic effects (or fail to produce a preponderance of good epistemic effects)',[8] Battaly then illustrates how, in the normal case, closed-mindedness does generally meet this criterion. However, she goes on to note certain cases where acts of closed-mindedness might count as virtuous on account of the effects they produce, before drawing the still more provocative conclusion that, in epistemically hostile environments, the *disposition* to be closed-minded might count as virtuous. She ends by noting that, despite the apparent hostility of aspects of our present epistemic environment, we should be wary about using this argument to justify closed-mindedness in the actual world.

A different set of vices underpin Alessandra Tanesini's discussion in 'Caring for Esteem and Intellectual Reputation: Some Epistemic Benefits and Harms', though again the question of when a certain trait or quality counts as virtuous and when it counts as vicious serves as a major theme. The central notion of her discussion is *esteem*, which she characterises as 'a positive or negative attitude, directed at a person, group or institution for their good or bad qualities'.[9] After providing some initial discussion of esteem and the related notions of reputation and admiration, Tanesini goes on to argue that it is epistemically valuable: it both helps us make 'reasoned judgements about who to trust' in situations where we are relying on the expertise of others,[10] and can also be helpful in acquiring knowledge of one's own good qualities. Moreover, she goes on to argue that

---

[6] Quassim Cassam, 'Vice Ontology', *Social Epistemology Review and Reply Collective* **6** (2017), 20–27, at 20.

[7] Heather Battaly, 'Can Closed-Mindedness be an Intellectual Virtue?', *Royal Institute of Philosophy Supplement* **84** (2018), 23.

[8] Battaly, 'Can Closed-Mindedness be an Intellectual Virtue?', 29.

[9] Alessandra Tanesini, 'Caring for Esteem and Intellectual Reputation: Some Epistemic Benefits and Harms', *Royal Institute of Philosophy Supplement* **84** (2018), 49.

[10] Tanesini, 'Caring for Esteem and Intellectual Reputation', 53.

Simon Barker *et al.*

desiring esteem provides an incentive to raise performance, and that, as a consequence, esteem can be virtuously pursued. Not all desires for esteem are virtuous, however, and the final sections of Tanesini's paper explore two familiar vices of esteem: intellectual vanity and intellectual timidity.

Epistemic Injustice

In the last few decades, the topic of *epistemic oppression* has attracted significant philosophical attention. Drawing on previous work on various dimensions of oppressive power relations in feminist, anti-racist, post-colonial, Marxist, and other theoretical frames and activist movements, theorists have identified epistemic oppression as involving 'persistent epistemic exclusion that hinders one's contribution to knowledge production...an unwarranted infringement on the epistemic agency of knowers'.[11] One significant form of epistemic oppression discussed in several contributions to this volume is *epistemic injustice*.[12] This term was coined by Miranda Fricker to describe a type of 'wrong done to someone specifically in their

[11] Kristie Dotson, 'Conceptualizing Epistemic Oppression', *Social Epistemology* **28** (2014), 115–38, at 115. Examples of early articulations of this kind of idea are found in Marilyn Frye, *The Politics of Reality: Essays in Feminist Theory* (Berkeley, CA: The Crossing Press, 1983); Audre Lorde, *Sister Outsider: Essays and Speeches,* (Freedom, CA: The Crossing Press, 1984); Gayatri Chakravorty Spivak, 'Can the Subaltern Speak?', in C. Nelson & L. Grossberg (eds.), *Marxism and the Interpretation of Culture* (Champaign, IL: University of Illinois Press, 1988), 271–313; Patricia Hill Collins, *Black Feminist Thought: Knowledge, Consciousness, and the Politics of Empowerment*, 2nd ed. (New York: Routledge, 2009), 1st ed. published 1991; Lorraine Code, *Rhetorical Spaces: Essays on Gendered Locations* (London: Routledge, 1995); Charles W. Mills, *The Racial Contract* (Ithaca, NY: Cornell University Press, 1999); María Lugones, *Pilgrimages/Peregrinajes: Theorizing Coalition Against Multiple Oppressions* (Lanham, MD: Rowman & Littlefield, 2003). Types of epistemic oppression other than epistemic injustice have been discussed in, for example, Kristie Dotson, 'Tracking Epistemic Violence, Tracking Practices of Silencing', *Hypatia* **26** (2011), 236–57; José Medina, *The Epistemology of Resistance: Gender and Racial Oppression, Epistemic Injustice, and Resistant Imaginations* (Oxford: Oxford University Press, 2013); Nora Berenstain, 'Epistemic Exploitation', *Ergo* **3** (2016), 569–90.
[12] For a comprehensive overview of work on epistemic injustice, see Ian James Kidd, José Medina, and Gaile Pohlhaus (eds.), *The Routledge Handbook of Epistemic Injustice* (London: Routledge, 2017).

capacity as a knower'.[13] Fricker describes two types of epistemic injustice. *Testimonial injustice* occurs where a speaker's testimony is understood but the hearer unfairly downgrades her credibility because of a prejudice against the speaker's social identity, wronging her in her capacity as a giver of knowledge.[14] *Hermeneutical injustice* occurs where a widespread absence of shared interpretive tools makes it difficult for the speaker's social experience to be understood in the first place, either by the hearer or even by the speaker herself, wronging her in her capacity as a giver or producer of knowledge.[15] Numerous other forms of epistemic injustice have been identified in connection with, for example, wilful ignorance of marginalised groups' hermeneutical resources, the distribution of epistemic goods, and the undermining of one's ability to participate in inquiry.[16] There has also been some significant work applying various concepts of epistemic injustice to concrete cases, such as educational justice, rape and domestic abuse myths, and healthcare practices concerning intersex patients.[17]

The usual focus in the epistemic injustice literature is on ways we can be wronged in our capacity as givers and producers of knowledge. In her contribution, 'Understanding Epistemic Trust Injustices and

---

[13]   Fricker, *Epistemic Injustice*, 1.

[14]   See also Jeremy Wanderer, 'Addressing Testimonial Injustice: Being Ignored and Being Rejected', *Philosophical Quarterly* **62** (2012), 148–169; Gaile Pohlhaus, 'Discerning the Primary Epistemic Harm in Cases of Testimonial Injustice', *Social Epistemology* **28** (2014), 99–114; Emmalon Davis, 'Typecasts, Tokens, and Spokespersons: A Case for Credibility Excess as Testimonial Injustice' *Hypatia* **31** (2016), 485–501.

[15]   See also Rebecca Mason, 'Two Kinds of Unknowing', *Hypatia* **26** (2011), 294–307; Charlie Crerar, 'Taboo, Hermeneutical Injustice, and Expressively Free Environments', *Episteme* **13** (2016), 195–207; Trystan S. Goetze, 'Hermeneutical Dissent and the Species of Hermeneutical Injustice', *Hypatia* **33** (2018), 73–90.

[16]   Gaile Pohlhaus, 'Relational Knowing and Epistemic Injustice: Toward a Theory of Willful Hermeneutical Ignorance', *Hypatia* **27** (2012), 715–35; Kristie Dotson, 'A Cautionary Tale: On Limiting Epistemic Oppression', *Frontiers: A Journal of Women's Studies* **33** (2012), 24–47; David Coady, 'Two Concepts of Epistemic Injustice', *Episteme* **7** (2012), 101–113; Christopher Hookway, 'Some Varieties of Epistemic Injustice: Reflections on Fricker', *Episteme* **7** (2010), 151–63.

[17]   Ben Kotzee, 'Educational Justice, Epistemic Justice, and Leveling Down', *Educational Theory* **63** (2013), 331–50; Katharine Jenkins, 'Rape Myths and Domestic Abuse Myths as Hermeneutical Injustices', *Journal of Applied Philosophy* **34** (2017), 191–205; Teri Merrick, 'From "Intersex" to "DSD": A Case of Epistemic Injustice', *Synthese* (forthcoming).

Their Harms', Heidi Grasswick inverts this approach, focussing instead on wrongs experienced in one's capacity as a *receiver* of knowledge. In the process, she identifies a new class of epistemic injustices: *epistemic trust injustices*. She concentrates in particular on the ways in which epistemic trust injustices arise in interactions between expert and lay communities, especially between scientists and marginalised social groups. As Grasswick argues, 'scientific knowledge is an especially important case to examine with respect to epistemic injustices... it is a dominant and powerful form of knowing in contemporary society, with deep significance for the structure of our social and material lives'.[18] Given the importance of scientific knowledge, and the division of intellectual labour that specialised knowledge production entails, relationships of epistemic trust are essential. In order to trust responsibly, we must exercise our epistemic agency by judging which speakers and which groups of putative experts deserve our trust. Doing so with regard to scientific communities, Grasswick argues, involves not just identifying their ability to provide us with significant knowledge, but also whether they sincerely care for our interests in producing and sharing their knowledge. Epistemic trust injustices arise when it is impossible to responsibly place one's trust in scientific experts on account of their having historically failed to meet the conditions of trust *vis-à-vis* one's social group, as is often the case for those in marginalised communities. As Grasswick shows, this harms the subjects of epistemic trust injustices in their capacity as receivers of knowledge, and produces a negative feedback loop where similar injustices recur because lay communities disengage from expert inquiry altogether. Grasswick closes with a few suggestions for addressing epistemic trust injustices by repairing expert–lay relations and increasing the participation of marginalized communities in scientific inquiry.

Alison Bailey's 'On Anger, Silence, and Epistemic Injustice' uses feminist theory, particularly work on epistemic oppression by feminists of colour, to explore the place and role of *anger* in epistemic injustice. Starting from the observation that 'anger is the emotion of injustice',[19] Bailey sketches the ways in which epistemic oppression provokes anger, how mechanisms similar to those that silence and dismiss marginalised speakers' testimony also work to cool and dismiss their anger, and how holding on to one's anger in the face

[18] Heidi Grasswick, 'Understanding Epistemic Trust Injustices', *Royal Institute of Philosophy Supplement* **84** (2018), 69.

[19] Alison Bailey, 'On Anger, Silence, and Epistemic Injustice', *Royal Institute of Philosophy Supplement* **84** (2018), 93.

of injustice is an important and useful tool for resisting oppression. In the process, she introduces a variety of vivid concepts and distinctions, such as María Lugones's distinction between anger that is hard-to-handle because it is *heavy* – frustrating and exhausting in the face of repeated failures to be taken seriously – and anger that is hard-to-handle because it is *rebellious* – disorderly because directed against existing social and epistemic structures that make it difficult to be taken seriously in the first place.[20] Other distinctions are Bailey's own, such as the difference between two ways in which the anger of oppressed people is managed: *tone policing,* which identifies moments of anger and silences them as irrational or improper, and *tone vigilance,* which looks for anger before it is even expressed on the basis of the speaker's social identity. Bailey stitches together these distinctions – what she calls different 'textures' of anger – to give a multifaceted picture of *knowing resistant anger,* a kind of righteous anger directed against oppression on the basis of one's knowledge of one's own social experience, despite persistent obstacles to having both one's knowledge and one's anger taken seriously within dominant interpretive frames.

Inter-Personal Epistemic Practices

One of the key insights that motivated the turn towards theorising the social dimensions of epistemology was the significance of familiar inter-personal interactions, communications, and exchanges for our epistemic lives and conduct. What is striking about the early analytic work in this area, however, is the extent to which discussion of our socio-epistemic practices initially focussed (and, to some extent, still focusses) upon the internal mental states of the agents involved in such interactions, and how little it explores the ways in which those interactions actually play out within public and social spaces. The literature on disagreement, for instance, has primarily concerned the question of how, and if, epistemic agents should revise their beliefs and other doxastic states in the face of disagreement.[21] Similarly,

---

[20] See Lugones, *Pilgrimages/Pereginajes.*
[21] For a snapshot of the debate on disagreement, see Richard Feldman and Ted Warfield (eds.), *Disagreement* (Oxford: Oxford University Press, 2010) and David Christensen & Jennifer Lackey (eds.), *The Epistemology of Disagreement: New Essays* (Oxford: Oxford University Press, 2013). For work on disagreement with and between *groups,* see J. Adam Carter, 'Group Peer Disagreement', *Ratio* **27** (2016), 11–28; Bryan Frances,

much of the work on testimony has focussed upon theorising the conditions and mechanisms by which knowledge or warranted belief can be acquired via the testimony of others.[22] Yet, if we are to fully appreciate the ways in which our social-epistemic practices not only benefit

---

Disagreement (Cambridge: Polity Press, 2014); Mattias Skipper and Asbjørn Steglich-Petersen, 'Group Disagreement: A Belief Aggregation Perspective', *Synthese* (forthcoming); David Christensen, 'Disagreement and Public Controversy', in Jennifer Lackey (ed.), *Essays in Collective Epistemology* (Oxford: Oxford University Press, 2014), 143–163. For work on *deep* disagreement, where disagreements in belief can be explained by underlying differences in the norms, principles, and commitments that shape the disputant's epistemic practices, see Klemens Kappel, 'The Problem of Deep Disagreement', *Discipline Filosofiche* **22** (2012), 7–25; Michael P. Lynch, 'Epistemic Circularity and Epistemic Disagreement', in Adrian Haddock, Alan Millar and Duncan Pritchard (eds.), *Social Epistemology* (Oxford: Oxford University Press, 2010), 262–277; Alvin Goldman, 'Epistemic Relativism and Reasonable Disagreement', in Feldman & Warfield (eds.), *Disagreement* 187–215. Four examples of recent work taking the debate in new directions are Helen De Cruz and John De Smedt, 'The Value of Epistemic Disagreement in Scientific Practice: The Case of Homo Floresiensis', *Studies in History and Philosophy of Science Part A* **44** (2013), 169–177; Paul Faulkner, 'Agency and Disagreement', in Patrick Reider (ed.), *Social Epistemology and Epistemic Agency: Decentralizing the Epistemic Agent* (London: Rowman & Littlefield, 2016), 75–90; Jonathan Matheson, 'Disagreement and the Ethics of Belief', in James H. Collier (ed.), *The Future of Social Epistemology: A Collective Vision* (London: Rowman & Littlefield, 2016), 139–147; Fabienne Peter, 'The Epistemic Circumstances of Democracy', in Miranda Fricker and Michael Brady (eds.), *The Epistemic Life of Groups* (Oxford: Oxford University Press, 2016), 133–149.

[22] For a summary of the debate on testimony, see Jennifer Lackey, 'Testimonial Knowledge', in Sven Bernecker and Duncan Pritchard (eds.), *The Routledge Companion to Epistemology* (New York: Routledge, 2011), 316–325. Recently, a number of robustly inter-personal accounts of testimony have been forwarded, including Richard Moran, *The Exchange of Words: Speech, Testimony, and Intersubjectivity* (Oxford: Oxford University Press, 2018); Paul Faulkner, *Knowledge on Trust* (Oxford: Oxford University Press, 2011); Sanford Goldberg, *Relying on Others: An Essay in Epistemology.* (Oxford: Oxford University Press, 2010). See also more general discussion of the inter-personal nature of trust, including: Annette Baier, 'Trust and Antitrust', *Ethics* **96** (1986), 231–260; Paul Faulkner, 'The Practical Rationality of Trust', *Synthese* **191** (2014), 1975–1989; Richard Holton, 'Deciding to Trust, Coming to Believe', *Australasian Journal of Philosophy* **72** (1994), 63–76; Katherine Hawley,

but also disadvantage (and even harm) those involved, then we need to pay attention to the fact that these practices do not occur in the cold calm of the perfect epistemic agent's mind. Rather, they occur 'out in the open': in public, social, sometimes vexed, and often complicated interactions and exchanges between people.

The three contributions to this section of the volume can all be seen as contributing to a reorientation of social epistemology to more avowedly grapple with the interpersonal aspects of epistemic practice in the ways just outlined. Casey Rebecca Johnson, in 'Just Say "No!": Obligations to Voice Disagreement', does so by bringing new focus to the debate on disagreement. Departing from the conventional approach to discussing disagreement, Johnson asks not what the individual's doxastic response to discovering disagreement should be, but what she should do in the public and social space in which she realises that disagreement. Is it permissible, in the face of disagreement, to stay quiet and keep her opinions to herself? Or, is she obliged to make her opinions a matter of public record? Johnson argues the case for the latter. Not only are we *obliged* to make it known that we disagree with others, but often we are *epistemically* obliged to do so. Drawing on David Lewis's conception of the 'conversational scoreboard', Johnson argues that, when in a situation of disagreement, one must express content that at least 'appears to be' incompatible with what one took to be objectionable; and, crucially, one must make that sentiment of disagreement clear to at least some of the other participants in the original conversation. Importantly, Johnson explains, the obligation to make one's dissent public in this way is defeasible and can be overridden by prudential and moral considerations, as well as epistemic ones. In the final section of the paper, Johnson considers four potential sources for this obligation: epistemic well-being; the nature of inquiry; commitments to joint action; and the nature of doxastic justification.[23]

Olivia Bailey turns our attention towards another fundamental epistemic practice – testimony – in her contribution 'On Empathy and Testimonial Trust'. Bailey's focus is upon testimonial exchanges

---

'Partiality and Prejudice in Trusting', *Synthese* **191** (2014), 2029–2045; Karen Jones, 'Trust as an Affective Attitude', *Ethics* **107** (1996), 4–25.

[23]   For other recent work on the public problem of disagreement, see Jennifer Lackey, 'The Duty to Object', *Philosophy and Phenomenological Research* (forthcoming); Casey Rebecca Johnson (ed.), *Voicing Dissent: The Ethics and Epistemology of Making Disagreement Public*, (New York: Routledge, 2018).

that involve speakers who belong to one or more oppressed groups. By drawing out the complex relationship between empathy and trust in these cases, Bailey reveals the importance of theorising testimony in terms of the personal and social dynamics between recipient and speaker, not only its narrow epistemic function of transferring knowledge and warranted belief. Empathy, in the sense that interests Bailey, is a 'form of emotionally-charged imaginative perspective-taking'.[24] It is a way to understand the world as others experience it, to 'walk a mile in their shoes', as the idiom goes. 'Testimonial trust', as Bailey understands it, is a robustly interpersonal stance whereby one comes to believe the content of another's testimony *at their word*, without independently verifying that what they say is true. In the first half of the paper, Bailey explores the ways in which empathy can support testimonial trust by providing evidence as to the speaker's epistemic competence, particularly in cases that involve what Bailey calls 'testimony about experience'. This support represents a clear upshot to empathy's role in testimony. In the second half of the chapter, however, Bailey carefully draws out the darker side to the relationship between empathy and testimonial trust. In cases where a speaker belongs to one or more oppressed groups, Bailey explains, an unwavering or incautious reliance on empathy can lead to a double failure on the part of the recipient of testimony: firstly, to recognise the limitations of their epistemic perspective and imaginative capacities; and secondly, to respect the personal and moral significance of the speaker's investment in the testimonial exchange. With this in mind, Bailey lays out the case that – for all of the benefits of empathy – it can sometimes be morally and epistemically responsible to 'trust without empathy'.[25]

In a departure from the previous two chapters' focus on the core socio-epistemic practices of testimony and disagreement, Miranda Fricker's 'Ambivalence About Forgiveness' explores the epistemic functions, and possible degradations, of two inter-personal *moral* practices: blame and forgiveness. Fricker explains that blame and other mechanisms of moral accountability have a social constructive power that functions *proleptically*. By treating a wrongdoer as if she already shares one's moral outlook, in other words, one can thereby effect a change in the wrongdoer's moral understanding such that she comes to share one's outlook. But, at the same time, blame can degenerate into moral-epistemic domination, where the blamer shuts

---

[24]   Olivia Bailey, 'On Empathy and Testimonial Trust' *Royal Institute of Philosophy Supplement* **84** (2018), 139.
[25]   Olivia Bailey, 'On Empathy and Testimonial Trust', 149.

down the possibility of dialogue over the nature of the wrong commit-ted, brow-beating the blamee into accepting the blamer's outlook. Similarly, forgiveness – particularly the form Fricker calls 'gifted forgiveness', where the wronged party lets go of her feelings of resentment without any redemptive change on the part of the wrong-doer – can also bring about a change in the wrongdoer's moral under-standing by treating her as if she already shares the forgiver's outlook. Again, this proleptic mechanism has the potential for abuse. A gift of forgiveness can shut down the alleged wrongdoer's ability to contest or question the nature of the harm, pre-empting moral dialogue and twisting the forgiven person into acquiescing to the forgiver's outlook. The potential for moral-epistemic domination is heightened when the forgiver and forgiven are on either side of an imbalance of social power, further undermining the forgiven person's ability to challenge the forgiver's moral understanding. Forgiveness can also mask or smuggle in feelings of blame, short-circuiting the normal processes by which such resentment is communicated and forsworn.

Applied Epistemology

Once one scratches beneath the surface, one often finds the distinc-tion between applied and non-applied philosophy (or, certainly, applied and 'theoretical' philosophy) to be a fairly spurious one. That is certainly the case for this volume, in which each of the papers included explores some recognisable way in which our epi-stemic lives, as individuals and as communities, malfunction or go wrong. Our choosing to demarcate a number of the papers specifically as applied epistemology should therefore be taken with more than a pinch of salt. Nonetheless, we do so because each of these papers con-tributes to a particular recent trend within epistemology: the bringing of epistemological insights to bear on important and detailed case studies. This has seen epistemologists turn their attention towards an increasingly diverse array of issues, including the use of the inter-net,[26] the nature of fake news,[27] and the epistemic standards of

[26] Hanna Gunn and Michael P. Lynch, 'Google Epistemology', in David Coady (ed.), *The Routledge Handbook of Applied Epistemology* (New York: Routledge, Forthcoming); Richard Heersmink, 'A Virtue Epistemology of the Internet', *Social Epistemology* **32** (2018), 1–12.
[27] Regina Rini, 'Fake News and Partisan Epistemology', *Kennedy Institute of Ethics Journal* **27** (2017) 43–64; Axel Gelfert 'Fake News: A Definition', *Informal Logic* **38** (2018), 84–117.

Anglo-American legal systems.[28] The three papers of this section each undertake a similarly insightful applied analysis.[29]

The section opens with Quassim Cassam's paper 'The Epistemology of Terrorism and Radicalisation', which explores some of the epistemic practices in operation within counter-terrorism theory and practice. Specifically, he considers two popular answers to the question, 'what leads a person to turn to political violence?':[30] the Rational Agent Model (RAM), according to which terrorists are rational agents who turn to violence as a means for pursuing their political ends; and the Radicalisation Model (RAD), according to which people turn to political violence because they have been radicalised. Both views, Cassam argues, are flawed. RAM, although of some value, is unable to explain cases where terrorism is inefficacious and it is patently irrational to believe that it could have been otherwise. RAD, more seriously, faces significant theoretical difficulties about what it means to be 'vulnerable' to radicalisation, since given the 'multiple highly personal and idiosyncratic pathways to behavioural radicalisation' it is highly unlikely there is any such thing as *the* radicalisation process.[31] Cassam's preferred alternative to RAM and RAD is a view he calls Moderate Epistemic Particularism (MEP), a view that seeks not to *explain* the turn to political violence in a way that will allow us to uncover general causal laws, but to *understand* particular instances of it. This view is 'moderate', Cassam notes, because it does not deny the possibility of drawing interesting generalisations about the turn to political violence. The point, instead, is that we should recognise the limitations of these generalisations in the face of human particularity.

Ian James Kidd and Havi Carel's 'Healthcare Practice, Epistemic Injustice, and Naturalism' applies insights from the literature on epistemic injustice to the field of healthcare, revealing a number of ways in which ill persons are wronged in their capacity as knowers. Drawing on works by phenomenologists of illness and biographical accounts of

---

[28]   Georgi Gardiner, 'In Defence of Reasonable Doubt', *Journal of Applied Philosophy* **34** (2017), 221–241.

[29]   For more contributions to applied epistemology, see: David Coady, *What To Believe Now: Applying Epistemology to Contemporary Issues* (Malden, MA: Wiley-Blackwell, 2012); David Coady and Miranda Fricker (eds.), Special Issue on Applied Epistemology, *Social Epistemology* **34** (2017); David Coady and James Chase (eds.), *The Routledge Handbook of Applied Epistemology* (New York: Routledge, 2018).

[30]   Quassim Cassam, 'The Epistemology of Terrorism and Radicalisation', *Royal Institute of Philosophy Supplement* **84** (2018), 188.

[31]   Cassam, 'The Epistemology of Terrorism and Radicalisation', 199.

the experience of illness, Kidd and Carel present a number of these *pathocentric epistemic injustices,* which are ultimately connected to the very conception of health at work in most healthcare settings. They show how ill persons experience testimonial injustice, because of prejudices arising from 'pathophobia', or negative attitudes towards illness or ill persons. Pathocentric testimonial injustice not only wrongs ill persons as givers of knowledge, but can also lead to serious harms when ill persons' testimony regarding their treatment in the healthcare system is not taken seriously by healthcare providers. The issue is compounded by pathocentric hermeneutical injustices, which arise because there is a lack of adequate shared vocabulary for discussing the experience of illness, and a common distaste, even among healthcare professionals, for discussing suffering and death. These injustices are persistent because ill persons are often excluded from participation in the processes by which healthcare professionals develop shared understandings of illness. One root of the problem, Kidd and Carel explain, is that our very concept of health is excessively naturalistic, focused on functional biological aspects at the expense of the lived experience of illness and health. They argue that naturalistic conceptions of health may promote or even necessitate the pathocentric epistemic injustices they describe.

In the final paper of the volume, Keith Harris contributes to ongoing discussion about the epistemic merits of belief in conspiracy theories,[32] as he asks 'What is Epistemically Wrong with Conspiracy Theorising?' Harris focusses his discussion on the subset of conspiracy theories that offer explanations of events that run counter to official accounts, as well as implicating the supposed architects of the events in question in the promotion of the official accounts. Outlandish as some theories of this sort might be, Harris is careful to point out, they sometimes turn out to be true. Likewise, it will be reasonable for at least some people to believe some theories of this sort. If there is a problem with belief in conspiracy theories so defined, then it seems reasonable to suppose that it lies with the practices and forms of reasoning by which those beliefs often came to be

---

[32] See, for instance, David Coady (ed.), *Conspiracy Theories: The Philosophical Debate,* (Aldershot: Ashgate, 2006); Dentith, Matthew, *The Philosophy of Conspiracy Theories.* (Basingstoke: Palgrave Macmillan, 2014); Feldman, Susan, 'Counterfact Conspiracy Theories', *International Journal of Applied Philosophy* **25** (2011), 15–24; M. R. X. Dentith and Brian Keeley. 'The applied epistemology of conspiracy theories: An overview' in Coady and Chase (eds.), *Routledge Handbook of Applied Epistemology.*

held, not in the content of the beliefs themselves. Harris considers three explanations of what the problem with such 'conspiracy theorising' might be: that it typically manifests epistemic vice; that it leads to belief in unfalsifiable theories; and that it is akin to adherence to 'degenerating research programmes' in science. All three explanations, Harris argues, are unsatisfying, since each fails to pick out any failing that is characteristic of 'conspiracy theorising' and not equally characteristic of the theorising that leads to belief in supposedly more acceptable theories. In the second half of the paper, Harris offers his own suggestions for where the errors in conspiracy theorising might lie. These are two. Firstly, conspiracy theorists may employ a fallacious probabilistic form of *modus tollens* that leads to placing undue weight upon data that is 'errant with respect to the official account'.[33] Secondly, conspiracy theorists may display 'a sort of higher-order epistemic vice' that comes when an otherwise admirable devotion to inquiry is combined with a lack of attention to one's own biases and possibilities for error.[34]

Other Themes in Non-Ideal Epistemology

Owing to its origins in a two-day conference, this volume regrettably could not touch on every issue within the ambit of non-ideal epistemology. However, given our ambition to highlight the breadth and range of excellent work in this area, several other major themes bear mentioning. Whilst several of these topics represent currently flourishing areas of research within non-ideal epistemology, others represent areas for growth as research in this field continues to develop.

In addition to investigations of epistemic injustice in interactions between scientists and lay communities, as explored in Grasswick's contribution to this volume, there is growing interest in *socially relevant philosophy of science* more generally. Much like epistemology, over the 20th Century philosophy of science broadly concentrated on theoretical issues divorced from the social contexts in which scientific inquiry proceeds and in which scientific knowledge is used. Contemporary philosophers of science, however, are increasingly concerned not only with giving accounts of the nature of scientific knowledge or its background metaphysics, but also with how scientific inquiry should be organized in order to serve the interests of local

---

[33]   Keith Harris, 'What's epistemically wrong with conspiracy theorising?', *Royal Institute of Philosophy Supplement* **84** (2018), 249.
[34]   Harris, 'What's epistemically wrong with conspiracy theorising?', 255.

communities and whole societies, as well as the moral, political, and epistemic problems that can arise when science fails in these roles.[35] As Carla Fehr and Kathryn Plaisance argue, doing more work of this kind stands to benefit society, scientific practice, and philosophical inquiry itself, but requires a re-orientation of philosophy of science as a field towards non-ideal theory and socially engaged research.[36]

Another topic neglected by mainstream epistemology until recently is the topic of *ignorance*. One important set of questions concerns the *nature* of ignorance; for example, is ignorance the contrary of knowledge, of true belief, or something different?[37] Merely leaving discussion of ignorance there, however, obscures many complexities. Whilst *culpability* for one's ignorance has been discussed in moral philosophy in connection with the epistemic condition on moral responsibility,[38] there is seldom any engagement with relevant epistemological questions, such as the availability of evidence to the agent and the extent of the agent's epistemic obligations in deciding how to act.[39] Moreover, under certain conditions, ignorant beliefs can flourish with all the same respect that ought to be carried by knowledge. Such ignorance is not merely a passive lack of knowledge but an active and persistent impediment to true belief. This is particularly concerning where social injustice and ignorance walk in stride, enabling and reinforcing one another. Charles Mills coined the term *epistemology of ignorance* to describe such structures as they arise in

---

[35] See, for example, Philip Kitcher, *Science, Truth, and Democracy* (Oxford: Oxford University Press, 2001); Janet A. Kourany, 'A Philosophy of Science for the Twenty-First Century', *Philosophy of Science* **70** (2003), 1–14; Kathryn Plaisance and Carla Fehr (eds.), Special Issue: Making Philosophy of Science More Socially Relevant, *Synthese* **177** (2010), 301–492; Nancy Arden McHugh, *The Limits of Knowledge: Generating Pragmatist Feminist Cases for Situated Knowing* (Albany, NY: SUNY Press, 2015).

[36] Carla Fehr and Kathryn Plaisance, 'Socially Relevant Philosophy of Science: An Introduction', *Synthese* **177** (2010), 301–316.

[37] For a recent collection discussing this and related questions, see Rik Peels and Martijn Blaauw (eds.), *The Epistemic Dimensions of Ignorance* (Cambridge: Cambridge University Press, 2016).

[38] See, among others, Holly M. Smith, 'Culpable Ignorance', *The Philosophical Review* **92** (1983), 543–71; Gideon Rosen, 'Culpability and Ignorance', *Proceedings of the Aristotelian Society* **103** (2003), 61–84; George Sher, *Who Knew? Responsibility Without Awareness* (Oxford: Oxford University Press, 2009).

[39] An exception is Rik Peels, 'What Kind of Ignorance Excuses? Two Neglected Issues', *Philosophical Quarterly* **64** (2014), 478–96.

societies implicitly or explicitly structured on racism.[40] Much remains to be done on the topic of ignorance, its various forms, and how this decidedly non-ideal topic connects with moral and political issues.[41]

In the present political situation of increased polarization of opinion, cynicism about the potential for rational dialogue between opposing viewpoints, politicisation of expertise, and propagandistic disinformation masquerading as reliable news, practices of *epistemic accountability* take on renewed importance. However, work in this area seems largely concerned with classical epistemological questions about epistemic obligations and justification, and questions inherited from moral philosophy about whether belief, like action, must be voluntary for us to be blameworthy for getting things wrong.[42] While the notion of epistemic blame and epistemic culpability as notions distinct from their moral counterparts are assumed in some of the literature on epistemic injustice and intellectual vices, accounts of the conditions for being blamed in a specifically epistemic way are uncommon.[43] Given the role of moral accountability in bringing us to shared moral understandings, we might expect its epistemic analogue to be similarly useful in overcoming differences of opinion in the political arena. At the very least, we may hope that in holding the epistemically irresponsible to account, we may prevent or mitigate the spread of false and misleading information. A non-ideal approach to these epistemological issues is sorely needed to address associated social and political problems.

---

[40]   Charles W. Mills, *The Racial Contract* (Ithaca, NY: Cornell University Press, 1997). See also Nancy Tuana and Shannon Sullivan (eds.), Special Issue: Feminist Epistemologies of Ignorance, *Hypatia* **21** (2006); Shannon Sullivan and Nancy Tuana (eds.), *Race and Epistemologies of Ignorance* (Albany, NY: SUNY Press, 2007).

[41]   See also Cynthia Townley, *A Defence of Ignorance: Its Value for Knowers and Roles in Feminist and Social Epistemologies* (Lanham, MD: Lexington, 2011).

[42]   See, for example, Margery Bedford Naylor, 'Epistemic Justification', *American Philosophical Quarterly* **25** (1988), 49–58; William Alston, 'The Deontological Conception of Justification', *Philosophical Perspectives* **2** (1988), 257–99; Richard Feldman, 'Voluntary Belief and Epistemic Evaluation', in Matthias Steup (ed.), *Knowledge, Truth, and Duty: Essays on Epistemic Justification, Responsibility, and Virtue* (Oxford: Oxford University Press, 2001), 77–92.

[43]   An exception is Lindsay Rettler, 'In Defense of Doxastic Blame' *Synthese* **195** (2018), 2205–26. An argument against there being a distinctively epistemic form of blame is in Antti Kauppinen, 'Epistemic Norms and Epistemic Accountability', *Philosophers' Imprint* **18** (2018), 1–16.

Some of the issues discussed above, such as hermeneutical injustice and the pernicious effects of a naturalistic conception of health, point to a way our epistemic practices can go wrong in a cognitively deeper way than issues arising at the level of knowledge production, testimony, or intellectual character traits. Namely, sometimes things go wrong at the level of the very *concepts* we use to construct our beliefs and other attitudes. As Alexis Burgess and David Plunkett argue, 'what concepts we have fixes what thoughts we can think... our conceptual repertoire determines... what beliefs we can have'.[44] But the issue goes well beyond the doxastic: the concepts we have limit 'what hypotheses we can entertain, what desires we can form, what plans we can make on the basis of such mental states, and accordingly constrains what we can hope to accomplish in the world'.[45] When our concepts go wrong, our epistemic practices and everything that follows therefrom can be radically misdirected. There is growing attention in analytic philosophy to questions regarding the critique and revision of our concepts, referred to variously as *conceptual engineering*,[46] *conceptual ethics*,[47] and *ameliorative inquiry*.[48] Such work has always been a part of philosophy, but conceptual analysis was for most of the 20th century conceived along similar abstract lines to ideal theory in epistemology. More recent work takes seriously the epistemic, social, and political effects of both the concepts we have inherited and our efforts to improve them, as can be seen in work on our concepts of gender,[49] sexual orientation,[50] and the law.[51] There is room for considerably more

[44]   Alexis Burgess and David Plunkett, 'Conceptual Ethics I', *Philosophy Compass* **8** (2013), 1091–1101, at 1096.
[45]   Burgess and Plunkett, 'Conceptual Ethics I', 1096–7.
[46]   Herman Cappelen, *Fixing Language: An Essay on Conceptual Engineering*, (Oxford: Oxford University Press, 2018).
[47]   Burgess and Plunkett, 'Conceptual Ethics I'.
[48]   Sally Haslanger, *Resisting Reality: Social Construction and Social Critique*, (Oxford: Oxford University Press, 2012).
[49]   Sally Haslanger, 'Gender and Race: (What) Are They? (What) Do We Want Them to Be?', *Noûs* **34** (2000), 31–55; Jenkins, Katharine, 'Amelioration and Inclusion: Gender Identity and the Concept of Woman', *Ethics* **126** (2016), 394–421.
[50]   Robin A. Dembroff, 'What Is Sexual Orientation?' *Philosophers' Imprint* **16** (2016), 1–27; Esa Díaz-León, 'Sexual Orientation as Interpretation? Sexual Desires, Concepts, and Choice', *Journal of Social Ontology* **3** (2017), 231–248.
[51]   Natalie Stoljar, 'What Do We Want Law to Be? Philosophical Analysis and the Concept of Law', in Wil Waluchow and Stefan Sciaraffa

work in this area, regarding both the development of theories of conceptual change and conceptual error, and detailed studies of further cases of concepts that have gone wrong.

Finally, a recurring issue in the background of most of the papers in this volume is the *epistemological relevance of social identity,* particularly where oppressive power relations are at work, as is nearly always the case in actual, non-ideal conditions. This theme reflects ongoing research in the critical epistemology of race, gender, sexuality, disability, indigeneity, and other axes of oppression.[52] Indeed, many movements within non-ideal epistemology are rooted in concerns brought to light by theory and activism in these various and often intersecting lines of inquiry. By critically examining how social identities and stereotypes influence the production of knowledge and belief, in both academic and lay settings, non-ideal epistemology from these perspectives can reveal biases that contribute to epistemic and other forms of oppression. However, these critical approaches have historically been marginalized within analytic philosophy, and to some extent remain so.[53] Improving the philosophical

---

(eds.), *Philosophical Foundations of the Nature of Law* (Oxford: Oxford University Press, 2013).

[52] See, in addition to works cited in fn. 11 above, Donna Haraway, 'Situated Knowledges: The Science Question in Feminism and the Privilege of Partial Perspective', *Feminist Studies* **14** (1988), 575–99; Lorraine Code, *What Can She Know? Feminist Theory and Construction of Knowledge* (Ithaca, NY: Cornell University Press, 1991); Charles W. Mills, 'Alternative Epistemologies', in *Blackness Visible: Essays on Philosophy and Race* (Ithaca, NY: Cornell University Press, 1998), 21–39; Linda Alcoff and Elizabeth Potter (eds.), *Feminist Epistemologies* (London: Routledge, 1993); Edward Said, *Orientalism* (New York: Pantheon Books, 1978); Eve Kosofsky Sedgwick, *The Epistemology of the Closet* (Berkeley and Los Angeles, CA: University of California Press, 1990); Willie Ermine, 'Aboriginal Epistemology', in M. Battiste and J. Barman (eds.), *First Nations Education in Canada: The Circle Unfolds,* (Vancouver, BC: University of British Columbia Press, 2000), 101–111; Anita Silvers, "Feminist Perspectives on Disability", *Stanford Encyclopedia of Philosophy* (Winter 2016 Edition), Edward N. Zalta (ed.), <https://plato.stanford.edu/archives/win2016/entries/feminism-disability/>, §3.

[53] Phyllis Rooney, 'The Marginalization of Feminist Epistemology and What That Reveals About Epistemology "Proper"', in Heidi Grasswick (ed.), *Feminist Epistemology and Philosophy of Science* (Dordrecht: Springer, 2011), 3–24; Kristie Dotson, 'How is This Paper Philosophy?', *Comparative Philosophy* **3** (2012), 3–29; Katharine Jenkins, '"That's Not

understanding of our epistemic practices and of the non-ideal conditions in which all of us exercise our epistemic agency requires serious engagement with the overlooked perspectives and experiences explored by these critical approaches.

Acknowledgements

We will close this introduction with a brief note of thanks to some of the many people and institutions who have provided help and support in the preparation of this volume, as well as in the organisation of the prior conference. First and foremost, we are very grateful to the Royal Institute of Philosophy for their generous financial support towards the organisation of the conference. We would also like to thank the Analysis Trust and the Society for Women in Philosophy, for making financial bursaries available to attendees, and the University of Sheffield, the Hang Seng Centre, and the Faculty of Arts and Humanities, for kindly offering various forms of material support. Thanks to Paul Faulkner, Miranda Fricker, Jules Holroyd, and Jenny Saul for advice and insights at various points along the way. Thanks also to Ahmad Fattah and Jaanika Puusalu, as well as numerous anonymous referees, for assisting with the review process. Finally, thank you to all those who spoke at, presented posters, or attended the *Harms and Wrongs in Epistemic Practice* conference, and who made it such a rich and supportive venue for epistemological discussion.

University of Sheffield
bbarker2@sheffield.ac.uk
University of Connecticut
charlie.crerar@uconn.edu
University of Sheffield
tsgoetze1@sheffield.ac.uk

Philosophy": Feminism, Academia and the Double Bind', *Journal of Gender Studies* **23** (2014), 262–74.

Can Closed-mindedness be an Intellectual Virtue?

HEATHER BATTALY

Abstract

Is closed-mindedness always an intellectual vice? Are there conditions in which it might be an intellectual virtue? This paper adopts a working analysis of closed-mindedness as an unwillingness or inability to engage seriously with relevant intellectual options. In standard cases, closed-mindedness will be an intellectual vice. But, in epistemically hostile environments, closed-mindedness will be an intellectual virtue.

Many of us know someone like Paul. Paul believes that people who commit crimes are simply irredeemable. He thinks they are broken human beings who can't be fixed. Paul has stuck with these beliefs throughout his life, and is unwilling to engage seriously with ideas or evidence to the contrary: he summarily dismisses any competing ideas that cross his path without evaluating their merits. Accordingly, when the conversation turns to educating the incarcerated, Paul deems it ridiculous and shuts down, closing himself off. When he sees an article supporting reentry programs, he thinks it silly and scrolls past it. Paul recognizes that such ideas compete with his own, and rejects them because they seem implausible. In short, Paul is closed-minded, at least when it comes to this issue.

What is closed-mindedness? Is closed-mindedness always an intellectual vice? Are there conditions in which it might be an intellectual virtue? This paper, the third in a series on closed-mindedness, focuses on whether it can be an intellectual virtue.[1] Section 1 adopts a working analysis of closed-mindedness as an unwillingness or inability to engage seriously with relevant intellectual options.[2] Paul has one familiar species of closed-mindedness: he is dogmatic. He is unwilling to engage seriously with relevant alternatives to a belief he already holds. Section 2 explains why the disposition of

---

[1]   Heather Battaly, 'Closed-mindedness and Dogmatism,' *Episteme* **15** (2018): 261–282; 'Closed-mindedness as an Intellectual Vice', in C. Kelp and J. Greco (eds.), *Virtue Theoretic Epistemology: New Methods and Approaches* (Cambridge: Cambridge University Press, forthcoming).

[2]   I argue for this account of closed-mindedness and contrast it with an account of open-mindedness in Battaly 'Closed-mindedness and Dogmatism'.

doi:10.1017/S135824611800053X

closed-mindedness is an intellectual vice in standard cases, like Paul's. The bulk of the paper explores whether closed-mindedness can be an intellectual virtue. Section 3 argues that there are instances of closed-minded action that are intellectually virtuous, and Section 4 suggests that the disposition of closed-mindedness can be an intellectual virtue in epistemically hostile environments. Throughout, I treat the analysis of the disposition of closed-mindedness, and its status as an intellectual vice, as separate questions. I do not assume that the disposition is always an intellectual vice. This approach can help us home in on what makes closed-mindedness a vice, when it is one.

1. What is Closed-mindedness?

Paul is unwilling to engage seriously with alternatives to his belief that 'once a criminal, always a criminal'. We can use Paul's case, which is a paradigm of both closed-mindedness and dogmatism, to identify the key features of each of these two dispositions. Dismissing relevant alternatives to a belief – as Paul does – is one way to be both closed-minded and dogmatic. But, it isn't the only way to be closed-minded, or even the only way to be dogmatic. To see why, let's consider four features of Paul's case, none of which are necessary for closed-mindedness, and two of which – (2) and (3) – are also unnecessary for dogmatism.[3]

(1) **Having beliefs about the topic.** Paul already believes that 'once a criminal, always a criminal', and in dismissing relevant alternatives to this belief, he is being closed-minded. But, closed-mindedness does not *require* already having beliefs about a given topic. Consider Pauline who has no beliefs about this topic and is being confronted with evidence for the very first time. Pauline can still arrive at an initial belief by conducting a closed-minded inquiry. For instance, she may ignore or be oblivious to evidence that supports the success of reentry programs. Accordingly, closed-mindedness doesn't require having extant beliefs about the given topic. But dogmatism does; it requires a belief about which the agent is dogmatic. Paul is both closed-minded and dogmatic; Pauline is closed-minded but not dogmatic.

(2) **The locus of ideas and evidence.** Paul is closed-minded with respect to ideas and evidence that compete with a belief he already holds. Pauline is closed-minded in the way that she handles ideas and evidence in the process of arriving at a belief – she

---

[3] The arguments in this section are further defended in Battaly, 'Closed-mindedness and Dogmatism'.

ignores relevant evidence. But, one can also be closed-minded in the ways that one conducts inquiries more generally. One can be closed-minded with respect to which questions one asks, which sources one consults, and which methods one uses. Accordingly, the locus of closed-mindedness isn't restricted to ideas and evidence. Its locus includes ideas and evidence, but also includes other intellectual options, like relevant questions, sources, and methods. The locus of dogmatism isn't restricted to ideas and evidence either. The dogmatic agent who willfully 'hides her head in the sand' closes herself off to any further evidence, but also to any further sources, questions, and methods that might be relevant.

(3) **Engaging with intellectual options.** In dismissing intellectual options that cross his path, Paul engages with those options, at least insofar as he recognizes and rejects them, but he doesn't engage seriously with them – he doesn't evaluate the merits of competing ideas or the arguments for them. His engagement is entirely superficial. But, closed-mindedness and dogmatism don't even require this much, since one can be closed-minded or dogmatic by *failing* (in various ways) to engage with intellectual options. For instance, (i) one could *ignore* (rather than dismiss) intellectual options that one recognizes. Or, (ii) one could be *oblivious* to intellectual options – e.g., one could fail to recognize relevant defeaters or sources in the first place. One way to be oblivious to relevant sources is to be testimonially unjust.[4] Alternatively, (iii) one could *fail to seek out* or generate intellectual options. For instance, an agent could fail to look beyond his own echo chamber, or only look for evidence that confirms his belief that 'once a criminal, always a criminal'.

(4) **Unwillingness.** Paul is unwilling to engage seriously with relevant intellectual options. Unwillingness is arguably required for dogmatism, but it isn't required for the broader category of closed-mindedness. One can be closed-minded by being unable, albeit willing, to engage seriously with intellectual options. Consider Oblivia, who shares Paul's belief that the incarcerated are irredeemable. Unlike Paul, Oblivia is perfectly *willing* to engage seriously with intellectual options to this belief; but she is also systematically oblivious to relevant options and thus fails to engage with them.[5] She may have passively inherited this impaired perception from her

---

[4] Miranda Fricker, *Epistemic Injustice: Power and the Ethics of Knowing* (Oxford: Oxford University Press, 2007).

[5] Wayne Riggs, 'Open-mindedness, Insight, and Understanding', in J. Baehr (ed.), *Intellectual Virtues and Education* (London: Routledge, 2016), 18–37.

surrounding society,[6] or it may have been actively indoctrinated in her. Whatever its cause, Oblivia's impaired perception makes her closed-minded. Importantly, our environments can make us closed-minded even when we don't want to be closed-minded. This has two consequences. First, people who are unable to engage with intellectual options because of bad luck in their environments or their constitutions are closed-minded, but aren't blameworthy (in the standard sense) for coming to possess closed-mindedness. Second, as an inability, closed-mindedness can be an environmentally produced impairment, and can even result from a hard-wired impairment – it need not be a character trait.[7]

The upshot of all this is that closed-mindedness (CM) is an unwillingness or inability to engage seriously with relevant intellectual options. Dogmatism is a sub-set of closed-mindedness: (DG) it is an unwillingness to engage seriously with relevant alternatives to a belief one already holds. There are three addenda.

First, though the examples above feature beliefs that are false, one can also be closed-minded and dogmatic with respect to beliefs that are true. This is because closed-mindedness and dogmatism do not pertain to the contents of beliefs. They pertain to the agent's unwillingness or inability to engage seriously with relevant options to her beliefs, whatever their content. Accordingly, an agent can be dogmatic with respect to her religious beliefs, whether those beliefs are true or false. She can be dogmatic with respect to her political beliefs, whether they are true or false. And, she can even be dogmatic with respect to true and relatively unimportant beliefs; e.g., that her pet is well behaved.

Second, an agent's closed-mindedness might be restricted to a particular domain. An agent might only be closed-minded about her pets (e.g., whether her pets are well behaved), or about her pets and her children (e.g., whether her pets and her children are well behaved), and not about anything else. She thus has a domain-specific disposition to be closed-minded, but lacks a general disposition to be closed-minded. It is also possible for an agent to perform a closed-minded action as a one-off – to do what a closed-minded person would do – while lacking either a domain-specific disposition or a general disposition to be closed-minded. To illustrate, on a particular

---

[6] Fricker (*Epistemic Injustice*, 37) argues that a card-carrying feminist, at the level of belief and motive, might have passively inherited prejudiced perception from her surrounding society.

[7] I further defend this claim in Battaly 'Closed-mindedness and Dogmatism'.

occasion our agent might dismiss evidence that her dog was behaving badly, even though she does not usually dismiss such evidence.

Third, the analyses above define closed-mindedness and dogmatism in terms of *relevant* intellectual options. To see why this restriction is needed, consider Priscilla, a police detective who is investigating a standard break-in. In ignoring the possibility that David Bowie's ghost (or Ronald Reagan's ghost, etc.) did it, Priscilla is *not* being closed-minded. She isn't being closed-minded because these options aren't relevant to her inquiry. To be closed-minded, she would need to ignore an option that *is* relevant (e.g., the teenager responsible for the break-in next door also conducted this one). This much should be clear: closed-mindedness and dogmatism require relevancy restrictions on intellectual options. What is not clear, and what warrants exploration, are the precise conditions on relevancy. To provide a complete picture of closed-mindedness and dogmatism, we would need to answer the question: which options are, and which are not, relevant for an agent in an inquiry, and why? Alas, I won't be defending any single answer to this question, though I take the viable candidates for relevancy conditions to be familiar enough. Epistemic externalists will define relevant/irrelevant options for an agent in an inquiry to be: those options that are objectively likely/unlikely to be true (or likely/unlikely to be helpful in reaching the truth). Externalists may also include options that the agent's community reliably believes to be likely/unlikely to be true (or to be likely/unlikely to be helpful in reaching the truth). Whereas, internalists will take relevant/irrelevant options to be those that the agent, or community, has good reason to believe are likely/unlikely to be true. I won't be plumping for either of these over the other. But, the good news is that whether we are internalists or externalists, intellectual options like '2 + 2 = 5', 'The Holocaust never happened', and 'The earth is flat' will be *irrelevant* in ordinary environments – since these options are in fact false, and we (and our communities) believe reliably, and with good reason, that they are false. This means that in ordinary environments we aren't closed-minded in ignoring these options, because they aren't relevant.[8]

---

[8] Above, I assume that there is no moral or pragmatic encroachment on conditions of epistemic relevancy. But, I allow for the possibility that moral and pragmatic concerns might sometimes trump epistemic concerns. One might have moral or pragmatic reasons to engage with an agent who is arguing for an epistemically irrelevant claim. When one refuses to so engage, one isn't closed-minded, but one might be callous or uncivil.

Let's now explore a different candidate condition on relevancy, one that will play a role in the discussion below. Call it the 'pervasiveness' condition. It claims that the widespread presence or absence of an option in an environment suffices to make that option relevant or irrelevant for the agent. It is a live question as to whether we should endorse the pervasiveness condition. On the one hand, we have reason to think that the absence of an option in the agent's environment is not enough to make it irrelevant to her inquiry. Consider George Orwell's Oceania, in which the Ministry of Truth re-writes options, disseminating fabrications that support the party line, and destroying facts that do not.[9] Arguably, the facts that it destroys are still relevant options for agents conducting inquiries. For instance, we see Winston Smith struggling to reconstruct the events of his childhood without the benefit of any external record of them. To put the point differently, the epistemic environment in Oceania makes its subjects *more* closed-minded, not less. It doesn't *decrease* the number of relevant options; it makes those relevant options harder to access. This counts *against* the pervasiveness condition.

On the other hand, we have reason to think that the ubiquity of an option in an environment might make it relevant to the agent's inquiry. This counts *in favour* of the pervasiveness condition. Return to Oceania – an epistemic environment that is thoroughly polluted with 'alternative facts'. Arguably, the ubiquitous presence of such options makes them relevant to the agent's inquiry in the same way that the widespread presence of fake barns makes that option relevant. The option that a barn was fake wasn't relevant until one stumbled into fake barn country, where it became relevant and stayed relevant, even though the agent's beliefs – 'That's a barn' – are true.[10] (The agent happens to look at the one real barn in the area.) Likewise, the option that 'ignorance is strength' wasn't relevant until one woke up in Oceania, where it became relevant and stayed relevant, even though the agent's beliefs – 'Ignorance is not strength' – are true. For our purposes below, the key issue will be this: in ordinary environments, options like 'The earth is flat', '2 + 2 = 5', and 'The Holocaust never happened' are not relevant, and thus we aren't closed-minded in ignoring them. But, *if* the pervasiveness condition proves viable, then in epistemically hostile environments, options like '2 + 2 = 5' will be relevant, and we will be closed-minded in ignoring them. Is such closed-mindedness intellectually vicious? Or, might it even be intellectually virtuous?

[9]   George Orwell, *1984* (New York: Harcourt Brace, 1949).
[10]   Alvin Goldman, 'Discrimination and Perceptual Knowledge', *The Journal of Philosophy* **73** (1976), 771–791.

2. Closed-mindedness as an Intellectual Vice

Thus far, I have adopted working analyses of the dispositions of closed-mindedness and dogmatism. These analyses do not presuppose that closed-mindedness and dogmatism are intellectual vices. To count as intellectual vices, they will need to meet further conditions. Which conditions? That depends on our analysis of intellectual vice. Arguably, there is more than one kind of intellectual vice: (a) effects-vice, (b) responsibilist-vice, and (c) personalist-vice. Roughly, closed-mindedness and dogmatism will be (a) effects-vices whenever they produce a preponderance of bad epistemic effects (or fail to produce a preponderance of good epistemic effects). They will be (b) responsibilist-vices whenever they are bad epistemic character traits for whose possession the agent is blameworthy (accountable). Finally, they will be (c) personalist-vices whenever they are bad epistemic character traits for whose possession the agent is not blameworthy (accountable). The distinction between effects-vice and responsibilist-vice should be familiar to virtue epistemologists, since it corresponds to that between reliabilist- and responsibilist-virtue. We need the additional category of personalist-vice to capture the bad epistemic character traits of the indoctrinated (e.g., graduates of Hitler's *Jugend*.) My view is that in standard cases, like Paul's, the dispositions of closed-mindedness and dogmatism are intellectual vices. At a minimum, Paul's closed-mindedness meets the conditions for an effects-vice. Since effects-vices can be epistemic character traits, Paul's closed-mindedness may also meet the conditions for a responsibilist-vice or a personalist-vice (depending on the details of its acquisition). Here, I focus on effects-vice.

Briefly, effects-vices are stable cognitive dispositions that either consistently produce a preponderance of bad epistemic effects, or consistently fail to produce a preponderance of good epistemic effects. If we understand vices to be the contraries of virtues – such that one could simultaneously fail to have either – then effects-vices will produce a preponderance of bad epistemic effects. Whereas, if we understand vices to be the contradictories of virtues – such that whenever one fails to have a virtue, one thereby has a vice – then effects-vices will fail to produce a preponderance of good epistemic effects.[11] Any stable cognitive disposition – be it a character trait, an environmentally produced impairment, or a hard-wired

[11]   Heather Battaly, 'Varieties of Epistemic Vice', in J. Matheson and R. Vitz (eds.), *The Ethics of Belief* (Oxford: Oxford University Press,

impairment – that meets these conditions will be an effects-vice. Accordingly, readers can take their pick: in the below, readers are (e.g.) welcome to operate on the assumption that closed-mindedness is a character trait.

Why think that in standard cases, like Paul's, the disposition of closed-mindedness will be an effects-vice? For starters, closed-mindedness can produce a heap of bad epistemic effects for the closed-minded agent, for other agents, and for the epistemic environment.[12]

(1) **Bad epistemic effects for the closed-minded agent.** Closed-mindedness enables the agent who possesses it: (i) to sustain false beliefs that he already has. Paul's closed-mindedness enables him to sustain his false belief that 'once a criminal, always a criminal.' Similarly, in failing to look for sources outside our own epistemic bubbles, we may be sustaining false beliefs that we already have. Indeed, repeated agreement among the 'friends' in our bubbles may even lead us to mistakenly strengthen our confidence in our beliefs.[13] Closed-mindedness can also: (ii) prevent the agent from acquiring true beliefs and knowledge. Paul's closed-mindedness prevents him from acquiring true beliefs about whether incarcerated people can change. Moreover, closed-mindedness can: (iii) compound and expand an agent's extant system of false beliefs. It can lead agents to doxastically double down. We see this in the case of Samuel A. Cartwright, a nineteenth century white American doctor who believed that slaves lacked agency. When confronted with contrary evidence – their attempts to escape slavery – Cartwright doxastically doubled-down: he judged escape attempts to be manifestations of a mental disorder peculiar to slaves, which he invented out of whole cloth. Relatedly, closed-mindedness can lead agents: (iv) to pursue irrelevant questions, projects, and inquiries, and thus to waste their epistemic resources.

2014), 60–62. For criticism, see Charlie Crerar, 'Motivational Approaches to Intellectual Vice', *Australasian Journal of Philosophy* (forthcoming).

[12] These arguments are defended in Battaly 'Closed-mindedness as an Intellectual Vice'. On the debate over whether open-mindedness requires reliability, see J. Adam Carter and Emma C. Gordon, 'Open-mindedness and Truth', *Canadian Journal of Philosophy* **44** (2014), 207–224; B.J.C. Madison, 'Is Open-mindedness Truth-Conducive?' *Synthese* (forthcoming).

[13] This misplaced confidence will be epistemically bad, whether our beliefs are true or false. See Christopher Thi Nguyen, 'Escape the Echo Chamber', *Aeon* (9 Apr, 2018). <https://aeon.co/essays/why-its-as-hard-to-escape-an-echo-chamber-as-it-is-to-flee-a-cult>.

(2) **Bad epistemic effects for other agents.** In being closed-minded with respect to sources, one might: (i) fail to see another agent as a source of knowledge when she is, assigning her a 'credibility deficit'.[14] As a one-off, the harm done by a single instance of such closed-mindedness may be relatively ephemeral. But, closed-mindedness with respect to sources can take the form of testimonial injustice, whereby the closed-minded agent systematically overlooks the credibility of women and people of color, wronging them as 'giver[s] of knowledge'.[15] Relatedly, such closed-mindedness can: (ii) impede the development of intellectual virtues in women and people of color, and facilitate their development of intellectual vices. Additionally, it can: (iii) result in their exclusion from educational institutions, obstructing their acquisition of knowledge. The closed-minded agent can also: (iv) assign too *much* credibility to sources within his epistemic bubble. He may see them as sources of knowledge when they are not, assigning them a credibility excess. This, too, can cause agents to develop intellectual vices.[16] Similarly: (v) the closed-mindedness of agents who set the intellectual agenda for others – school boards, journalists – can be 'epistemically corrupting'; i.e. it can 'encourage the development and exercise of epistemic vices' in others.[17]

(3) **Bad epistemic effects for the environment.** Closed-mindedness can also lead to: (i) the intentional or unintentional pollution of the epistemic environment. Closed-minded agents who pursue irrelevant inquiries and do so sincerely, e.g., 'true believers' like Cartwright (above), can unintentionally disseminate falsehoods in their environments. Closed-minded agents who re-post the claims of their 'friends' without seeking independent corroboration, can likewise populate their feeds with unwitting falsehoods. By inadvertently polluting their epistemic environments with false claims, these closed-minded agents may also be: (ii) obfuscating truths and knowledge, making them harder to find. Of course, pollution will be a matter of degree: the wider the dissemination of falsehoods, the more polluted the environment; at extreme levels of saturation, polluted environments will be hostile. Arguably, closed-mindedness can also lead to intentional pollution and obfuscation. Let's grant

---

[14]   Fricker, *Epistemic Injustice*, 27.
[15]   Fricker, *Epistemic Injustice*, 44.
[16]   José Medina, *The Epistemology of Resistance* (Oxford: Oxford University Press, 2013), 60.
[17]   Ian James Kidd, 'Epistemic Corruption and Education', *Episteme* (forthcoming).

that intentionally polluting the environment with claims one *knows* to be false, and intentionally concealing claims one *knows* to be true, involve dishonesty and deceit rather than closed-mindedness. Even so, dogmatic 'true believers' can still intentionally hide or erase competing ideas (that they incorrectly believe to be false) in an effort to prevent others from believing them. We see this repeatedly in book-burnings, and also in the EPA's 2017 decision to delete or move information about anthropogenic climate change from its main webpage into its archive.[18] Dogmatic 'true believers' can also intentionally populate the environment with options that will divert agents who would otherwise endorse competing views. 'True believers' may do this in a sincere effort to 'control the message', or to disseminate what they think are truths, or to manufacture doubt. For instance, they may publicize studies on the role of natural variability in climate change.[19]

In short, the disposition of closed-mindedness can produce a ream of bad epistemic effects. Now, to be an effects-vice, it must produce a *preponderance* of bad epistemic effects, or fail to produce a *preponderance* of good epistemic effects. Does it meet these conditions? Below, I argue that the disposition of closed-mindedness will minimize the production of bad effects in *hostile* epistemic environments. But, in *ordinary* epistemic environments like ours,[20] it is still reasonable to think that the disposition of closed-mindedness (usually) meets the conditions of an effects-vice. As a failure to seek out sources beyond our bubbles, it leads to misplaced confidence and credibility excess. As testimonial injustice, it obstructs the intellectual virtues of other agents, facilitating intellectual vice. As dogmatism about a belief that is false, it results in the maintenance, strengthening, and compounding of false beliefs. And, in all of these forms, it obstructs the acquisition of knowledge. That is a plethora of bad epistemic effects. Even at our most conservative, we can conclude that

---

[18] L. Friedman, 'EPA Scrubs a Climate Website of "Climate Change"', *New York Times* (20 Oct, 2017) <https://www.nytimes.com/2017/10/20/climate/epa-climate-change.html>.

[19] Naomi Oreskes and Erik M. Conway, *Merchants of Doubt* (New York: Bloomsbury, 2010).

[20] Our current epistemic environment is still several magnitudes away from Orwell's 1984. Some of us can still find (relatively) ordinary environments to occupy, though this will be much harder for some agents than others. It is possible for a single environment to be hostile for some agents (e.g., members of non-dominant groups) but not others; and for a single agent to move through different environments, some of which are hostile and others of which are (relatively) ordinary.

closed-mindedness sometimes, perhaps often, fails to produce a preponderance of good epistemic effects. That's enough to make it an effects-vice.

The disposition of closed-mindedness also meets the conditions for an effects-vice when the belief one is being closed-minded about is *true*.[21] Suppose I believe that my pet is well behaved, and that this belief is true but doesn't constitute knowledge (I am unjustified in believing it). In ignoring relevant options – I refuse to engage with relevant evidence to the contrary or with relevant sources who criticize my pet's behavior – I am ignoring options that are indeed false and unreliable. My closed-mindedness enables me to sustain a true belief. But, in ignoring these relevant options, I am not engaging with them seriously – I am not evaluating them on their merits. Accordingly, I may be sustaining a true belief that my pet is well behaved while blocking my ability to gain related epistemic goods, like knowledge that my pet is well behaved, or an understanding of what makes her well behaved. Here, too, closed-mindedness may obstruct the acquisition of knowledge. And, of course, it may do this while simultaneously producing many of the other bad effects mentioned above, including misplaced confidence. Here, too, we can at least conclude that closed-mindedness sometimes, perhaps often, fails to produce a preponderance of epistemic goods.

3. Closed-mindedness as an Intellectual Virtue: One-off Instances of Closed-minded Action in Ordinary Environments

I have argued that the disposition of closed-mindedness is an intellectual vice in standard cases like Paul's, and more generally, that it is an intellectual vice in ordinary epistemic environments. But, is it *always* an intellectual vice? In epistemically hostile environments, might the disposition of closed-mindedness even be an intellectual-virtue, albeit a 'burdened' virtue of some sort?[22] I explore that question in the concluding section. Here, I address a worry about my analysis of closed-mindedness as it applies to ordinary environments.

[21] Eamonn Callan and Dylan Arena, 'Indoctrination', in H. Siegel (ed.), *The Oxford Handbook of Philosophy of Education* (Oxford: Oxford University Press, 2009), 117. I address closed-mindedness about knowledge below.
[22] Lisa Tessman, *Burdened Virtues: Virtue Ethics for Liberatory Struggles* (Oxford: Oxford University Press, 2005).

Heather Battaly

My analysis of closed-mindedness (CM) is broad. It encompasses closed-minded *actions* in addition to dispositions, and entails that closed-mindedness will be more common than we might have thought. It even entails that we act in closed-minded ways with some frequency. The worry is that (CM) is so broad that instances of closed-minded action will outstrip instances of intellectually vicious action. Hence, closed-mindedness won't always be intellectually vicious. I embrace this worry and its implications. The below argues that there *are* instances of closed-minded action that are intellectually virtuous (though these may not be quite as common as the objector thinks). Indeed, I think there are advantages to approaching the analysis of closed-mindedness, and its status as an intellectual vice, as distinct questions. Namely, this approach can help us home in on what makes closed-mindedness a vice when it is one, and on what makes it a virtue when it is one.

Here, as above, let's restrict the discussion to *effects*-virtues and vices. Accordingly, our question is: are there any one-off instances of closed-minded action that produce more good epistemic effects than bad ones in ordinary environments? Clearly, there are instances of *ignoring* options – e.g., that the earth is flat, that 2 + 2 = 5, that the Holocaust never happened – that produce a preponderance of good epistemic effects. But, at least in ordinary environments, cases like these are beside the point because in ignoring *these* options one isn't being closed-minded. Closed-mindedness requires ignoring relevant options, and the options above are not relevant in ordinary environments. Whatever relevancy conditions we adopt – internalist, externalist, pervasiveness – these options will fall short. What we need are instances of ignoring *relevant* options that produce more good epistemic effects than bad ones.

There are at least three sorts of candidate cases to address. First, consider being closed-minded with respect to knowledge you already possess. In his 'Dogmatism Paradox', Saul Kripke asks whether possession of knowledge that p could justify ignoring future evidence against p.[23] His answer is that it sometimes can.[24] Ernest Sosa describes Kripke's reasoning as follows:

> Once you know that p, you can deduce...that any evidence contrary to p would be misleading, whereas positive evidence would probably do you little good. After all, by hypothesis you

---

[23]   Saul Kripke, *Philosophical Troubles: Collected Papers, vol. 1* (Oxford: Oxford University Press, 1972), 42–45.
[24]   Kripke, *Philosophical Troubles*, 49.

already know that p! Given this, you should close your mind to any new potential evidence to the question whether p. If positive, the evidence will do little for you; if negative, it will harmfully pull you away from the truth, and may even cost you the knowledge that you have.[25]

Might the closed-minded actions described here enable the agent to sustain her knowledge, and prevent her from devoting epistemic resources to relevant but ultimately misguided options? Do these instances of closed-mindedness produce an overall preponderance of good epistemic effects? In my view, the jury is still out. Ignoring options that are relevant but misguided will prevent the agent from devoting resources to those options, thus freeing up those resources for more promising epistemic pursuits. It will also preserve her true belief that p. The question is whether it causes her to lose her knowledge that p. Quassim Cassam thinks it does, Jeremy Fantl thinks it doesn't, and Ernest Sosa takes the road between. Cassam argues that when an agent is confronted with relevant evidence against p, which she can't refute and closed-mindedly dismisses, she loses her justification for p and thus loses her knowledge that p.[26] In direct contrast, Fantl contends that the agent can sometimes retain her knowledge that p when she dismisses a relevant counterargument that she can't refute.[27] Whereas, Sosa thinks the agent retains her animal knowledge that p, but is prevented from having reflective knowledge that p. For Sosa, the closed-minded agent is still 'apt', but not 'fully apt':

> If knowledge is a matter of apt intellectual performance in pursuit of truth…we get the result that negligence can deny us knowledge, or at least knowledge of a certain epistemically desirable level. We are denied fully apt attainment of the truth when we attain truth despite intellectual negligence. We are negligent when we should be open to verifying evidence, but close our minds instead.[28]

---

[25] Ernest Sosa, 'Knowledge and Time: Kripke's Dogmatism Paradox and the Ethics of Belief', in J. Matheson and R. Vitz (eds.), *The Ethics of Belief* (Oxford: Oxford University Press, 2014), 78.

[26] Quassim Cassam, 'Vices of the Mind' (book manuscript).

[27] Jeremy Fantl, 'A Defense of Dogmatism', in T. Gendler and J. Hawthorne (eds.), *Oxford Studies in Epistemology* 4 (Oxford: Oxford University Press, 2013), 34–5; *The Limitations of the Open Mind* (Oxford: Oxford University Press, 2018).

[28] Sosa, 'Knowledge and Time', 87.

Heather Battaly

We can say at least this much: closed-mindedness with respect to knowledge you already possess produces some good epistemic effects (it preserves truth). But, the jury is still out on exactly which bad epistemic effects it produces. Accordingly, it is an open question as to whether it produces a *preponderance* of good epistemic effects. We can also conclude that *if* knowledge is lost rather than preserved, then closed-mindedness with respect to knowledge won't be a clear advance on closed-mindedness with respect to unjustified true belief (e.g., that my pet is well-behaved). And, so, if closed-mindedness with respect to unjustified true belief fails to produce a preponderance of good epistemic effects (as argued above), so will closed-mindedness with respect to knowledge.

Second, it is worth considering whether the closed-minded behavior of a group-member might contribute to the production of epistemic goods by the group as a whole. In this vein, Christopher Hookway suggests that 'a research team may benefit from having some members who are dogmatic, and unwilling to take on board new possibilities, while others are much more ready to take seriously seemingly wild speculations'.[29] The suggestion is that the closed-minded behavior of a group-member might help a group of diverse agents produce a preponderance of epistemic goods. Relatedly, it is worth considering whether a group composed entirely of closed-minded agents might produce a preponderance of epistemic goods. Adam Morton is optimistic about this possibility. In his words:

> There are combinations of degraded motivation that result in the entrenchment of prejudice, the ignoring of evident fact, and the suppression of promising ideas. Some, probably most, combinations...have these bad effects. But not always: some virtuous combinations of vices result in more knowledge, of greater predictive and explanatory power, than we can have from the enterprises of dispassionate sages.[30]

Relatedly, Miranda Fricker employs the example of a debating club, all of whose members are prejudiced, but whose prejudices cancel one another out, rendering the group as a whole neutral.[31] Though it is

---

[29]   Christopher Hookway, 'How to be a Virtue Epistemologist', in M. DePaul and L. Zagzebski (eds.), *Intellectual Virtue* (Oxford: Oxford University Press, 2003), 189.

[30]   Adam Morton, 'Shared Knowledge from Individual Vice', *Philosophical Inquiries* **2** (2014), 171.

[31]   Miranda Fricker, 'Can there be Institutional Virtues?', in T. Gendler and J. Hawthorne (eds.), *Oxford Studies in Epistemology* **3** (Oxford: Oxford

unclear whether the closed-minded behavior of one or more group-members would help a group produce a preponderance of epistemic goods, this question is worthy of exploration.

Even if the jury is still out on the two considerations above, I think the third consideration is decisive. Think about the most recent article you wrote, or about what it took to actually start *writing* your dissertation. At some point, you likely ignored relevant options, in order to focus on developing your own answer – not because it was your own, but because it was *the answer*! Because you thought it was true. You stopped reading alternative views – you tuned them out. You knew that another article had just been published on your topic, but you ignored it, in an effort to make progress on the solution you thought was correct. According to (CM), this behavior is closed-minded. Moreover, there will be *some* cases where it produces a preponderance of good epistemic effects; e.g., where researchers on the verge of a big discovery (e.g., the cure for a disease) ignore relevant (but different) work that has just been published in order to push forward and successfully complete their own line of inquiry. They may even (causally) *need* to ignore that work in order to make their discovery. Note that the goods here produced are epistemic – the researchers produce knowledge. The method of production is also epistemic – they push forward in their own inquiry. Their motives are likewise epistemic – they are motivated to attain knowledge. So, the values in play are epistemic and not, or not merely, pragmatic.[32]

Granted, some cases of ignoring relevant options will produce a preponderance of *merely* pragmatic goods, or moral goods, but not epistemic goods. As when closed-mindedly avoiding inquiries into one's own health, and sustaining the false belief that one is fine, actually helps one heal. This category may also include cases of closing off inquiry after one has gained just enough knowledge, though these cases can be tricky. For starters, consider the graduating senior who waits until the last minute to write a term paper. He addresses only two sources on the topic, ignoring other sources and closing off his inquiry in order to meet the deadline. Arguably, his closed-minded behavior helps him produce pragmatic goods – shutting down his inquiry helps him produce, in this case, a barely passing paper, which is a necessary condition for graduating. But, it should be

---

University Press, 2009). Hookway, Morton, and Fricker address dispositions. I am shifting the focus to actions.

[32] We could describe the case so that it produces a preponderance of pragmatic bads – imagine that the researchers are subject to verbal abuse, etc.

fairly clear that shutting down his inquiry doesn't help him gain any epistemic goods. Unlike the researchers above, the graduating senior doesn't continue his inquiry – he turns the paper in and walks away from the subject. For him, ignoring relevant options isn't a necessary step in the production of epistemic goods; it is an impediment to the production of further or better epistemic goods. Epistemically, he would be much better off if he kept his inquiry open. Consider a more complicated case. Suppose I have promised a friend that I will make pavlova for her party tomorrow. Having never made it before, I read the recipes of twenty celebrity bakers. I ignore the remaining 10 million recipes turned up by Google and close off my inquiry, in order to keep my promise and get the pavlova done. Here, too, closed-minded action arguably helps me produce a pragmatic good – closing off my inquiry helps me produce, in this case, a good pavlova. Closed-minded action also helps me produce a moral good – keeping a promise. Does it help me produce any epistemic goods? Perhaps, not – ignoring other recipes may be an impediment to the production of further or better epistemic goods. It may be the twenty-fifth recipe that gets me special insight into baking meringue. On the other hand, perhaps I have hit the point of diminishing epistemic returns – after having read twenty recipes (which seems like a lot!), keeping my inquiry open may not produce further or better epistemic goods. Accordingly, ignoring other recipes may prevent me from devoting further epistemic resources and amassing epistemic opportunity costs.

In sum, however we end up classifying these tough cases, there will be some instances of closed-minded action – e.g., of the researchers above – that *are* epistemically virtuous. The other candidate cases above also warrant further exploration.

4. Closed-mindedness as an Intellectual Virtue: The Disposition of Closed-mindedness in Epistemically Hostile Environments

What about the *disposition* of closed-mindedness? Is it always an intellectual vice, or could it be an effects-virtue in epistemically hostile environments? Could it be a 'burdened' virtue of some sort – or at least a disposition that is only useful for surviving in environments that are hostile or oppressive?[33] Recall the pervasiveness

---

[33]   Tessman, *Burdened Virtues*, 2. Tessman argues that burdened virtues are both useful for surviving in oppressive environments, and negatively

condition on relevant options – let's assume, for the sake of argument, that it holds. Accordingly, the widespread presence of an intellectual option in an environment will suffice to make that option relevant. Further, let's suppose that an epistemically *hostile* environment is not minimally or moderately polluted, but extremely polluted – it is utterly saturated with intellectual options that are false, unreliable, or aimed at misdirection.[34] Some of these options will be explicit statements (e.g., 'ignorance is strength'), some will be unreliable sources (e.g., the dimwits in the film *Idiocracy*), and some will be implicit norms (e.g., that discredit women and people of color as sources of knowledge). The pervasiveness condition renders these options *relevant* in epistemically hostile environments.

So, what is a knowledge-possessing agent to do when she finds herself in an epistemically hostile environment? My proposal is that there are *epistemic* reasons for her to be closed-minded – to be unwilling to engage seriously with relevant intellectual options that conflict with what she already knows. That is, if she knows that, e.g., '2 + 2 = 4', 'ignorance is not strength', and 'the earth is round', then there are externalist epistemic reasons for her to refuse to engage with the options that, e.g., '2 + 2 = 5', 'ignorance is strength,' and 'the earth is flat.' *Why* should she be closed-minded? Because, in an epistemically hostile environment, closed-mindedness is an effects-virtue. When a knowledge-possessing agent is stuck in an epistemically hostile environment, surrounded by falsehoods, incompetent sources, and diversions, closed-mindedness about options that conflict with what she knows will minimize the production of bad epistemic effects for *her*.

To explicate, suppose the knowledge-possessing agent wakes up in Mike Judge's *Idiocracy*[35], which is flooded with incompetent sources, or in Orwell's Oceania, which is flooded with lies. Closed-mindedness about options that conflict with what she knows will avert at least one bad epistemic outcome and produce at least two epistemic goods for *this agent*. First, it will enable her to sustain the true

---

impact the agent's flourishing. In an epistemically hostile environment, does CM negatively impact an agent's epistemic flourishing? It may, if (for example) it prevents the agent from attaining knowledge. If it doesn't, then I am departing from Tessman's use of 'burdened'.

[34] The sources of hostility vary: some environments will be hostile by design (the Ministry of Truth deliberately lies); others will be hostile due to neglect (the Idiocracy).

[35] *Idiocracy*, Dir. Mike Judge, (20th Century Fox, 2006).

beliefs she already has. That is one good, and it is not insignificant – there is considerable risk of her coming to believe what the Ministry of Truth wants her to believe (its control is totalizing, its slogans appear on every screen, etc.) Second, closed-mindedness will prevent her from devoting epistemic resources to options that are relevant (due to pervasiveness) but misguided and from amassing epistemic opportunity costs. It averts that bad outcome. It thus frees up those resources for more promising epistemic pursuits; it enables her to continue to pursue her own intellectual projects and options (e.g., Winston Smith keeps a journal). That is a second good. Should she closed-mindedly forego opportunities to understand *why* the 'idiots' in the *Idiocracy* believe what they do? I think she can, though the answer will partly depend on whether such understanding could effect change in the hostile environment. Suppose it couldn't, and suppose she would be amassing epistemic opportunity costs in pursuing 'idiot-diagnosis' instead of other projects. Closed-mindedness would avert those epistemic opportunity costs.

Some agents – members of non-dominant groups – don't have to imagine being in an epistemically hostile environment. They already live in one. Our current epistemic environment routinely discredits women and people of color as sources of knowledge. It does this even though it isn't entirely over-run with misinformation – despite Kellyanne Conway's 'alternative facts' and Facebook's dissemination of Russian propaganda, our current epistemic environment is not saturated with falsehoods about every topic. On this score, it falls several magnitudes shy of Orwell's Oceania. But, it is thoroughly saturated with norms that discredit women and people of color – these norms run deep and systematically track agents across domains. Hostility can take different forms, and our environment *is* hostile for these agents. Accordingly, closed-mindedness might be an important resource for members of non-dominant groups. Here, too, it will enable knowledge-possessing agents to hold onto their true beliefs, avert epistemic opportunity costs, and pursue their own intellectual projects. Importantly and ironically, it might also help them ward off the vice of intellectual servility – closing themselves off from denials of their credibility might prevent them from losing confidence in their intellectual strengths and over-attributing limitations to themselves.[36]

[36] Dennis Whitcomb, Heather Battaly, Jason Baehr, and Daniel Howard-Snyder, 'Intellectual Humility: Owning Our Limitations' *Philosophy and Phenomenological Research* **94** (2017), 509–539.

Can Closed-mindedness be an Intellectual Virtue?

One important unanswered question is whether closed-minded agents in epistemically hostile environments retain their knowledge. Hostile environments compound this problem because they are unsafe; i.e. they are environments in which any agent – closed-minded or not – could easily go wrong when revisiting her belief.[37] In short, hostile environments may themselves rob an agent of knowledge, whether or not she is closed-minded; they are hostile, after all. Suppose an agent knows that countries X and Y are at war, but then wakes up in Oceania, in which the Ministry of Truth has replaced all references to the war with a sanitized history. When the agent revisits his belief, he can now easily go wrong. Is he thereby robbed of knowledge? If so, can he somehow inoculate himself against this unsafe environment by being closed-minded – by ignoring the falsehoods spouted by the Ministry of Truth? Alternatively, suppose we were to claim that the agent retains his knowledge despite his unsafe environment (knowledge doesn't require safety). Does his closed-mindedness then cause him to lose his knowledge (in a manner similar to that described by Cassam above)? Whatever conclusions we draw about knowledge, I submit that in epistemically hostile environments, the disposition of closed-mindedness still succeeds in minimizing bad epistemic effects for the agent himself, even if it doesn't produce an outright preponderance of good epistemic effects for the agent. In such environments, we may have to sacrifice knowledge in order to avoid even worse epistemic effects. Such is the power of hostile environments.

Does the closed-mindedness of the knowledge-possessing agent minimize bad epistemic effects for *other agents* in the hostile environment? One might worry that it does not. Indeed, an objector might argue that in order to minimize bad epistemic effects for deluded or incompetent others in Oceania and the *Idiocracy*, the knowledge-possessing agent should be somewhat open-minded. Even if she is ultimately unwilling to revise her *own* beliefs (2 + 2 = 4), she should still engage seriously with deluded or incompetent others, and the options they endorse, in an effort to change *their* minds and practices.[38]

I want to suggest an avenue of reply. Deluded or incompetent others in *hostile* environments like Oceania and the *Idiocracy* are

---

[37] Michael Lynch, 'Epistemic Arrogance and the Value of Political Dissent', C. Johnson (ed.), *Voicing Dissent* (London: Routledge, forthcoming).
[38] I am inclined to think this isn't open-mindedness, since the agent is unwilling to revise her beliefs. It is something like charity or civility.

unlikely to change their minds and practices as a result of one-on-one engagements with a knowledge-possessing agent. Such engagements are unlikely to produce the desired epistemic goods. They are also likely to produce bad epistemic outcomes for the knowledge-possessing agent herself (see above). Accordingly, the combined outcome of such engagements – likely epistemic bads for the agent herself and unlikely epistemic goods for others – also favors closed-mindedness.[39]

By way of further reply, it is worth considering whether serious engagement with deluded or incompetent others in a hostile environment might do *them* or the *environment* an epistemic disservice. When the knowledge-possessing agent engages seriously with deluded or incompetent others, might she be inflating their epistemic credibility, or at least signaling to them that they are credible enough to be taken seriously (though they aren't)? José Medina argues that credibility excess facilitates the development of intellectual vices, and can begin to do so over the course of a single conversation.[40] Accordingly, we can ask whether engaging with deluded or incompetent others facilitates, or sustains, intellectual vices via credibility excess. If it does, this would be a further strike against engagement. Relatedly, in engaging seriously with the Ministry of Truth and its fabrications, might our knowledge-possessing agent make the epistemic environment worse, rather than better? One might argue that our agent would need to choose her engagements strategically, in an effort to avoid the Ministry's smear campaigns (and avoid being executed). But, in a hostile environment like Oceania, that might not be feasible. Our agent's engagements might unavoidably be fodder for the Ministry's manipulations; in which case, they would inadvertently contribute to making the environment *more* polluted, not less. This would also count against engagement.

To sum up, I have argued that in an epistemically hostile environment, closed-mindedness on the part of the knowledge-possessing

---

[39]   Open-mindedness is a disposition to engage seriously with relevant intellectual options; closed-mindedness is an unwillingness or inability to so engage. There are situations in which a knowledge-possessing agent can simultaneously fail to be open-minded and fail to be closed-minded – when the options aren't relevant. But, in the hostile environment, the options *are* relevant. Accordingly, in the hostile environment, choosing not be open-minded entails being closed-minded. The question of whether this is virtuous or vicious is independent.

[40]   Medina, *The Epistemology of Resistance*, 60.

agent would minimize bad epistemic effects for the agent herself. This is enough to make her closed-mindedness an effects-virtue, since her engagement with other agents is unlikely to benefit them, and might even do them and the epistemic environment a disservice. To put the point differently, this is enough to make her closed-mindedness a 'burdened' effects-virtue in a hostile epistemic environment.

Now, for some caveats. First, I am not arguing that the knowledge-possessing agent in a hostile environment should be closed-minded in *every* domain or possess the *general* disposition of closed-mindedness. Rather, I am arguing that she should be closed-minded about relevant intellectual options that conflict with what she already knows. That will cover *many* domains, since the environment is hostile. Still, she can be largely *open*-minded in the way she conducts her own intellectual projects or her projects with epistemically reliable allies – here, she should still brainstorm relevant options. Nor must she give up open-mindedness as a valued goal for herself or the environment. Even if she can't make her hostile environment more open-minded by being an exemplar of open-mindedness herself – by engaging seriously with deluded or incompetent others and the fabrications they endorse – she may try to facilitate open-mindedness in other ways. (Perhaps, populating the environment with truths, to compete with the received falsehoods, would be a start.)

Second, I am not arguing that the knowledge-possessing agent should abandon her motivation for truth or develop epistemic motivations that are intrinsically bad. I am not advocating that she develop the responsibilist vice of closed-mindedness. I am only arguing that in hostile environments, her disposition of closed-mindedness will minimize the production of bad epistemic *effects*.

Nor, third, am I arguing that morally, pragmatically, or politically, the knowledge-possessing agent should be closed-minded. Rather, I am merely arguing that she has epistemic reasons to be closed-minded. Closed-mindedness on the part of the knowledge-possessing agent minimizes bad *epistemic* effects for the agent herself, and may also minimize bad epistemic effects for other agents, and the environment. If closed-mindedness produces bad moral, pragmatic, and political effects in hostile environments (or our *current* environment), those will need to be weighed against, and may trump, its epistemic effects.

Fourth, importantly, I advise caution in any attempts to apply the claims above to our current epistemic environment. Our current epistemic environment is not 'hostile' (for members of dominant groups), as I am using that term. It may be moderately polluted, but it isn't extremely polluted – it isn't utterly saturated with false and unreliable options in the way that Orwell's Oceania and Judge's Idiocracy are. This has two repercussions for attempts to apply the claims above. First, options like 'the earth is flat' may not be pervasive enough in our current environment to count as epistemically relevant. If they don't count as epistemically relevant, then in ignoring them, we aren't being closed-minded. Accordingly, the claims above would fail to apply: since we wouldn't be closed-minded in ignoring flat-earthers, the issue of whether we should be never gets off the ground. But, second, even if some misguided options ('Donald Trump is a good President') are pervasive enough in our current environment to count as relevant, and even if we are closed-minded in ignoring them, our closed-mindedness might produce different epistemic effects than it did above. We will need to ask whether, *in our current environment*, closed-mindedness on the part of the knowledge-possessing agent will minimize bad epistemic effects for other agents. It may not. After all, a proportion of Trump-voters can be convinced otherwise – engaging with them may ultimately produce a preponderance of good epistemic effects *for them*. Likewise, we will need to ask whether closed-mindedness on the part of knowledge-possessing agents will minimize bad epistemic effects *for our current environment*. Again, it may not; if it is corrupting – if it facilitates closed-mindedness – it may not minimize bad epistemic effects.

Fifth, one might worry that the reasoning above could be used by far-right conservatives to justify their closed-mindedness. Consider, for instance, religious fundamentalists who deny the rights of women. Such conservatives, believing that they are in a hostile environment and that they have knowledge, could defend their closed-mindedness on those grounds. In reply, their beliefs would be false. They are not in a hostile environment, nor are they knowledge-possessing agents – their beliefs about women are false. Nor would their closed-mindedness minimize the production of bad epistemic effects. Quite the contrary! It would be akin to Paul's closed-mindedness, and to epistemic injustice, which are effects-*vices*, not effects-virtues. Recall that effects-virtues and effects-vices are defined externally (along reliabilist lines). So, even if these conservatives *believed* that their closed-mindedness was an effects-virtue, they would be wrong. This is a strength of epistemic externalism. Granted, those of us on the progressive end of the political spectrum (who are in dominant groups) aren't in a hostile environment either (see point four). This means we also need to exercise caution (even when we have knowledge) – we, too, should avoid jumping to the conclusion that we are in a hostile environment that justifies our closed-mindedness.

This brings us to a final set of open questions, which are well worth exploring. How does one *know* whether one is in a hostile environment? And, relatedly, how does one *know* whether one's closed-mindedness would be intellectually virtuous or vicious – how does one *know* when one should be closed-minded? The virtue epistemologist's answer is that one will need to do what an open-minded person would do – engage with relevant options – in order to know whether one is in a hostile environment. Likewise, for knowing the epistemic effects of one's closed-mindedness (where this is an admitted weakness of epistemic externalism and of consequentialist views more broadly.) This doesn't mean that such knowledge requires possessing the general disposition of open-mindedness. But, it does mean that those who already possess the general disposition of closed-mindedness will have a tough time gaining such knowledge. Breaking that cycle might require finding a cure for closed-mindedness.

In sum, I have argued that in standard cases, including Paul's, the disposition of closed-mindedness is an intellectual vice. But, I have also argued that closed-mindedness can be intellectually virtuous. In ordinary environments, some one-off instances of closed-minded action will produce a preponderance of good epistemic effects. Moreover, in epistemically hostile environments, the disposition of closed-mindedness will be an effects-virtue, albeit a 'burdened' one.[41]

University of Connecticut
heather.battaly@uconn.edu

[41] Thanks to Teresa Allen, Simon Barker, Sven Bernecker, Noell Birondo, Paul Bloomfield, Charlie Crerar, Amy Flowerree, Trystan Goetze, Heidi Grasswick, Thomas Grundmann, Raja Halwani, Michael Lynch, Toby Napoletano, Christopher Thi Nguyen, Ryan Nichols, Howard Nye, Alicia Patterson, Clifford Roth, Catherine Saint-Croix, Lionel Shapiro, Alessandra Tanesini, Etsuko Taylor, Jon Taylor, Cody Turner, Lani Watson, Dennis Whitcomb, Sarah Wright, an anonymous referee, and audiences at the Epistemic Harms and Wrong Conference (Sheffield 2017), the 2018 Central APA, the Political Polarization and Epistemic Arrogance Conference (UConn 2018), Azusa Pacific University, Vanderbilt University, the Fake Knowledge conference (Cologne 2018), and the University of Connecticut.

Caring for Esteem and Intellectual Reputation: Some Epistemic Benefits and Harms

ALESSANDRA TANESINI

Abstract

This paper has five aims: it clarifies the nature of esteem and of the related notions of admiration and reputation (sect. 1); it argues that communities that possess practices of esteeming individuals for their intellectual qualities are epistemically superior to otherwise identical communities lacking this practice (sect. 2) and that a concern for one's own intellectual reputation, and a motivation to seek the esteem and admiration of other members of one's community, can be epistemically virtuous (sect. 3); it explains two vices regarding these concerns for one's own intellectual reputation and desire for esteem: intellectual vanity and intellectual timidity (sect. 4); finally (sect. 5), it offers an account of some of the epistemic harms caused by these vices.

The desire to be esteemed and have a good reputation is a common feature of academic life. Intellectuals are often obsessed with being acknowledged, cited, read and discussed. Such concerns are not surprising since several aspects of academic careers depend on reputation. Markers of esteem figure implicitly or explicitly in promotion decisions, and in the award of research grants. Information about these is collected by universities, requested by governments, and used to produce reputational rankings. Hence, *ceteris paribus*, being esteemed and having a good reputation are of prudential value to those whose professional lives are dedicated to the acquisition and transmission of knowledge and understanding. It is therefore no surprise that intellectuals seek to obtain these accolades.

Being esteemed and having a good reputation are also epistemically valuable because they are evidence of the quality of one's performance, the reliability of one's abilities or the trustworthiness of one's opinions. Individuals often rely on others' judgments, as manifested in expressions of esteem and admiration, to gauge the value of their own achievements. For example, a scientist may develop an appreciation of the full significance of her discovery by first noting that it has earned her the esteem of other scientists whom she admires.

Facts about the esteem and reputation in which individuals are held can also be valuable evidence when trying to ascertain whom to

doi:10.1017/S1358246118000541

believe among disagreeing parties. When one is not able to judge independently the likely truth of the views expressed in a debate, one may rationally rely on the reputations of the conflicting parties to decide whose opinion, if any, to accept. Hence, the existence within a community of a practice of esteeming is of epistemic value to its members.

The desire to be esteemed, however, can be at the root of vicious, including intellectually vicious, behaviour. It has a prominent place in the psychology of those who are best described as vain, who suffer from envy and are inordinately keen to impress. However, deliberate concealment to prevent others from making esteem-based judgements about oneself is also vicious. I label this vice 'timidity'. Both vanity and timidity have distorting influences on the relations of dependence that hold among members of epistemic communities. Vain individuals, unless exposed, may be taken to be more reliable, trustworthy or intellectually excellent than they are; those who are timid may not be called upon, because presumed to be ignorant, when they could supply valuable information. In this and other ways, vanity and timidity are obstacles to effective and responsible enquiry. That is, enquiry which is knowledge-conducive, sensitive to the evidence, careful and in other ways respectful of the obligations that bind epistemic subjects.[1]

This paper has five aims. The first is to clarify the nature of esteem and of the related notions of reputation and admiration (sect. 1). The second is to argue that communities which possess practices of esteeming individuals for their intellectual qualities are epistemically superior to otherwise identical communities lacking this practice (sect. 2). The third is to show that a concern with one's own intellectual reputation, and a motivation to seek the esteem and admiration of other members of one's community, can be epistemically virtuous (sect. 3). The fourth is to discuss two vices regarding these concerns for one's own intellectual reputation and desire for esteem. They are intellectual vanity and intellectual timidity (sect. 4). Finally (sect. 5), the paper explains some of the damaging effects of these vices on the relations of epistemic dependence among members of epistemic communities.

---

[1]   See Q. Cassam, 'Vice Epistemology', *The Monist* **99** (2016), 159–180 for a defence of the view that intellectual character vices are character traits that are an impediment to effective and responsible enquiry. Although I do not fully endorse his account, it provides a useful way to approach the issues with which I am concerned in this paper.

Caring for Esteem and Intellectual Reputation

1. Esteem, Reputation, and Admiration

In this section I define esteem as a positive or negative attitude, directed at a person, group or institution for their good or bad qualities.[2] I distinguish it from related notions such as reputation and admiration. I discuss some of its manifestations and bring to light some of the ways in which being esteemed is of prudential value.[3]

Observing people who seem good (or bad) in some respect, or are performing some action to a high (or low) standard, generally moves us to respond in positive or (negative) ways. We are impressed by the person who can skilfully juggle five balls; we applaud those who can overcome adversity; and we are full of admiration for those who excel in academic pursuits. These responses are typically based on comparative evaluations of another's performance with our own abilities.[4] I take these reactions to be expressions of esteem or disesteem.[5]

The qualities that attract esteem are diverse. Some are categorical: e.g., having sailed single-handedly around the globe. Only few people have achieved this feat. Those who have are generally held in high esteem by the many who have not, as well as by their peers. Other qualities belong to continua and attract esteem in proportion to the perceived nature of the accomplishment. For example, professional players of musical instruments are generally held in esteem by members of the public, but virtuoso players attract higher levels of esteem since they are esteemed more highly and by a larger group of people that includes highly accomplished players. Further, esteem can be bestowed because of positional features such as being the winner of a race, or the first to make a discovery.

---

[2]   My focus in this paper is exclusively with esteem conferred by individuals upon other individuals.

[3]   Conferring esteem upon others may also be of prudential value when, for example, it induces them to reciprocate. My discussion in this section is indebted to the account of the economy of esteem developed by G. Brennan and P. Pettit, *The Economy of Esteem: An Essay on Civil and Political Society* (Oxford: Oxford University Press, 2004).

[4]   There is empirical evidence that humans assess other people's qualities by comparing them to oneself rather than by adopting objective standards of evaluation. See D. Dunning and A. F. Hayes, 'Evidence for Egocentric Comparison in Social Judgment', *Journal of Personality and Social Psychology* **71** (1996), 213–29.

[5]   In what follows, for the sake of brevity, I shall often use 'esteem' as a shorthand for 'esteem or disesteem'.

Alessandra Tanesini

So understood, esteem is a psychological state of taking a positive or negative stance toward other people based on the judgment that they possess qualities perceived as good or bad that make them a model or exemplar to imitate or to distance oneself from.

Esteem and reputation have normative dimensions since their conferral or withdrawal can be warranted or unwarranted. Esteem may be misguided when it is based on judgments which are false or inaccurate. For example, a plagiarist, whose fraud lies undiscovered, might be esteemed by many for his originality because they wrongly rate him highly in this regard. Conversely, it is possible that someone is not esteemed because her abilities are underestimated.

Esteem is closely associated with admiration. Both are directed at individuals whom one represents as models or exemplars that are worthy of emulation.[6] The attitude of admiration, however, differs from esteem in at least two respects. Firstly, admiration is a more positive attitude than mere esteem. We admire those we hold in high esteem. Secondly, admiration, unlike esteem, can accrue to people for features, such as some aspects of physical appearance or (if such a thing exists) natural talent, that are not even the indirect long-range result of voluntary activities designed to bring them about. Esteem, and its self-regarding equivalent proper pride, seems instead to be exclusively directed at qualities for which the agent can take credit.[7]

Esteem can be a fleeting attitude since it can be directed toward someone whom we would be unable to re-identify. For example, one may esteem an anonymous donor. Anonymity, however, prevents the gesture from contributing to the person's reputation. This latter is the socially shared equivalent of being the recipient of esteem. In general, a person may be said to possess a (good or bad) reputation when numerous members of the community esteem her, and at least some of these members base their esteem at least in part on the testimony of others.[8] Hence, attributions of esteem are not

---

[6] The connection between admiration and the desire to emulate is defended by L. Zagzebski in 'I – Admiration and the Admirable', *Aristotelian Society Supplementary Volume* **89** (2015), 205–21. Similarly, those who are held in disesteem are singled out as cautionary bad examples.

[7] Much more would need to be said to defend these claims. See Brennan and Pettit, *The Economy of Esteem*, 21–22, and A. Tanesini, 'Intellectual Humility as Attitude', *Philosophy and Phenomenological Research* **96**.2 (2018), 399–420, at 403–4.

[8] I use 'testimony' here rather broadly to include assertions testifying that one holds someone in esteem and other speech acts such as expressions of admiration.

always exclusively based on independent evaluations of others' qualities; they can also be partly based on information about whom others esteem. Learning that a person, whom we esteem in some regard, holds someone else in esteem for the same feature, gives us some defeasible evidence for esteeming the person who has this reputation. It also offers some evidence that such person is likely to be excellent in the relevant respect since she is held as a standard by someone who is herself a model for some.[9]

While esteem itself is a psychological state, it finds its expression in several verbal and non-verbal behaviours. I shall refer to these varied outward expressions of esteem and reputation as their markers.[10] I have chosen this term, rather than the commonly used 'indicator', to distinguish clearly actions and statuses which are marks of esteem and reputation from esteem itself as a psychological state which is an indicator of the presence of some notable feature. In short, markers of esteem are twice removed from the properties they are intended to track.[11]

Individuals mark the esteem in which they hold other people through their words and actions.[12] These include speech acts such as expressing one's admiration and asserting that the individuals in question are excellent or exceptional. Other markers of esteem in conversation include deference to the opinions of esteemed individuals. Those who are powerful and possess a good reputation also have other means at their disposal to bestow markers of esteem. They may invite esteemed individuals to become members of a research group; they may seek their views on a given topic.[13]

Often these gestures are reciprocated so that networks are created that enhance the reputation of all the agents involved. For example, the author of a book may suggest to the publisher that another

---

[9] When good or bad reputations become common knowledge, they can be described as fame or infamy. See, Brennan and Pettit, *The Economy of Esteem*, 57.

[10] Brennan and Pettit, *The Economy of Esteem*, at 55 and *passim* refer to these markers as esteem services.

[11] Barring insincerity, esteem markers manifest esteem. Esteem itself, however, may fail to track qualities that are worthy of it. This happens when one esteems someone, although this person is not worthy of esteem or vice versa.

[12] Markers of admiration are often also as markers of esteem.

[13] Other kinds of esteem markers include prizes, honours, credentials and giving credit to someone for a discovery or an innovation. See K. J. S. Zollman, 'The Credit Economy and the Economic Rationality of Science', *Journal of Philosophy* **115** (2018), 5–33, for a discussion of the epistemic value of the credit motive in science.

specialist is asked to write the blurb. The endorsement by an esteemed specialist clearly would enhance the reputation of the writer of the monograph; but it also strengthens and reaffirms the reputation of the author of the blurb as someone whose opinion of other people's work counts. In this manner, both parties gain reputational enhancement from the transaction. This example also illustrates an instance when markers of esteem do not merely track pre-existing attitudes of holding a person in esteem. Instead, the presence of esteem markers can also contribute to enhancing reputation by broadcasting that a person is esteemed by esteemed individuals.

It should by now be obvious that there are numerous advantages to being esteemed and having a good reputation. Some are straightforwardly financial. Some esteem markers such as prizes and promotions involve monetary gains, these markers track (to some extent) pre-existing attributions of esteem which it is therefore advantageous to have. The prudential benefits that accrue to being esteemed go beyond financial incentives. People who are held in esteem are generally better treated by others who are therefore more attentive to their needs, and more forgiving. Fame and reputation also open doors so that one may find it easier to get what one wants. In addition, people who are held in esteem are more trusted, and thus likely to gain the cooperation of others when they need it. In sum, being esteemed is, in normal circumstances, a prudential good.

2. The Epistemology of Esteeming

In this section I argue that the practice of esteeming each other is generally epistemically valuable in epistemic communities whose members have finite resources and limited abilities. In many of our activities we rely on reputation to make choices and achieve our goals. For instance, we depend on word of mouth to select a dentist or an electrician. This kind of information is of great assistance because knowing that another person holds a third in esteem is defeasible evidence that that individual is worthy of the accolade. In what follows, I restrict my discussion of the epistemic value of the practice of esteeming to activities whose goal is distinctively epistemic such as the acquisition of understanding or knowledge, the transmission of information, or the formulation of good and precise research questions.

When engaging in enquiry or in other activities whose goals are epistemic, individuals often rely on other people for pertinent information, for informed and constructive challenges to their views, or for suggestions about avenues of further enquiry. Such reliance is both widespread and inevitable. It is also becoming more extensive with the rise in the specialisation of knowledge. Since no single person can be an expert even about all topics within one's own discipline, reliance on the results achieved by others, and trust in their testimony are pervasive features of contemporary intellectual lives.

Increasing specialization intensifies the reliance of members of epistemic communities on each other at the same time as it makes it harder to make reasoned judgements about whom to trust.[14] Individuals are often faced with the task of adjudicating between contradictory testimonies, or of deciding whether to change their pre-existing opinions in the light of the views expressed by their critics. It is not always feasible or possible to proceed by assessing independently the likely truth of the views themselves. One may lack either the resources or the knowledge required rationally to evaluate the positions at hand. Further, one may also be unable to evaluate the competence of the disagreeing would-be experts.

In some of these cases esteem supplies evidence that assists one's evaluation. Often we need to assess the testimony of so-called experts about whom we have not ourselves formed any evaluative belief at all. Markers of esteem, admiration and of reputation are especially helpful in these cases. For example, if I know that a colleague admires another researcher for her expertise or intellectual integrity because I have heard him praise her for these qualities, I have some additional evidence to accept, or at least take seriously, the views of the esteemed individual. Praise is evidence that the colleague esteems this researcher; and the colleague's esteem is evidence that the researcher is worthy of it. Such evidence is defeasible. My colleague may be a bad judge of people's abilities and intellectual characters. He may be biased or insincere. Even so, relevant esteem markers often provide some evidence for trusting the claims made by an esteemed person.

One may wonder whether we should rely on our practices of attributing esteem and reputation since we may suspect them to be marred by self-serving motives and by systemic biases and prejudices, both conscious and not.[15] In response I wish to make two related points.

---

[14] A. I. Goldman, 'Experts: Which Ones Should You Trust?', in A. I. Goldman and D. Whitcomb (eds.), *Social Epistemology: Essential Readings* (Oxford: Oxford University Press, 2011), 109–133.

[15] The presence of these problems is well-established. For a review of bias in peer review see C. J. Lee, C. R. Sugimoto, G. Zhang and B. Cronin, 'Bias in Peer Review', *Journal of the American Society for Information Science and Technology* **64** (2013), 2–17. For a powerful argument that less powerful individuals receive less credit or esteem than they

First, I acknowledge that in communities, where individuals' concern for esteem is vicious, the practice of esteeming can go badly awry by becoming utterly unreliable. In such cases, the harms generated by the practice may outweigh the benefits it brings in its trail. When this occurs, it may be epistemically prudent to suspend one's reliance on the practice. In this paper, I shall not try to ascertain whether one should adopt this stance toward the practices of esteeming in use in current academic communities, for instance. Instead, I leave this empirical issue as an open question. It is a question that is partly to be settled by establishing whether the vicious traits discussed in the fourth section below are widespread.

Second, I defend the claim that an epistemic community of individuals who have finite cognitive powers, care for knowledge and understanding, but also for esteem and reputation, without attempting to earn undeserved accolades, is superior to another otherwise identical community in which people have no concern for others' opinion of them. Several considerations speak in favour of this claim. The difficulties highlighted above faced by lay persons when assessing conflicting claims by self-proclaimed experts are pressing and not easily resolvable. The presence of a practice of esteeming others in a community offers a solution to this problem. Since esteem markers are more easily observable than the features they indicate, they prove to be epistemically valuable especially in communities characterised by highly specialised knowledge domains. So, if attributions of esteem are somewhat reliable, an epistemic community that has a practice of esteeming is superior to one without this practice.

In addition, we should expect esteeming practices to be reasonably reliable whenever individuals care to be esteemed but also to be worthy of that esteem. The argument for this claim depends on the intermediary conclusion that the esteem motive supplies a prudential reason that favours basing one's esteem of others at least partly on independent evaluations. Hence, widely shared reputational judgments deserve the trust that befits consensual, yet independent, opinions.

These points are based on the observation that reputation and esteem are scarce goods. Firstly, they are scarce because to earn them, one must be noticed. Since attentional resources are finite, the more attention is given to one person or group, the less is available

---

are due for their contributions to collaborative research see J. Bruner and C. O'Connor, 'Power, Bargaining, and Collaboration', in T. Boyer, C. Mayo-Wilson and M. Weisberg (eds.), *Scientific Collaboration and Collective Knowledge*, (Oxford: Oxford University Press, 2017), 135–157.

for others. Secondly, esteem and reputation are also scarce because they are essentially based on favourable comparisons. Since to esteem someone is to think of her as a model, typically esteem is conferred by each person only to a limited number of individuals.[16] Further, reputation requires the one is esteemed by many in a community and that at least some of these evaluations are partly based on knowing that other esteemed individuals hold that person in esteem. Knowing that a person whom I esteem for a given quality takes another person to be an example gives me a reason not only to esteem this individual but also to presume that she is likely to be excellent in the relevant respect since she is held as an example by those whom I take to be exemplar. Hence, as a person's reputation rises, that of some others is likely to fall since the group of those who are thought to be among the best for some quality or ability cannot indefinitely increase. Thirdly, sometimes esteem is allocated for one's position in a ranking such as being the winner in a context. When esteem is explicitly positional, one gains it to the exclusion of all others.[17]

Esteem testimonials sometimes can raise the reputations of the person who confers the esteem and of the one receiving it. Hence, the scarcity of esteem does not entail that if I express my esteem for you, the esteem in which I am held by others must automatically suffer. However, unless the context is such that the granting of esteem is mutually advantageous, competition entails that when one bestows esteem upon another for possessing some good feature, one runs the risk of seeing that the extent to which one is esteemed for the same quality is somewhat reduced.[18] For example, if I heap admiration on a colleague for his original ideas, I may be instrumental in drawing attention to his work and away from mine. I could thus contribute to lessening my reputation.

These considerations show that any marking of esteem in words or deeds can lead to shifts in the distribution of esteem in which people are held with some emerging as winners and others as losers. This feature of the economy of esteem indicates that, barring evidence of mutual recognitional gain, when individuals express their esteem

---

[16] It is extremely unlikely that any one person would regard everyone else as their model regarding a relevant good feature.
[17] See Ch. 1 of Brennan and Pettit, *The Economy of Esteem*. The notion of credit as discussed by Zollman, 'The Credit Economy' is also positional.
[18] It is worth noting therefore that esteem is different from attributions of credibility or of authority. If I find a person more credible or authoritative than I did before, there need not be another person whose standing by my lights is therefore diminished.

Alessandra Tanesini

for others with whom they are in competition for reputation, they defeasibly can be presumed to be sincere and their relevant judgments, if in agreement, can be assumed to be reasonably reliable.

Suppose a person A conveys to another D, that she (A) holds an individual C in esteem and that B does too, what should D conclude based on this information? Given competition among A, B and C over being esteemed with regard to the same quality, D has reasons to believe that A is sincere in her claim that she esteems C for that feature and that she believes that B does too. By conveying her esteem for C, and by offering further support that C is worthy of esteem by reporting B's attitude, A knowingly runs the risk of lessening her own reputation. Given these incentives, A's testimony is likely to be sincere since in giving it she is going against her self-interest.

Facts about competition also give D a reason to believe that A's esteem of C is at least partly independent of B's attitude toward C under the assumption that A cares for her reputation. Since A has a concern for her reputation, learning that B esteems C, she learns of a fact that potentially puts at risk something that she cares about. The presence of risk means that much is at stake for A in B's testimony. Therefore, A is unlikely to accept uncritically that C is worthy of esteem on B's saying-so. These considerations give D a defeasible reason to believe that A and B's evaluations of C are at least in part independently arrived at. Therefore, reports about a person's reputation coming from various sources can be presumed not to be entirely derivative. So, the audience of such reports, especially if they are numerous, has a defeasible reason to believe that they are not in the position of the person who checks the reliability of a newspaper report by buying another copy of the same edition of the same newspaper. This feature of judgements about esteem means that one can presume that when an assessment of esteem is shared and grows into a reputation, one can put some trust in numbers since the incentives of competition make it probable that the agreeing sources are somewhat independent of each other in their assessments.

These considerations do not rule out the possibility of run-away backscratching through the creation of communities of mutual admiration. Such situations can always occur especially when individuals in an epistemic community are motivated to seek to be esteemed regardless of whether they are worthy of it. However, the arguments above show that these epistemically negative results are not inevitable. In addition, there are reputational risks to bestowing esteem in a self-serving manner. The person, who writes a positive endorsement to a book which is subsequently widely judged to be terrible, would see her reputation suffer since she may be thought to

have bad judgement or disreputable intentions. In sum, since bestowing esteem in a self-serving manner is widely disapproved,
there are self-serving reasons not to engage openly in this kind of behaviour. Dissimulation, of course, remains a possibility but it is a
strategy that makes one vulnerable to being found out. This is a
serious risk since dissimulation itself attract further disapprobation.

The argument so far seeks to establish that epistemic communities
where people care about reputation and have thus developed practices
of esteeming others are epistemically superior to similar communities
in which the practice has not developed because agents do not care for
reputation. The argument is based on the incentives provided by
competition over esteem and reputation. Provided individuals seek
to be esteemed only to the extent to which they are worthy of it, the
esteem motive promotes both the sincerity and the reliability of reputational claims about which there is broad consensus.

3. The Value of Being Esteemed

In this section I discuss the epistemic value of being esteemed before
arguing that desiring to be the object of others' esteem is also epistemically valuable. Finally, having established that being esteemed and
having a reputation are epistemic goods, I argue that they can be rationally and virtuously pursued, and explain what such pursuit may
involve.[19]

While there are community-wide epistemic advantages that result
from adopting a practice of esteeming, being the object of others'
esteem is of epistemic value to the individual in two further distinctive ways. First, others' esteem supplies information about oneself that
aids the acquisition of self-knowledge. Second, the desire to be esteemed by others provides an incentive to raise performance and
become a better epistemic agent.[20]

---

[19] Aristotle makes this point when he states that loving honours in the
right amount and when conferred by the right people is a virtue which
is flanked by two vices: that of the honour-lover who aims at 'honour
more than is right, and from the wrong sources', and that of the person
who is indifferent to deserved honour. Aristotle, *Nichomachean Ethics*,
T. Irwin (trans.) (Cambridge: Hackett Publishing Company, 1985),
1125b 1–25.
[20] This desire is likely to be qualified along several dimensions. One
may desire to receive positive evaluations for some features, whilst not
caring very much about other qualities. One may seek the esteem of some

Alessandra Tanesini

First, in normal circumstances, when a person discovers that she is esteemed by others for some quality, she acquires evidence about others' opinion of her and also about herself. That is, she can treat their marks of esteem as expressing their esteem (disesteem) for her, which is to say their belief that she possesses some good or bad feature. Further, she can take their esteem as offering some defeasible evidence that she possesses the quality for which they esteem her. Therefore, knowing about the esteem in which others hold one promotes the acquisition of self-knowledge.

Second, wanting to be esteemed is an incentive to raise one's performance and improve since others esteem only good performances and admire excellence. It may be objected that although the desire to be esteemed is an additional motive for performing, it leads to raised performance only if the agent would otherwise lack sufficient motivation to strive to improve. Whilst this objection is well-taken, its scope is somewhat limited. Human agents, even when motivated to seek knowledge and understanding, are often prone to temptations to cut corners. Given this generally accepted fact about human psychology, the desire to be esteemed is a powerful incentive to raise one's game.

If this is right, the practice of esteeming is, at least in the absence of systematic self-serving biases and prejudices, epistemically valuable to those communities that adopt it. In addition, both being the object of esteem and having a desire to be esteemed are of epistemic value to individuals because they are instrumental to self-knowledge and to improved performance.

Yet it may seem that esteem and reputation cannot be virtuously (or even rationally) pursued.[21] There is a difference between demonstrating one's abilities in front of an audience and behaving in a way that is designed to attract approval or praise. The person who is seeking to be esteemed engages in behaviour of the second kind as well as of the first. It is precisely this desire to be praised or admired that is said to be not impressive. In short, despite the prudential and epistemic values that accrue to being esteemed and having a reputation, it would seem that one cannot rationally take their acquisition to be an explicit goal of one's activities unless one, at the same time,

---

people but not value the opinion of others. Finally, and most importantly, one may desire esteem only if it is deserved, rather than at any cost.

[21]   See J. Elster, *Sour Grapes: Studies in the Subversion of Rationality* (Cambridge: Cambridge University Press, 1983).

conceals one's motivations. The desire for esteem, therefore, appears to be essentially self-stultifying.

This conclusion is premature. There are cases in which behaviour that is transparently motivated by the desire to be esteemed attracts no disapproval. For example, the woman who draws attention to her, unjustly neglected, contribution to a collective success may be admired for her courage and gain a larger share of esteem without suffering any reputational damage because of her self-publicity. More generally, at least in contemporary Western societies, there is no automatic disapprobation for presenting oneself in one's best light in front of an audience with the intention that one's good features are noticed. What is frowned upon is the desire to draw attention to one's own good features in an unfair attempt either to divert attention from the achievements of others, or to showcase our successes in a manner that is at least likely to mislead about their significance.

The desire to be esteemed goes hand in hand with the desire to gain others' evaluative respect which is respect that accords with one's admirable features.[22] Demanding that one is accorded respect which is calibrated to one's actual intellectual worth is not vicious; rather, it may be a requirement of self-respect. Since it is impossible to receive this kind of respect when one is unnoticed, behaving in a way designed to highlight one's good features in front of others, is compatible with possessing a virtuous psychology. However, this is so only when the desire to be esteemed is accompanied also by the desire to be worthy of the esteem one seeks.

One might object that, since positive esteem is allocated only to performances and qualities that are highly rated, to desire to be esteemed is to want to be seen to be better than some other people. However, one may add, the possession of this desire is incompatible with humility. True; wanting to be thought to be better than others can lead to bragging. It is also generally considered unimpressive. However, to seek to be esteemed is to want a positive evaluation because of one's qualities. This is not the same as wanting to appear to be better than others. One may have the first desire without the second. This might be true even though one may also realise that unless one's

---

[22] For a discussion of distinct kinds of respect see R. S. Dillon, 'Kant on Arrogance and Self-Respect', in C. Calhoun (ed.), *Setting the Moral Compass: Essays by Women Philosophers*, (Oxford: Oxford University Press, 2004), 191–216. For some connections between arrogance and disrespect see also A. Tanesini, 'I – "Calm Down, Dear": Intellectual Arrogance, Silencing and Ignorance', *Aristotelian Society Supplementary Volume* **90** (2016), 71–92.

Alessandra Tanesini

audience thinks that one is better than some people, its members are not going to hold one in high esteem. Hence, to want to be esteemed is not clearly incompatible with humility and may at least in some circumstances be required by proper pride.[23]

One may also object to the view that esteem can be virtuously desired on the grounds that virtue requires that one is motivated by the desire for some final or intrinsic good whilst esteem would seem to be prudentially valuable and its epistemic value is at best instrumental. In response one may reject the presumption that good motives are a requirement of virtue. The identification of intellectual vices as obstacles to effective and responsible enquiry that I have adopted in this paper invites exactly such a response. That is, one may propose that esteem is virtuously pursued whenever in ordinary circumstances it reliably leads to good epistemic effects.[24]

However, a supporter of a motivational account of virtue can also address this objection by drawing attention to the connection between esteem and evaluative respect. Respect, like esteem, requires that one is paid attention to, since to demand respect is to demand that one is noticed rather than ignored. The connection between esteem and respect is even deeper since the latter can be thought of as the tribute that others attribute to merit, and those who receive it acquire a good whose value is arguably not purely prudential or instrumental. Therefore, when - and to the extent in which - seeking esteem is desiring only that one is given credit for those among one's features which are worthy of esteem, it can be thought as a desire for an intrinsic good. In short, the desire to be esteemed can be virtuous when it consists in desiring other people's evaluative respect.[25]

---

[23] More needs to be said to support this claim. It is opposed by R. C. Roberts and W. J. Wood, *Intellectual Virtues: An Essay in Regulative Epistemology* (New York: Oxford University Press, 2007), 239. See Tanesini, 'Intellectual Humility as Attitude' for a defence.
[24] This position would be a kind of virtue reliabilism. For a useful characterisation see H. Battaly, 'Epistemic Virtue and Vice: Reliabilism, Responsibilism, and Personalism', in C. Mi, M. Slote and E. Sosa (eds.), *Moral and Intellectual Virtues in Western and Chinese Philosophy* (London: Routledge, 2016), 99–120.
[25] I wish to thank Charlie Crerar for pushing me to consider these issues. There are further complications here since virtue may require that not only one desires esteem in the right way but also from the right people. I shall ignore this issue here.

Caring for Esteem and Intellectual Reputation

4. The Vices of Esteem: Vanity and Timidity

Some desires for esteem are vicious. In this section I focus on the kinds of desire for esteem associated with two vices of self-presentation. These are: intellectual vanity and intellectual timidity. Vanity involves a positive evaluation of one's own intellectual character, an unwillingness to accept or own one's limitations, and an engrossing desire to be held in high esteem.[26] Intellectual timidity is the opposite of vanity since it is associated with a negative self-evaluation, and a resigned acceptance of one's real or presumed limitations. It finds expression in a desire not to be noticed and a fear of others' evaluation of the self.[27]

To get a grip on intellectual vanity, it is helpful to highlight some of its behavioural manifestations. The intellectually vain person constantly compares herself to others. Consider, for example, a person who often checks her h-index on the software *Publish or Perish*, or who always first opens a book in her area of research at the index pages merely to check whether she is cited in it. Not everyone who checks these things is vain, but those who are overwhelmingly preoccupied with them usually are. These people clearly are prepared to trade-off knowledge and understanding for their reputations.[28]

One of the defining features of intellectual vanity is an inability to accept one's intellectual limitations.[29] This inability is not the same as a tendency to have false beliefs which underestimate one's limitations or overestimate one's intellectual strengths. Rather, it is manifested either by obsessing about defects that others would consider to be trivial, or by being in denial about the existence of any such

---

[26]   Vanity may not be the only vice characterised by a consuming desire to be esteemed. There might be others which do not share the other two features of vanity highlighted here.

[27]   Fear may not be the only motive. Thus, there may be vices of deficient concern for others' esteem other than timidity.

[28]   A. T. Nuyen, 'Vanity', *The Southern Journal of Philosophy* **37** (1999), 613–627; V. Tiberius and J. D. C. Walker, 'Arrogance', *American Philosophical Quarterly* **35** (1998), 379–390; and S. L. Bartky, 'Narcissism, Femininity and Alienation', *Social Theory and Practice* **8** (1982), 127–143 offer some discussion of the topic. None focus on the intellectual variety of this vice. An exception is M. Kieran, 'Creativity, Vanity, Narcissism', in B. Gaut and M. Kieran (eds.), *Creativity and Philosophy* (London: Routledge, 2017), 74–92.

[29]   It is therefore opposed to humility as the latter is understood by D. Whitcomb et al. 'Intellectual Humility: Owning Our Limitations', *Philosophy and Phenomenological Research* **94** (2017), 509–39.

Alessandra Tanesini

faults. A vain person, for example, may become obsessed with a small defect and feel very embarrassed and ashamed by it. At the root of this obsession is the fear that others may notice this limitation and evaluate her accordingly. Her reaction to this blemish may seem to all others totally out of proportion.[30] For example, a person during a talk to an audience of fellow philosophers may fail to give an adequate answer to a question from the audience. In the days ahead, she may focus on this small failure and instead of thinking of a better answer to the question to use on future occasions, she continually revisits the episode, worrying about how it reflects on her reputation.

At the same time, the intellectually vain often seek the spotlight because they want to be the centre of attention. If they succeed in receiving the praise they crave, they may gradually come to believe that they have very few intellectual shortcomings; they may then tend to ignore their defects or suppress any evidence of their existence. When it is motivated by a desire to wish away any limitations so that one can gain the admiration of one's peers, behaviour of this sort exemplifies another way in which vanity as a lack of acceptance of one's limitations can manifest itself.

In sum, there are three aspects to intellectual vanity. The first is a sense of self-regard or self-importance which results from a high estimation of one's own qualities shaped by a need to be socially valued or esteemed. The second is an inability to accept one's shortcomings which results in attempts to hide them from view. The third is an all-consuming desire to be admired without caring whether one is worthy of the admiration, which leads to an excessive focus on comparing oneself with others. Vain individuals therefore often are envious of those who are successful and engage in spiteful behaviour designed to prevent others from receiving the praise that one craves for oneself.[31]

The characterisation offered above helps to distinguish virtuous concern for the esteem of others from vain concern for the same. What characterises the latter is not necessarily the intensity of the

[30] Thanks to J. Adam Carter for this example of vanity.
[31] Theories about the nature of vanity have generally selected one of these aspects as fundamental. For example, Roberts and Wood, (*Intellectual Virtues*, 237) define vanity 'an excessive concern to be well regarded by other people'; Walker and Tiberius ('Arrogance', 383) think of it as 'having an excessively high self-estimation'. In my view, vanity is not a matter of thinking too well of oneself or of being too concerned that others' think highly of one, instead it is a matter of developing a positive self-assessment which is driven by others' alleged perception of the self.

62

desire for esteem. Rather, the distinguishing features of this desire are: its disregard for being worthy of the admiration one seeks;[32] its related willingness to receive this admiration at the cost of others' receiving unfair treatment; and an envious attitude that gives rise to spiteful behaviour.[33] In addition, vanity is often accompanied by dissimulation; since envy and the desire to be admired without caring to be admirable are, if uncovered, likely to attract disapproval, vain individuals are unlikely to be open about their motivations.

If vanity is characterised by a desire to grab the spot light of attention, timidity has the opposite effect. Intellectual timidity manifests itself as unwillingness to express one's own opinions, to trust one's own hunches, to show adventurousness in exploring one's trains of thought. The timid lacks conviction in her own opinions, and in her ability to discover the truth. She is riven with doubt and anxiety about the correctness of her views, and she is afraid that her alleged shortcomings might be exposed. For these reasons, she remains silent in conversation, and exhibits conservative dispositions in enquiry. The person who exhibits these tendencies is also likely to be aware that others may form a negative estimation of her intellectual abilities because of her silence. Despite this awareness, the timid keeps herself to herself since she would rather pass unnoticed and unappreciated than risk failure and disapproval.[34]

Although individuals who are timid may believe that they are intellectually inferior to other agents, beliefs of this kind are neither necessary nor sufficient for timidity. Instead, what characterises timidity is fear of criticism which trumps regard for one's intellectual standing in the community. This anxiety gives rise to feelings of self-doubt which in turn heighten anxiety. Thus, timidity is primarily a negative affective stance toward one's own cognitive abilities rather than a set of beliefs about one's intellectual capacities.

---

[32]   Some, including Hume and more recently Kieran 'Creativity' argue that vanity is a vice close to virtue since one can use the desire to be esteemed that is characteristic of vain individuals and rely on it to educate them to care about being worthy of esteem. Hence, vanity can be instrumentally valuable. Nevertheless, the vain desires esteem irrespective of whether it is proportional to the evaluative respect that is due to one.

[33]   On how the desire to be admired can turn into envy see L. Zagzebski, 'I – Admiration and the Admirable'.

[34]   Intellectual timidity is therefore a vice which is also opposed to intellectual courage. It seems possible and plausible that one vice may be opposed to more than one virtue. Timidity is opposed to courage in so far as it exemplifies excessive risk aversion and to proper concern with one's intellectual standing because it exhibits insufficient care for esteem.

Alessandra Tanesini

To appreciate this dynamic, consider the predicament of many young girls when doing mathematics in school. They may have heard that boys are meant to be better than girls at this subject. Hence, girls may experience a certain amount of self-doubt and anxiety in class which may lead to timid attitudes. Thus, imagine one such girl who refrains from raising her hand when the teachers ask questions to the class. Even when she thinks that she may know the answer, her fear of criticism prevents her from putting herself forward. Thus, she avoids being the centre of attention since she perceives the opportunity to be noticed as a risk of being exposed as lacking in talent. Her timidity may be partly the product of her temperament, partly the result of her interpretation of gender norms, and partly still due to the contingencies of her experiences. More darkly, it may also have been in part the result of acts of intimidation. She may have been mocked when she made a mistake in the past or she may have simply sensed that her contributions were not welcomed by classmates or teachers. Either way she has developed a tendency to bite her tongue and hide away.

Unsurprisingly over time this same person may have acquire the belief that she has nothing to say.[35] She may come to the conviction that she lacks ability and that she cannot improve. Once she has moved from mere intellectual timidity to defeatism and resignation that she has little in the way of intellectual strengths she will have become fatalistic in her outlook.[36] Her inability to demand evaluative respect is thus instrumental in her loss of self-respect.

5. Some Epistemic Harms Resulting from Vanity and Timidity

In this closing section I draw on the conclusions defended above to highlight some of the epistemic harms that flow from intellectual vanity and timidity. I presume that everyone has an interest in the acquisition of epistemic goods such as knowledge, information or understanding. When these interests suffer setbacks, individuals are harmed. Some of these harms may be systematic rather than due to

[35]   On this point see Tanesini, '"Calm Down, Dear"'. For a contrasting higher-order evidence account of this psychological transition see Sanford Goldberg, 'Arrogance, Silence, and Silencing', *Proceedings of the Aristotelian Society* **90** (2016), 93–112.
[36]   It should be clear to the reader versed in the literature on implicit bias and stereotype threat that the vice of intellectual timidity is one to which individuals who suffers from stereotype threat may be particularly prone.

the peculiar aspects of a given situation. Further, some harms may also be wrongful; when they are, the person who is harmed epistemically also suffers a wrong. In this paper my focus is exclusively on the systematic epistemic harms caused by vanity and timidity; I set aside all questions of wrongness.

Some of these harms are self-inflicted. Each person has an interest in knowing herself or himself. Both intellectual vanity and timidity are obstacles to the pursuit of self-knowledge. For instance, intellectual vanity promotes the formation of false beliefs about oneself. It is therefore an obstacle to effective and responsible enquiry. To see why this is so, consider that vain individuals seek to be praised. Therefore, they learn to value above all those aspects of themselves that attract the most praise. Thus, their sense of self-worth is excessively bound up with others' esteem of them. However, were they to become aware that they do not deserve the esteem that they have accumulated, the acquisition of this information would make it difficult to sustain their own positive conception of the self. Discovering that others are mistaken in their positive evaluations of the self would undercut one's positive self-esteem because it is largely based on others' positive estimations of the self; but if these are believed to be wrong, it would be unreasonable to rely on them. Therefore, when praise is not commensurate to desert, vain individuals are motivated to ignore any evidence to this effect.

Intellectual timidity is also an impediment to self-knowledge. Those who are timid, and shy away from others' estimation of their features, deny themselves access to relevant evidence about their own intellectual characters. Insofar as others' opinions of us, as manifested in their esteem, are a valuable source of information about the self, intellectual timidity is an obstacle to both effective and responsible enquiry since it makes those who are timid less likely to know truths about themselves and less sensitive to the evidence relevant to acquire such knowledge. In addition, for reasons outlined in section 4 above, intellectually timid individuals are also likely to form several false beliefs about their abilities or expertise. To rationalise their fear of others' judgments, they are likely to underestimate their good qualities.

In sum, intellectual vanity and timidity are sources of epistemic self-harm. Those who possess these traits are likely to engage in wishful thinking and rationalisation; they ignore relevant evidence or deprive themselves of the opportunity to access it. As a result, these individuals harbour numerous false beliefs about themselves, and are limited in their self-knowledge. These setbacks to their epistemic interests are systematic and stubborn because, if the dynamics described above are correct, both vanity and timidity are to some degree stealthy. Vanity blocks in vain individuals the realisation that their sense of self-importance may be due to their vanity rather than to an honest self-assessment of their abilities. Similarly, timidity is an obstacle to the realisation that one's pessimistic assessment of one's intellectual character is the result of timidity. Thus, both vanity and timidity can evade detection in those who suffer from them. It is not impossible for people to come to realise that they are vain or timid, rather it is difficult because of the self-occluding nature of these vices.[37]

Intellectual vanity and timidity are also sources of epistemic harms inflicted upon other members of an epistemic community. I have argued in the second section of this paper that esteem is a valuable, albeit imperfect, indicator of key features of epistemic agents such as reliability and trustworthiness. Markers of esteem, barring dissimulations, are the outward expressions of esteem and are therefore an important source of information about whom to trust and believe. Both vanity and the timidity cause the mis-calibration of esteem so that it becomes a less reliable indicator of those features which would be worthy of esteem. Hence, they degrade the quality of the evidence available to members of the community to assess when they are warranted in relying on others in their enquiries. Vain individuals may engage in dissimulation to big themselves up or they may, out of spite, describe the actions of another person in the worst possible light. Unless exposed, they may succeed in gaining more esteem than they deserve and in depriving others of some esteem to which they are entitled. Consequently, other members of the community may treat some as reliable, who are not, and others as unreliable, when they are reliable. Either way, intellectual vanity is an impediment to effective enquiry since it may lead agents to trust unreliable testimony and distrust testimony which is reliable. Therefore, the widespread presence of vanity in an epistemic community has such a negative impact on its practice of esteeming that it might make it unwise to rely on it.

Intellectual vanity is corrosive of relations of epistemic dependence in other ways. Epistemic communities work better if their members can presume a degree of co-operation and good will. Intellectual

---

[37]   See Q. Cassam, 'Stealthy Vices', *Social Epistemology Review and Reply Collective* **4** (2015), 19–25 and 'Vices of the Mind' (book manuscript) for the point that some vices are stealthy. Stealth is a matter of degree. Other vices, e.g., intellectual arrogance, may be stealthier than either vanity or timidity.

vanity is especially harmful because it is corrosive of these. The harms inflicted by vanity are not nullified by exposure, since other agents' may not trust the apparent esteem that surrounds the vain, but do not thereby acquire the means to assess how reliable or knowledgeable the vain individual may be. Some supremely vain individuals may be genuine authorities in their field, but the lay person is unable to assess this fact, if they cannot independently evaluate track records, and cannot trust reputations.

Individuals who are intellectually timid are reticent to share information or answer questions out of fear to make a mistake or appear stupid. Yet, it is possible that they may alone possess information which would be valuable to other agents. Thus, timid individuals are likely to deprive others of knowledge which is otherwise hard to acquire. In addition, individuals who are timid are unlikely to criticise or question the opinion of other people. Their uncritical stance is a further hindrance to the pursuit of effective and responsible enquiry. These considerations lead to two further questions which I must leave for future research. The first concerns the conditions under which these harms are wrongful. The second regards whether those who wrong others in these ways should always be blamed for these outcomes.

In conclusion, the desire to be held in others' esteem can, contrary to what one may think, be part of a virtuous psychology and yield genuine epistemic benefits to individuals and their communities. When this desire, however, is distorted as is the case for those who are vain and those who are timid, it contributes to traits which, in so far as they are impediments to effective and responsible enquiry, are epistemically vicious.[38]

Cardiff University
tanesini@cardiff.ac.uk

[38]   My thanks to the editors of this volume and an anonymous referee for helpful comments on earlier versions of this paper.

Understanding Epistemic Trust Injustices and Their Harms

HEIDI GRASSWICK

Abstract
Much of the literature concerning epistemic injustice has focused on the variety of harms done to socially marginalized persons in their capacities as potential *contributors* to knowledge projects. However, in order to understand the full implications of the social nature of knowing, we must confront the circulation of knowledge and the capacity of epistemic agents to take up knowledge produced by others and make use of it. I argue that members of socially marginalized lay communities can suffer *epistemic trust injustices* when potentially powerful forms of knowing such as scientific understandings are generated in isolation from them, and when the social conditions required for a *responsibly-placed trust* to be formed relative to the relevant epistemic institutions fail to transpire.

1. Introduction

Much of the literature concerning epistemic injustice has focused on the variety of harms done to persons in their capacities as potential *contributors* to knowledge projects. For example, recognizing that knowledge generation is a social endeavour, feminist epistemologists and critical race theorists have articulated and analyzed the idea of testimonial injustice arguing that social prejudices and implicit bias can result in members of certain groups suffering credibility deficits that interfere in their ability to participate in joint epistemic projects.[1] Similarly, arguments have been made that dominant conceptual frameworks favouring the experiences of the privileged can play a role in wronging members of groups through a lack of culturally available hermeneutical resources that would be necessary for the marginalized

---

[1] Kristie Dotson, 'Tracking Epistemic Violence, Tracking Practices of Silencing', *Hypatia* **26** (2011), 236–57; Miranda Fricker, *Epistemic Injustice: Power and the Ethics of Knowing* (Oxford and New York: Oxford University Press, 2007); José Medina, *The Epistemology of Resistance: Gender and Racial Oppression, Epistemic Injustice, and Resistant Imaginations* (Oxford and New York: Oxford University Press, 2013); Gaile Pohlhaus, 'Relational Knowing and Epistemic Injustice: Toward a Theory of *Willful Hermeneutical Ignorance*', *Hypatia* **27** (2012), 715–35.

doi:10.1017/S1358246118000553   ©The Royal Institute of Philosophy and the contributors 2018
Royal Institute of Philosophy Supplement **84** 2018   69

Heidi Grasswick

to come to fully understand their experiences, as well as have those experiences given uptake within society.[2] These kinds of wrongs, along with others, have been conceptualized as wrongs that thwart one's ability to participate in epistemic projects of generating knowledge.[3]

But the variety of ways in which one's ability to participate in the generation of knowledge can be unjustly thwarted do not exhaust the epistemic injustices that marginalized inquirers can suffer. If we are to understand the full implications of the social nature of knowing, we must confront another dimension of the knowing enterprise: the circulation of knowledge and the capacity of epistemic agents to take up knowledge produced by others and make use of it. Not enough philosophical attention has yet been devoted to understanding ourselves as potential *receivers* of knowledge and understanding. As epistemic agents, we have the potential both to be responsible *contributors* to knowledge production and responsible *recipients* of knowledge. Furthermore, our abilities to act as responsible receivers of knowledge and understanding are crucially linked to our abilities to serve as contributors to knowledge: receiving knowledge well places us in a better position to both generate further knowledge and participate in passing on knowledge to others. To be trustworthy contributors to the endeavours of our epistemic communities, we must be good at judging the trustworthiness of those who offer knowledge claims to us.[4] The interaction of these two components of epistemic responsibility – contributor and recipient – makes clear the philosophical importance of investigating our epistemic responsibilities as recipients of knowledge, and relatedly, the nature of epistemic injustices that might occur on this front.

In what follows I first examine the important role of epistemic trust given the cognitive division of labour and the presence of communities of expertise in modern society. Although what I argue is relevant to many different contexts of knowing through trust, I focus on the case of scientific knowledge and understanding, examining the relationship between those communities and institutions that generate and communicate such knowledge and situated lay communities

[2] Dotson, 'Tracking Epistemic Violence, Tracking Practices of Silencing'; Fricker, *Epistemic Injustice*; Medina, *The Epistemology of Resistance*; Pohlhaus, 'Relational Knowing and Epistemic Injustice'.
[3] Christopher Hookway, 'Some Varieties of Epistemic Injustice: Reflections on Fricker', *Episteme* **7** (2010), 151–63.
[4] Nancy Daukas, 'Epistemic Trust and Social Location', *Episteme* **3**, (2006), 109–24.

who are in a position where, as non-experts, trust is the only way to access such knowledge. Scientific knowledge is an especially important case to examine with respect to epistemic injustices; because it is a dominant and powerful form of knowing in contemporary society, with deep significance for the structure of our social and material lives, it has the potential to pose a greater threat to the epistemic capacities and opportunities of the socially marginalized than other less pervasive epistemic practices. I argue that members of socially marginalized lay communities can suffer epistemic trust injustices when potentially powerful forms of knowing such as scientific understandings are generated in isolation from them, and when the social conditions required in order to generate reasons that would support a responsibly-placed trust in the relevant epistemic institutions fail to transpire. Significant epistemic and other harms can result from such injustices.

2. Epistemic Injustice and Trust

In Miranda Fricker's characterization of an epistemic injustice, an epistemic injustice is a wrong 'done to someone specifically in their capacity as a knower'.[5] Others have used slightly different language. Elizabeth Anderson characterizes epistemic injustices as involving impediments to one's capacity 'as an inquirer'[6] and Christopher Hookway discusses epistemic injustices in terms of obstacles to *activities* (my emphasis) that are 'distinctly epistemic'.[7] These descriptions are used to specify the characteristics of an epistemic injustice as distinct from other forms of ethical injustice. The emphasis of these theorists is clearly on the activities of inquiry; when Fricker refers to the wrong of an epistemic injustice with reference to one's 'capacity as a knower', the term 'knower' must be understood as someone engaged in the activities of knowing, not a 'knower' in the sense of someone who is already in possession of knowledge. This is an important feature to note because for the idea of epistemic injustice to be taken seriously, it cannot simply amount to the denial of an opportunity to access a piece of knowledge. Since 'knowing

---

[5]   Fricker, *Epistemic Injustice*, 1.
[6]   Elizabeth Anderson, 'Feminist Epistemology and Philosophy of Science', *The Stanford Encyclopedia of Philosophy* (Spring 2017 Edition), Edward N. Zalta (ed.), <https://plato.stanford.edu/archives/spr2017/entries/feminism-epistemology/>.
[7]   Hookway, 'Some Varieties of Epistemic Injustice'.

everything' is not a viable goal of epistemic life, simply missing out on bits and pieces of knowledge cannot carry the seriousness required of the concept of epistemic injustice. This is not to say that being prevented from accessing certain knowledge, or having it hidden from one, could not constitute an epistemic injustice, but the case would have to be made for the seriousness of this particular instance of knowledge. The knowledge would have to be of particular significance to one's well-being overall, or its lack must more generally negatively affect one's epistemic abilities, such as one's capacity to obtain other knowledge extremely relevant to one's life. This is why science is an important case to examine: if in today's society scientific knowledge is a dominant source of significant knowledge relevant to people's lives, and social conditions and historical relations with scientific communities block members of some marginalized communities from having the ability to access such knowledge claims in a responsible way, then epistemic trust injustices and their associated harms result.

Given that epistemic injustices are typically defined as affecting one's capacities as an active knower or inquirer, it is reasonable to understand epistemic injustices as impeding (unjustly) on the exercise of one's *epistemic agency*. Moreover, we engage our epistemic agency not only when trying to actively generate new understandings or convey them to others. We also engage our epistemic agency when we are on the receiving end of others' attempts to convey their understandings of the world to us. When we take someone else's word on trust, or when we trust others to produce a certain kind of knowledge for us (via a cognitive division of labour), we are engaging our epistemic agency, and this can be done either well or poorly. In what follows I first address how one's epistemic agency is engaged when we take epistemic matters on trust, and then explain how that epistemic agency can itself be stymied by histories of certain social conditions that result in marginalized groups having reason to distrust dominant knowledge sources.

Many philosophers and sociologists of knowledge who take seriously the social nature of knowing have taken up issues concerning the relationship between experts and non-experts[8] and have

---

[8] H. M. Collins and Robert Evans, *Rethinking Expertise* (Chicago: University of Chicago Press, 2007); John Hardwig, 'The Role of Trust in Knowledge', *The Journal of Philosophy* **88** (1991), 693–708; Philip Kitcher, 'The Division of Cognitive Labor', *The Journal of Philosophy* **87**, (1990), 5–22; Philip Kitcher, *Science, Truth, and Democracy* (New York: Oxford University Press, 2001).

recognized the fact that a cognitive division of labour requires that epistemic agents trust other knowers to a great extent. However, fewer have worked explicitly with the likes of a *situated analysis* such as what we see in the epistemic injustice literature specifically, and more generally in many versions of feminist epistemology.[9] A situated analysis of expert/non-expert trust relations considers the social relations between knowledge providers and knowledge recipients and the histories of interactions between them. The philosophical work that has identified epistemic injustices that impede on one's participation in the generation and communication of knowledge has stemmed from an awareness of the deep ways in which power relations and the social biases that are a part of relations between inquirers have epistemic effects. In arguing the case for epistemic trust injustices, I likewise attend to the power-infused social relations between scientific communities as authoritative generators of knowledge and socially marginalized lay communities.

3. The Role of Trust in Knowing, and Responsible Trust

One of the reasons epistemologists have worried about people's dependence on others for knowing through trust is that trust makes one vulnerable, and may appear to remove epistemic agency from us as individual knowers, or suggest an abdication of epistemic responsibility. In John Hardwig's phrasing, trust is 'at least partially blind' and as he notes, for many epistemologists who focus on the need for evidence in order to have knowledge, the problem is not simply that knowledge does not involve trust, but rather that trust and knowledge are conceptualized as antithetical to each other.[10] But it is far from clear that trusting others for knowledge incapacitates us as epistemic agents or involves an abdication of epistemic agency, and if our epistemic agency is still involved in trusting others in our epistemic pursuits, then epistemic injustices involving trust are possible and need to be examined.

---

[9]   Lorraine Code, *What Can She Know?: Feminist Theory and the Construction of Knowledge* (Ithaca: Cornell University Press, 1991); Donna Haraway, 'Situated Knowledges: The Science Question in Feminism and the Privilege of Partial Perspective', *Feminist Studies* **14** (1988), 575–99; Sandra Harding, *Whose Science? Whose Knowledge?: Thinking from Women's Lives* (Ithaca, N.Y: Cornell University Press, 1991).

[10]   Hardwig, 'The Role of Trust in Knowledge', 693.

When it comes to a general theory of trust, numerous trust theorists have argued that in addition to its cognitive dimension, trust has an affective and attitudinal dimension that goes beyond simply relying on someone to deliver the goods with which one is entrusting them. To trust someone is to hold an attitude of optimism toward their fulfillment of your expectations.[11] Trust relations have a moral dimension to them, and the difference between trust and reliance is what explains the feelings of betrayal that can occur under circumstances when a trusted one fails you. Further, we can trust people for many different things, and we rightfully place boundaries on our trust: to trust someone is shorthand for person A trusting person B for Z (where Z is some kind of good that A cares about). I can easily trust a friend to not steal from me, but at the same time, because I know that they also are forgetful, I may not trust them to care for and feed my dog for the weekend. Given this, we need to identify the kind of trust and the boundaries of that trust that are of interest for understanding cases of *epistemic trust*.

I take it as uncontroversial that in many circumstances, trusting another epistemically is the most epistemically virtuous course of action. The need for trust makes each of us *vulnerable* to others who claim expertise. I hope it is also uncontroversial that in the case of highly specialized and large scale epistemic endeavours such as those involved in many forms of contemporary scientific knowledge, it would be epistemically unwise to offer a blanket trust to anyone and anything purporting to be scientific or that one takes to be scientific. One can lack discernment in whom to trust for knowledge, but that is not something we should strive for. The issue is not whether we do or do not place trust in others, but rather whether and when such trust can be relatively well-grounded. For ideal epistemic success, trust relations would be such that the degree of trust one grants would always be balanced by the degree of trustworthiness of the source. In the case of epistemic trust, the balance of epistemic trust and trustworthiness would still not guarantee epistemic success; even a trustworthy source who is doing their best can end up failing to deliver the epistemic goods, or can (out of character) betray the trust one has given them, upending their history of trustworthiness. Grounding our trust, to whatever degree that we do, does not mean we escape the vulnerability that we expose ourselves to when we trust. Additionally, the truster is never in a position to fully determine the trustworthiness of their source.

[11]   Annette Baier, 'Trust and Antitrust', *Ethics* **96** (1986), 231–60; Karen Jones, 'Trust as an Affective Attitude', *Ethics* **107** (1996), 4–25.

Thus, we cannot expect ideally placed trust that is always perfectly balanced with the source's trustworthiness. Even so, it remains possible to distinguish *responsibly-placed trust* – trust granted in cases in which one has good reason to take one's source as trustworthy – from trust which might fail to be responsible, such as might occur if one ignores the reasons right in front of them for thinking that a source is not trustworthy, but trusts anyways.[12] If the options are an inability to access the knowledge (by resisting trust), or to trust in the claims irresponsibly (when the reasons direct you otherwise), we might (with further specified conditions) be facing a case of an epistemic trust injustice.

Although trust necessarily makes one vulnerable and one can go wrong in trusting others, building robust trust relations is a very important part of a fruitful epistemic life, and thus participation in well-developed trust relations constitutes an important exercise of epistemic agency. A responsibly-placed trust is not a result of an abdication of one's epistemic responsibilities of assessment, or being closed to re-assessment should further evidence come one's way. Hardwig's note that trust is '*partially* blind' (my emphasis) is not the same as claiming that trust is fully opaque or that we have turned off our capacities as epistemic agents in resorting to trust. Placing epistemic trust in another is an exercise in epistemic agency, even though these trust placements and the reasons supporting them function quite differently from the ways we engage in the collection of evidence during individual inquiry. Trust relations are formed with others in part through histories of interactions with them, and these histories give a broad set of relevant reasons for trust in particular circumstances, and give reason for doubt, skepticism, and distrust in others. When those reasons inform in whom, for what, and to what degree one places one's epistemic trust, this trust (or distrust) can be said to be responsibly-placed. It is in part because of this breadth of relevant reasons for trust and distrust that histories of social marginalization can result in epistemic trust injustices.

The most simplified version of epistemic trust concerns trusting a single person's testimony. Most straightforwardly, epistemic trust

---

[12] More could be said about what constitutes 'irresponsibly-placed trust'. It could range from ignoring evidence, to negligence with respect to seeking out evidence to support one's trust assessments. The standards for seeking such reasons will vary dramatically depending on the stakes involved, but I do not take up these issues here. My primary concern is with social conditions that could *prevent* the formation of a responsibly-placed trust.

concerns one's willingness to take the word of another – to trust in their testimony, form beliefs on the basis of that testimony, and act in accordance with such beliefs. As many testimony theorists have pointed out, conditions of acceptable trust in testifiers involve judgements that the testifier is *competent* and *sincere*.[13] It only makes sense to rely on someone's testimony if I have reason to think that the person is competent in the area in question – that is, likely to be in possession of the knowledge I am interested in, and sincere – that is, likely to be trying to convey to me what they take to be true beliefs rather than dupe me, lie to me, play a joke on me, or mislead me in my beliefs. While the competency requirement focuses on the testifier's relationship to the knowledge in question, the sincerity requirement emphasizes the ethical dimension of successful testimony practices; it signals a relationship between the speaker and the hearer, and an attitude toward the knowledge recipient. Competency and sincerity are necessary for a testifier to be trustworthy, and a truster can responsibly place their trust in a testifier who appears to satisfy these requirements, relative to the context at hand.

In simple and isolated cases of testimony, the above interpretations of competence and sincerity may do the trick for inquirers determining their placements of epistemic trust. However, in order to understand our ongoing epistemic trust relations with communities of experts, especially in cases where the stakes are more significant, these initial interpretations need to be broadened and I take this up in the next section.

Additionally, although the personal testimony work helps us identify core features of epistemic trust, further issues emerge when we consider trust in communities and institutions of knowledge production, such as scientific communities. Most trust theorists agree that interpersonal trust remains the paradigmatic form of trust, with institutional trust being modeled after it.[14] Epistemic trust in institutions and communities share core features of interpersonal epistemic trust: vulnerability of the truster, an attitude of optimism toward the institution and its ability to fulfill certain expectations related to providing

---

[13] Jonathan Adler, 'Epistemological Problems of Testimony', *The Stanford Encyclopedia of Philosophy* (Summer 2015 Edition), Edward N. Zalta (ed.), <https://plato.stanford.edu/archives/sum2015/entries/testimony-episprob/>.

[14] Carolyn McLeod, 'Trust', *The Stanford Encyclopedia of Philosophy* (Fall 2015 Edition), Edward N. Zalta (ed.), <http://plato.stanford.edu/archives/fall2015/entries/trust/>.

the truster with reliable knowledge, the possibility of being betrayed, and the possibility of the trust being more or less well-grounded.

What is different about the 'impersonal' trust in institutions and communities compared with trust in persons, however, is that the trustworthiness of the specific *practices* of the institution[15] plays a more significant role in determining well-placed trust than in the case of individual testifiers. It may be less important that every participant in the institution be perfectly trustworthy if an institution operates with robustly trustworthy practices that help protect against the undue influence of untrustworthy individual members. But this can work the other way as well; when historically an institution has been failing to operate with trustworthy practices, and there is a track record that demonstrates this, these failures will be more relevant to assessments of the institution's trustworthiness than would be the sincere efforts at trustworthiness exhibited by particular individuals within the institution. Grasping the relevance of the practices of the institutions and communities themselves beyond the epistemic efforts of their individual members in assessments of trustworthiness allows us to appreciate the impact that such institutional features as embedded racism and sexism can have on epistemic trustworthiness. Lay persons and their communities have historical relations with enduring institutions of knowledge production and dissemination that outlive connections with individual members of those institutions, and evidence of histories of untrustworthy practices due to embedded racism and sexism can place responsibly-formed trust out of reach for some marginalized lay persons, resulting in epistemic trust injustices and their associated harms.

4. Complicating the Grounding of Epistemic Trust 1: The Competence Condition as 'Providing Significant Knowledge'

In anything more than a mundane case of testimony, the relevant epistemic competencies are likely broader than simply that the testifier has the background to 'know what they are talking about'. The idea in the standard case of testimony was that if a hearer has reason to think that the speaker knows what they are talking about, that

[15]   Karen Frost-Arnold, 'Imposters, Tricksters, and Trustworthiness as an Epistemic Virtue', *Hypatia* **29** (2014), 790–807. See also Miranda Fricker, 'Can There Be Institutional Virtues?' in Tamar Szabo Gendler and John Hawthorne (eds.), *Oxford Studies of Epistemology* **3** (Oxford: Oxford University Press, 2013).

counts as a reason (*ceteris paribus*) to believe them. But one of the problems with using the standard testimony analysis as a model for epistemic trust across expertise, either generally or specifically in cases of scientific experts, is that it focuses on a very narrow form of epistemic trust: simply trusting another's word in a given instance, without taking account of how that version of epistemic trust is embedded in a collection of competency expectations that are crucial to longstanding trust relations that operate in the service of our epistemic goals. In the case of scientific experts (and other large institutions of expert knowledge production) we (rightly) place upon our speakers a set of expectations that cover a broader range of epistemic goods than simply delivering a claim of knowledge.[16] Their competence as a testifier depends crucially on many other epistemic skills and capabilities.

For example, in his discussion of public trust, David Resnik points out that members of the public trust scientists to do many different things.[17] Identifying what members of the public trust scientists to do is a way of articulating the public's *expectations* of scientists. Resnik provides a partial list of public expectations including: trusting researchers with public resources, trusting researchers to provide knowledge and expertise that can inform policy debates, trusting researchers to provide knowledge that will 'yield beneficial applications in medicine, industry, engineering, technology, agriculture, transportation, communication, and other domains', and trusting researchers to make informed judgments about new technologies. Many other activities could be added to the list, but two I want to explicitly draw attention to are first, trusting researchers to filter information for us, determining what the best understandings of the day are and omitting poorer quality, less important, or outdated research,[18] and second, trusting researchers to treat stakeholder populations, including research subjects, ethically and not place them at too great a risk in the pursuit of knowledge. In the first, we expect experts to be able to offer expert *judgement* on the current status of

---

[16]   Katherine Hawley notes that we can sometimes impose too much on others in the expectations that lie behind our trust in 'Trust, Distrust and Commitment', *Noûs*, **48** (2014), 1–20. My discussion focuses on what we might rightfully expect.

[17]   David B. Resnik, 'Scientific Research and the Public Trust', *Science and Engineering Ethics* **17** (2011), 399–409.

[18]   Heidi Grasswick, 'Scientific and Lay Communities: Earning Epistemic Trust through Knowledge Sharing', *Synthese* **177** (2010), 387–409.

knowledge, and in the second, we expect them to conform to certain societally-held ethical norms as they make judgements concerning limits in the pursuit of knowledge.

Clearly, not everything laypersons trust scientists to do will be relevant to an assessment of their overall *epistemic* trustworthiness; the work of scientists involves them in social practices which may have non-epistemic goals as well. For example, the public may expect scientists to use their funds appropriately, not embezzle them and not to use them carelessly or inefficiently. If they fail in this, it is not immediately clear that this failing is relevant to one's assessment of their *epistemic* trustworthiness, though it certainly is relevant to their financial trustworthiness and potentially their general personal trustworthiness as well. Similarly, many may consider that the point concerning whether or not scientists treat their research subjects ethically may be relevant to their *ethical* trustworthiness, but not relevant to their *epistemic* trustworthiness. I will argue against this position shortly, but many will find it an initially plausible position. Even acknowledging that there will be some public expectations of activities that are not epistemically relevant, a strong argument can be made that the epistemic competencies members of the public expect of expert communities include a broad range of activities that need to be done well in order for scientists to serve as trustworthy testifiers of scientific knowledge, and failure in some of those may affect their overall core role as trustworthy providers of knowledge. These activities include skillfully undertaking their research activities, conveying their results in an epistemically responsible manner, avoiding research and publication misconduct throughout their professional activities, and filtering and assessing results within their field of expertise to allow them to convey robust judgements of the current state of knowledge in a field.

Particularly in the case of organized epistemic communities, such as scientific communities, when we trust these communities, we are not just trusting their specific *claims*. We are in fact (and quite rightly) trusting them to undertake a variety of valuable epistemic work: to *engage in inquiry* for us, to *produce knowledge* for us, to *orient their research in ways that will be useful,* or at least not harmful for us, and to *make judgements concerning which claims need communicating.* This clustering of epistemic expectations means that when there are reasons to suspect that such communities have failed in some of these expectations, these failures should be relevant to our assessment of their epistemic trustworthiness, in effect lowering the trust levels we grant them.

Heidi Grasswick

In determining which activities are relevant for these trust assessments, it is helpful to characterize the overall function of epistemic work of communities of experts in more general terms. Importantly, when we turn to communities of experts, we have an interest in certain kinds of knowledge. It is, of course, *significant* knowledge that we are after, not just any collection of trivial facts about the world,[19] and if the knowledge was not important to us, there would not be much motivation to place one's trust in the experts. We turn to experts when and if we consider that they are well positioned to produce such knowledge, recognize its significance for us, and communicate that knowledge to us. This involves expecting them to run robust and sound research programs, be able to filter results such that they can offer us a sound judgement on the best knowledge available, and also attend to our particular epistemic needs (which may not be shared by all) so that what they are providing is actually *significant knowledge for us*. Furthermore, given that each of us is socially situated, we cannot assume that what is significant knowledge for us will be significant for all other knowers.

In short, a general characterization of the epistemic role of experts is one of being a *provider of significant knowledge*. In order to succeed in this, many activities are involved, but this overarching characterization can give us a foothold into determining how these various activities contribute to the epistemic function with which lay persons seek to trust them. From there, we will be able to identify when a history of failures in certain activities may be surprisingly relevant to creating a blockage in possibilities for responsibly-placed trust for particularly situated lay persons, especially the socially marginalized.

5. Complicating the Grounding of Epistemic Trust 2: The Sincerity/Care Condition

Similarly, although the sincerity requirement as previously described can work well in identifying the moral component of the trust relation for simple cases where the testimonial trust relationships are quite limited and short-lived (such as when I ask a stranger for directions to the nearest bus stop) it is insufficient for richer relations of epistemic dependence. When the knowledge in question is much more

---

[19]   Elizabeth Anderson, 'Knowledge, Human Interests, and Objectivity in Feminist Epistemology', *Philosophical Topics* **23** (1995): 27–58; Kitcher, *Science, Truth, and Democracy*.

than trivial, the relationship between the speaker and the hearer will need to be more robust in order to sustain the depth and breadth of trust that would support making oneself vulnerable by taking someone's word for it on an issue of grave importance. Consider the case of my physician giving me news of a serious disease, alongside a recommendation for experimental treatment as my best course of action. I have interests in coming to understand both my health condition and the recommended options and their risks so that I can make treatment decisions. My medical interests in pursuing good health include epistemic interests; there are things I need to know. In trusting my physician with my relevant epistemic needs, I will expect (with optimism) that she will have a stronger attitude of care toward me than simply being sincere in her statements (i.e. telling me the truth). I will expect that she has enough care directed towards me and my medical interests that she will attempt to offer me the specific knowledge that I need in order to make reasonable decisions – perhaps outlining the range of available options. For her to be trustworthy, sufficient care for my interests will need to override competing concerns, such as her potential need to feel socially secure by offering a definitive diagnosis (even if she is not completely confident of the diagnosis), or her need to satisfy other interests of hers, such as finding enough research subjects for the experimental treatment. My trust might be bolstered in part by my understanding that the professional standards of medical practice stipulate caring for the medical interests of one's patients, including their epistemic interests of accessing the necessary knowledge to help them take care of themselves and make appropriate treatment decisions. My history of interactions with my physician, and with the medical establishment more generally, can also offer me reasons for trust: have I been well-served in the past by them on different medical issues? Or are there past instances in which either my physician or other doctors failed to display the relevant care (and competency) towards my interests and needs?

In rich and important cases of ongoing epistemic exchange, 'sincerity' in itself is insufficient to capture the attitude of care that is needed to support the kind of extensive and lasting trust for satisfying the ongoing epistemic needs of a nonexpert. I propose renaming this general requirement as the 'sincerity/care' condition. The sincerity/care condition notes that a trustworthy expert must embody some degree of a moral attitude of care toward the recipient. Sincerity captures a minimal requirement of care, but the degree of care required to form and sustain trust will be context-dependent, in part depending on the stakes of the epistemic situation and the scope of the epistemic trust placed in the expert.

Heidi Grasswick

6. Epistemic Trust Injustices

A brief recap is in order. Having begun with a narrow understanding of the sincerity and competence requirements for making reasonable judgements for trust in cases of mundane testimony, I expanded these requirements, arguing that in cases of higher stakes knowing, and cases where we need to trust communities and institutions for expert knowledge on an ongoing basis over time, the relevant competencies are multiple and broad in terms of the activities that must be undertaken to be epistemically trustworthy. I offered a core description of these competencies as consisting in the experts' ability to provide significant knowledge to the non-expert, which, in the case of science, includes both producing it and conveying it. Additionally, I argued that the sincerity requirement is better understood as a broader 'sincerity/care' condition, in recognition that trust relations are ongoing and exist in complex epistemic environments. In order to depend upon an expert community for their ongoing and sometimes high stakes epistemic needs, a lay person needs to trust that in undertaking and conveying the epistemic work, the expert embodies an appropriate degree of care for their interests, most importantly their epistemic interests, though caring for one's other central interests can be crucial to identifying and serving those epistemic interests. One needs to trust that the ongoing judgements of the expert account for one's concerns.

Both of these conditions draw attention to the relevance of differences in social situation. If competencies are understood under the larger heading of being a provider of significant knowledge, attention must be paid to differences in situation that make some knowledge significant to some, but not necessarily all. Differently situated lay persons will differ on at least some epistemic interests, and histories of the provision of knowledge from various institutions and communities may or may not demonstrate patterns of having addressed such epistemic interests. Similarly, the sincerity/care requirement can only be fulfilled if there is an awareness of the relevant interests of the particular non-expert in question. If an expert community is unaware of the needs of a particular lay community and the epistemic dimensions of those needs, it will be challenging for it to offer, let alone demonstrate the appropriate level of care for those needs. To be trustworthy for particularly situated lay persons, an expert or expert community must be able to satisfy these conditions.

From the perspective of the potential truster, what is relevant to determining cases of epistemic trust injustices is whether, through past histories of interaction, there have emerged reasons to distrust these experts, or at least withhold trust.[20] When there is historical evidence available concerning how well suited a community of experts is to satisfy the competency and the sincerity/care conditions, we need to use it. A history through which an epistemic community has served us well as a provider of significant knowledge leads us to reasonably and responsibly continue in that trust relationship, learning lots of things on the basis of that trust, without further checking.[21] But in cases where there is evidence that the competency and sincerity/care conditions have not been well satisfied over time, a lay person may fail to have adequate grounds from which they could responsibly place their trust in the expert community on an ongoing basis. This is a situation where they actually have reasons to distrust or withhold trust from the expert community. This may not stop them from trusting, but, if *responsibly-placed trust* is prevented under such conditions, then regardless of whether they trust or distrust, their capacity to inquire and attain knowledge in a responsible way is stymied.

When faced with such reasons for distrust, there are various possible outcomes. Lay persons may reject the claims, or they may end up merely 'relying' on an expert community out of desperation, having no better options than to proceed without any expectation or optimism that the expert will be able to deliver the epistemic goods. They also may consciously take the risk of trusting in the hopes of improving the trust relationship, engaging a long-haul strategy of bettering epistemic relations. However, the relevant point here is that although reaching for the poorly grounded trust or mere reliance strategy might work out for them in a particular case, at this juncture (given that they have reasons to distrust) they are faced with the unsatisfying situation of being unable to partake in a healthy trust relation in an epistemically responsible manner, due to the way the socially embedded epistemic practices have been functioning.

We have now reached a point where we can articulate the idea of an epistemic trust injustice and connect it to a failure to satisfy the

---

[20] See Katherine Hawley, 'Trust, Distrust and Commitment', for an important distinction between distrust and non-reliance (a form of lack of trust). Epistemic trust injustices could result in either case, but space limitations prevent any extended discussion here.

[21] Cynthia Townley points out that when we trust someone, we actually commit to not checking up on them. See her *A Defense of Ignorance: Its Value for Knowers and Roles in Feminist and Social Epistemologies* (Lanham, Md: Lexington Books, 2011).

conditions of responsibly-placed trust. We will recall that in the case of epistemic injustices that concerned epistemic agents as contributors to the production and circulation of knowledge, it was the thwarting of their capacities as inquirers and epistemic agents that constituted the epistemic nature of the injustice. I have demonstrated that the ways in which we place and sustain trust in others for expert knowledge also involves our epistemic agency; though we trust, our epistemic capacities are not set aside but rather play a role in forming and sustaining our attitudes of trust and distrust. When the conditions are such that the available evidence points in the direction of distrust, making it difficult or impossible to *responsibly* trust in expert communities such that I could receive knowledge and understandings of the world through responsibly-placed trust, there is a sense in which my epistemic agency is being thwarted.

Of course, one might argue that withholding trust in such a situation is actually a case of well-exercised epistemic agency; after all, I've noted that this person has reasons for distrust. One could say that the epistemically responsible thing to do in such a hostile environment is to withhold trust. However, my point in emphasizing the threat to epistemic agency is that the described circumstances that give reasons for distrust do not just pop up for an isolated case. As a relationship of distrust that has grounding, it will apply to many interactions with this expert community over time. As I pointed out early on, the incapacity to acquire a particular piece of knowledge does not itself threaten one's epistemic agency. But if social conditions are such that this incapacity is either quite far-reaching (by blocking my access to large swaths of knowledge) or concerns understandings central to my self-understanding (blocking knowledge that is of crucial importance to my overall life and ability to continue as an active epistemic agent) at some point we can make sense of this blockage as actually threatening one's epistemic agency. Such blockages in one's ability to form responsibly-placed trust constitutes an epistemic injustice when such thwarting is systemic, and involves my capacity (more specifically, my lack thereof) to access areas of knowledge that are significant for me. Epistemic trust injustices occur in situations of substantial social marginalization by having a significant dampening effect on the abilities of members of subordinated groups to function well epistemically in a social world with widespread divisions of cognitive labour. The epistemic capacities of these inquirers are systematically stymied, even when what the experts are reporting might qualify as cases of reliable knowledge, or useful understanding.

7. Indicators of Epistemic Untrustworthiness

Building on my discussion of the competence and sincerity/care conditions, there are at least three different types of indicators that could suggest a lack of trustworthiness on the part of a community of scientific experts from the perspective of a specifically situated lay person. The first concerns a history of failing to provide significant knowledge for a particular lay community by having gotten things wrong, especially with respect to areas of knowledge that are particularly relevant for a marginalized group. When this becomes evident, the reliability of the community and its research practices are called into question. For example, feminists have drawn attention to the fact that sexist biases and background assumptions have played a significant role in the history of research on women's sexuality, an area of research that could produce significant knowledge for women. The use of such assumptions has resulted in a pattern of mistaken understandings and areas of ignorance that have been damaging to women.[22] Similarly, in spite of the repeated discrediting of projects of scientific racism that purport to explain away economic disparities between those of European descent and those of African descent by undertaking and referencing poor quality scientific studies, such projects keep popping up throughout the history of the human and biological sciences.[23] Evidence that scientists have repeatedly produced theories and results that turn out to be mistaken, especially when this pattern occurs more frequently with respect to particularly relevant knowledge for a specific group, offers reasons for the group's distrust of the relevant scientific community, especially on topics of specific concern for the group. Over time, such scientific communities show themselves to be poorly suited as trustworthy providers of significant knowledge for these groups.

Second, there may be an identifiable history of a community of experts ignoring the interests and concerns of a particular lay community. Often, areas of ignorance are not just gaps in knowledge, but are

---

[22]   Elisabeth A. Lloyd, *The Case of the Female Orgasm: Bias in the Science of Evolution* (Cambridge, Mass: Harvard University Press, 2005); Nancy Tuana, 'The Speculum of Ignorance: The Women's Health Movement and Epistemologies of Ignorance', *Hypatia* **21** (2006), 1–19.

[23]   Stephen Jay Gould, *The Mismeasure of Man*, Revised & Expanded edition (New York: W. W. Norton & Company, 1996); Sandra Harding (ed.), *The 'Racial' Economy of Science: Toward a Democratic Future* (Bloomington: Indiana University Press, 1993).

actively constructed to serve the interests of the dominant.[24] When there are patterns of the research priorities of scientific communities being consistently directed toward the needs of the dominant, without attention to the needs of subordinated groups, again, there is reason for members of such groups to distrust those communities epistemically. Histories of androcentric assumptions in medical science, such as the research on heart disease that was performed on all male subjects rather than researchers attending to the possibility of sex-specific manifestations of the disease offers an example here.[25] Again, researchers have been failing as successful providers of significant knowledge for the group (women), but this time the failure is due to the inability to generate knowledge that is of particular significance for the group in question.

These first two indicators that might support the distrust of a marginalized community both stem from failures in the core competency condition of being a provider of significant knowledge. The second indicator – ignoring the epistemic needs of a particular group – can also be said to fail to satisfy the sincerity/care condition. Particularly in cases where the history of the expert community's knowledge-making indicates a gross amount of care and attention offered to other (more dominantly situated) people relative to the attention offered to epistemic concerns of the marginalized, the question arises of whether there has been adequate care and attention directed toward the epistemic interests of the marginalized in order to generate the types of knowledge that are important for them.

In contrast, the third type of indicator I suggest primarily involves the sincerity/care requirement. This indicator concerns actual histories of ethical and social injustices involved in the production of knowledge. If there is evidence that members of one's group have been mistreated within the institutions and practices of knowledge production (particularly if there is a historical pattern), this offers some reason to think that these institutions lack a sufficient dose of the moral attitude of care required to sustain making oneself vulnerable by trusting them epistemically on matters of importance. I noted early on that many will find it initially implausible that ethical injustices perpetrated by epistemic institutions (such as the ethical abuse of research subjects, or more generally placing stakeholder populations at risk) should be relevant to the basis one has for forming or

---

[24]   Shannon Sullivan and Nancy Tuana (eds.), *Race and Epistemologies of Ignorance* (Albany: State University of New York Press, 2007).
[25]   Sue Vilhauer Rosser, *Women's Health – Missing From U.S. Medicine* (Bloomington: Indiana University Press, 1994).

maintaining epistemic trust. However, through the articulation and expansion of the conditions of competency and sincerity/care, the connection between a history of ethical injustices and the epistemic case is now more apparent.

Though her work is not framed in terms of epistemic injustices, Naomi Scheman has drawn attention to the 'systematically trust-eroding effects of various forms of social, political, and economic injustice'[26] all of which can be identified in a variety of the institutions and practices of science. For Scheman, social injustices within the communities and social practices of knowledge generation that have epistemic relevance can include histories of particular groups having suffered ethical abuses as research subjects, or having being discriminated against in the entry to and participation in the institutions of science. As she writes, 'the credibility of science suffers, and, importantly, ought to suffer…when its claims to trustworthiness are grounded in the workings of institutions that are demonstrably unjust – even when those injustices cannot be shown to be responsible for particular lapses in evidence gathering or reasoning'.[27] Her point is not that the ethical injustices she cites imply that scientific institutions cannot serve as reliable truth trackers, but rather that what matters for grounding trust is whether or not variously situated laypersons outside of science can justifiably think they can serve as such.[28] The cases Scheman describes are cases of epistemic trust injustices, whereby a history of social conditions suggest the epistemic untrustworthiness of an expert community toward a marginalized group, thereby significantly diminishing opportunities for group members to gain important knowledge through a responsibly-formed trust.

8. The Harms of Epistemic Trust Injustices

There is in fact evidence that certain social groups are more distrustful of some scientific communities than others: many indigenous groups distrust geneticists and their research that seeks to

---

[26] Naomi Scheman, 'Epistemology Resuscitated: Objectivity as Trustworthiness', in *Engendering Rationalities*, ed. Nancy Tuana and Sandra Morgen (Albany: SUNY Press, 2001), 34.
[27] Scheman, 'Epistemology Resuscitated: Objectivity as Trustworthiness', 36.
[28] Scheman, 'Epistemology Resuscitated: Objectivity as Trustworthiness', 35.

identify genetic markers affiliated with their groups,[29] and African Americans are more distrustful of medical researchers than are whites, often citing the history of research abuses of African Americans as reasons for their distrust.[30] I have focused on how, from the point of view of epistemological analysis, some of such socially located distrust can be warranted. Where histories of oppression and social marginalization create conditions that do not support a judgement of the expert community's trustworthiness as a sincere and caring provider of significant knowledge for a marginalized group, the possibility of responsibly-placed trust may elude the group, amounting to its members suffering epistemic trust injustices.

The most obvious harm that results from epistemic trust injustices are the epistemic losses that are incurred by members of these marginalized communities when current expert communities actually *are* capable of providing significant knowledge for them, but where the poor track record of historical interactions leads the marginalized lay persons to dismiss the experts (and reasonably so). Quite simply, such social conditions that result in poor trust relations make it harder for members of such communities to obtain knowledge that is otherwise in circulation.

More prominently, I have argued that compounding those independent epistemic losses is the harm of impediments to one's epistemic agency. When the epistemic losses are systemic, one's epistemic agency can itself be threatened or diminished. As I outlined earlier, epistemic agency itself can only be said to be thwarted when the effects of the warranted distrust prevent significant areas of knowledge acquisition – areas crucial to one's ability to understand oneself and one's situation. But in such cases, these conditions of injustice can begin to undermine one's general capacity to succeed as an independent inquirer within the maladapted social network. Though any expert community might fail to be trustworthy, or could face a situation where a particular lay community lacks reasons to trust it, the harm of thwarting epistemic agency is reserved for cases where such expert communities dominate the social networks of knowledge production and circulation. In modern society, communities of scientific expertise are plausible candidates.

Furthermore, beyond the losses that can occur in one's role as a recipient of knowledge, epistemic trust injustices can circle back, with

---

[29] 'After Havasupai Litigation, Native Americans Wary of Genetic Research', *American Journal of Medical Genetics Part A* **152A**, (July 1, 2010), ix.

[30] Scheman, 'Epistemology Resuscitated: Objectivity as Trustworthiness'.

recurrent effects on the participation of members of marginal groups in the production of knowledge – that is, in their contributory roles. For example, if a member of a marginalized community is distrustful of a scientific research community, they are less likely to be eager to participate in the practices of that community. This will make it more challenging for research communities to correct some of the social and epistemic injustices that played a role in creating the very situation of the epistemic trust injustice in the first place! Those who don't trust medical research communities are less likely to pursue such a research career, and they are unlikely to be eager to take on the role of a research subject. Indeed, as medical researchers have recognized the importance of a diverse human subject pool for robust knowledge generation, they have found it challenging to encourage greater research subject participation across diverse populations, something that is necessary if they are to correct for some of the subject biases in their research.[31] Distrust of scientific institutions may even lead to a dissociation from educational opportunities (such as high school or college level STEM classes) that could be important for significant epistemic endeavours besides research careers (as teachers, policy makers, or engineers for example). In these and other ways, epistemic trust injustices can interact with the kinds of participatory epistemic injustices I mentioned at the outset, all of which can combine to create quite a difficult situation for the social production and circulation of knowledge, with certain groups bearing the burden of the losses and harms more than others.

Though I have focused on epistemic harms, there are of course innumerable social harms that can also result from epistemic trust injustices. When trust in knowledge-producing institutions is low within one's community, the practical benefits of putting those knowledge results into use are lost. If one does not trust the knowledge claims being circulated by the medical community, or one rejects the claims of government environmental regulators concerned about pollutants in local drinking water, one could even be putting one's life at risk if in fact these expert communities are reliable sources. Such social harms offer another reason why trust relations in the epistemic realm need to be taken seriously; epistemic trust injustices can re-inscribe social inequities when the opportunities that knowledge acquisition can foster are not taken advantage of by the victims of epistemic injustices.

---

[31] Steven Epstein, *Inclusion: The Politics of Difference in Medical Research* (Chicago: University of Chicago Press, 2007).

Heidi Grasswick

9. Addressing Epistemic Trust Injustices

As epistemic agents, we inherit our places within a network of social epistemic practices that have histories of successes and failures – histories that shape our own epistemic capacities and opportunities. The various epistemic injustices that result from these practices make epistemic success harder on some than others, and epistemic success is often tied to other forms of flourishing.

The variety of harms associated with epistemic trust injustices, and the feedback loops between recipient-based epistemic trust injustices and contributory epistemic injustices create a challenging situation for those who seek to correct both epistemic and broader social injustices. Yet the same connections between the different forms of epistemic injustice that make the problem so difficult also offer pathways forward. Though historical patterns of institutional failures as providers of significant knowledge for particular groups serve as evidence against offering up epistemic trust to these institutions, evidence is defeasible, and there other sources of evidence could arise that would push in a different direction. What is needed to counter warranted distrust is evidence that the epistemic practices have somehow changed, or that the previously untrustworthy epistemic community has taken on new commitments that suggest a greater epistemic accountability to one's marginalized communities. For example, on the participatory side, many scientific communities are beginning to take seriously the need to diversify both their practitioners, and their pools of research subjects. If members of marginalized groups see improvement in these institutions in terms of participation by similarly situated persons, or if they see increased efforts to involve their community in determining the direction and parameters of its research goals, this could mark a difference in the institution's practices that could be relevant to trust relations. A research community that increases diversity within its ranks could plausibly develop a greater awareness of the epistemic needs of relevant groups, and demonstrate greater care, concern and motivation for addressing these epistemic needs. No doubt, the burden is on the institutions themselves to not only make the changes to their practices, but to communicate new evidence that their practices have shifted so as to be better positioned to serve specifically situated communities.

One thing that should be clear from my discussion of epistemic trust injustices is that they are highly contextual. I have not argued that any and every marginalized group in society suffers from epistemic trust injustices. In fact, my argument depends on the social conditions that produce the reasons for distrust being fairly systemic and wide-ranging, but they can be quite specific to a particular group. We must look closely to the specific historical context of the relations between particularly situated lay communities and specific epistemic institutions, seeking out the failures and trust betrayals that have resulted in epistemic trust injustices and made it challenging to turn those trust relations around to foster healthier and more epistemically fruitful networks of epistemic trust. This is difficult work. Yet given that for each of us, the vast majority of knowledge that is significant to us can only be accessed through trust, it should be clear that working against epistemic trust injustices is an important part of achieving epistemic justice for all, and social justice for all.

Middlebury College
grasswick@middlebury.edu

On Anger, Silence, and Epistemic Injustice

ALISON BAILEY

Abstract

If anger is the emotion of injustice, and if most injustices have prominent epistemic dimensions, then where is the anger in epistemic injustice? Despite the question my task is not to account for the lack of attention to anger in epistemic injustice discussions. Instead, I argue that a particular texture of transformative anger – a *knowing resistant anger* – offers marginalized knowers a powerful resource for countering epistemic injustice. I begin by making visible the anger that saturates the silences that epistemic injustices repeatedly manufacture and explain the obvious: silencing practices produce angry experiences. I focus on *tone policing* and *tone vigilance* to illustrate the relationship between silencing and angry knowledge management. Next, I use María Lugones's pluralist account of anger to bring out the epistemic dimensions of knowing resistant anger in a way that also calls attention to their histories and felt textures. The final section draws on feminist scholarship about the transformative power of angry knowledge to suggest how it might serve as a resource for resisting epistemic injustice.

1. Introduction

Anger is the emotion of injustice.[1] Historically, members subordinated groups have defended our anger as a morally and politically appropriate response to daily injustices. Our anger surfaces quickly pulling us back into our bodies. This is how injustice *feels*. Those of us who live in *epistemic twilight zones*, that is, in worlds where testimony about our lived experiences is repeatedly silenced, dismissed, distorted, or gas lighted, are familiar with the ever-present anger these constant erasures trigger.[2] Historically, discussions of anger

---

[1] As Aristotle says, 'anger is an appropriate response to perceived injustice'. *Nicomachean Ethics* V.8 1135b28–9.

[2] Alison Bailey, 'The Unlevel Knowing Field: An Engagement with Dotson's Third-Order Epistemic Oppression.' *Social Epistemology Review and Reply Collective* **3**.10 (2014), 62–68 <http://wp.me/p1Bfg0-1Gs>. 'Epistemic twilight zones' are undefined or intermediate conceptual areas where there are insufficient or inadequate epistemic resources. Here, epistemic resources are not shared as much as people think.

doi:10.1017/S1358246118000565   ©The Royal Institute of Philosophy and the contributors 2018
Royal Institute of Philosophy Supplement **84** 2018   93

and injustice have focused on the political uses of anger; but, as Kristie Dotson once remarked, 'All injustices are epistemic at root'.[3] So, I'm curious: if anger is the emotion of injustice, and if injustices have prominent epistemic dimensions, then where is the anger in epistemic injustice? Despite the question, my project is not to explain the lack of attention to anger in the epistemic injustice literature. Instead I argue that a particular texture of anger – a *knowing resistant anger* – offers marginalized knowers a powerful resource for countering epistemic injustices. I begin by making visible the anger that saturates the complex silences that epistemic injustices repeatedly manufacture. I outline four silencing practices to illustrate the obvious point that social practices of silencing produce angry experiences. Next, I introduce two additional silencing practices – *tone policing* and *tone vigilance* – because they best illustrate the intimate relationship between silencing and angry knowledge management. My fourth section uses María Lugones's pluralist account of anger to bring out the epistemic dimensions of knowing resistant anger in a way that also calls attention to the histories and textures of this anger. Anger is powerful resource for resisting epistemic injustice. Anger does things. Anger can be a claim to respect. It offers us clarity. And, it is useful for mapping epistemic terrains. Anger calls attention to bad epistemic habits. It prompts us to seek out resistant epistemic communities and new worlds of sense where our epistemic confidence can be restored.

2. Anger is a Justified Response to Social Practices of Silencing

Social practices of silencing produce angry experiences. So, my first task is to make visible the overlooked and undertheorized resistant anger saturating the silences that epistemic injustice repeatedly manufactures. All testimonial exchanges take place on an *unlevel knowing field*; that is, 'on contested terrains where knowledge and ignorance

---

[3]   Kristie Dotson, in conversation. Dotson's claim is intentionally strong. Unpacking the 'all' is beyond the scope of this project. I ask readers to feel the weight of the *all* in Dotson's claim by considering how the epistemological dimensions of violence are integral to the process of dehumanization: Reducing knowing subjects to dehumanized subjects or objects (i.e. non-citizens, property, animals, savages, criminals, etc.) is the first step toward doing violence to them. Charles W. Mills makes a weaker claim: the historical production of the racial contract has *prominent* epistemic dimensions. See his *The Racial Contract* (Ithaca, New York: Cornell University Press, 1997).

circulate with equal vigor, and where dominant groups have a deep and abiding interest in maintaining their epistemic home turf advantage'.[4] Dominant groups use silencing practices to defend their epistemic home terrain. Silencing does epistemic violence to marginalized epistemic communities not only by undermining speakers' epistemic credibility, but also by causing them to doubt their ability to make judgements about their moral worth.[5] Effective silencing practices make it difficult for marginalized knowers to hold their epistemic ground.

The epistemic injustice scholarship identifies a variety of silencing practices. Knowers can be silenced *pre-emptively,* when they are excluded in advance from participating in a testimonial exchange. Miranda Fricker describes this as 'a tendency for some groups simply not to be asked for information in the first place'.[6] Consider how women have been accidently-on-purpose excluded from U.S. government committees on reproductive healthcare policy. Silencing practices also treat knowers as *epistemic objects, or as truncated subjects.*[7] Here, knowers are treated as (re)sources, from whom so-called 'legitimate inquirers' glean information to produce proper knowledge. Here, speakers *are* asked for information in the first place, but their knowledge is co-opted in support of the asker's project, undermining their capacity as givers of that knowledge.[8] Think about how universities co-opt the resistant work done by gender studies programs and use it market their commitment to diversity in ways that don't threaten institutional comfort. Kristie Dotson's scholarship on epistemic violence identifies two additional

---

[4]   Bailey, 'The Unlevel Knowing Field: An Engagement with Dotson's Third-Order Epistemic Oppression', 63.

[5]   Dotson distinguishes between episodic, non-repetitive *instances of silencing* and deeper systemic and socially functional *practices of silencing* that concern 'a repetitive *reliable* occurrence of an audience failing to meet the dependencies of a speaker that finds its origins in a more pervasive ignorance'. I focus on Dotson's repetitive reliable occurrences. See 'Tracking Epistemic Violence, Tracking Practices of Silencing', *Hypatia* **26**.2 (2011), 236–57.

[6]   Miranda Fricker, *Epistemic Injustice: Power and the Ethics of Knowing* (New York and Oxford: Oxford University Press, 2007), 130.

[7]   'Epistemic objectification' is Fricker's term. See, *Epistemic Injustice: Power and the Ethics of Knowing,* 133. The term 'truncated subjects' comes from Gaile Pohlhaus, Jr., 'Discerning the Primary Epistemic Harm in Cases of Testimonial Injustice', *Social Epistemology* **28**.2 (2013), 99–114.

[8]   Fricker, *Epistemic Injustice: Power and the Ethics of Knowing,* 133.

silencing practices.[9] *Testimonial quieting* happens when an audience fails to recognize the speaker as a knower whose testimony is worth hearing. The speaker does not just suffer a credibility deficit. The speaker's credibility deficit is so severe, that her words are not heard at all. It's as if she never spoke. Consider the court scene in *To Kill a Mockingbird*. Tom Robinson doesn't simply suffer a credibility deficit because he's a Black man. His testimony is 'worth nothing to the jury. As if he did not testify at all'.[10] Finally, *testimonial smothering* is a coerced self-silencing that happens when 'the speaker perceives her immediate audience as *unwilling or unable to gain the appropriate uptake of proffered testimony*'. The speaker's knowledge from previous conversations teaches her to shape or truncate her testimony to 'insure that [it] contains only content for which [her] audience demonstrates testimonial competence'.[11] People of colour, for example, tactically limit the conversations they are willing to have with white people about race, knowing that white audiences typically lack the epistemic competence to judge those experiences accurately.

So, where is the anger in social practices of silencing? It's *everywhere*. Silence is a condition of oppression, and part of resisting oppression is finding a voice that effectively pushes back against the weight of imposed silences. Silence is saturated with anger because injustice is painful. Anger is an audible expression of resistance to the sufferings of injustice. Our anger pushes back against the complex silences that injustice repeatedly manufactures. When Audre Lorde says: 'My response to racism is anger', she means that her anger is a justified response to the social and cultural habits, ideologies, institutions, and laws that dehumanize, erase, and do violence to her.[12] Anger is a justified response to all subordination injuries, even epistemic ones. When a speaker's testimony is smothered, silenced, or rendered inaudible, her anger is smothered, silenced, or rendered inaudible. Silencing anger exacerbates the harms of epistemic injustices because silencing neutralizes or renders invisible

---

[9] Dotson, 'Tracking Epistemic Violence, Tracking Practices of Silencing', 242–45.

[10] Rachel McKinnon, 'Epistemic Injustice', *Philosophy Compass* **11**.8 (2016), 240.

[11] Dotson, 'Tracking Epistemic Violence, Tracking Practices of Silencing', 244.

[12] Audre Lorde, 'On the Uses of Anger: Women Responding to Racism', *Sister Outsider: Essays and Speeches by Audre Lorde* (Trumansburg, New York: The Crossing Press, 1984), 124.

the knowledge speakers have of the injury their anger communicates. To be angry is to make a claim on respect.[13] Silencing is disrespectful precisely because it communicates to the speaker that her testimony is not worth hearing, that she is incapable of making accurate judgements about how she has been wronged, or that the emotional injuries she sustains during a testimonial exchange are unworthy of consideration. The audience's failure to give the speaker's testimony and anger uptake illustrates a failure to respect the speaker as a credible knower; and, like all discredited knowers, she is denied the right to social participation.[14]

3. Tone Management as Angry Knowledge Management

My task so far has been to make visible the resistant anger that saturates social practices of silencing. The fact that silencing practices produce angry experiences should now be evident. This section suggests that resistant angry experiences have epistemic content and that the aim of silencing is to manage resistant anger's epistemic content. To illustrate this, I examine two anger-silencing practices – *tone policing* and *tone vigilance* – aimed at directly managing subordinate groups' angry knowledge. My discussion highlights the epistemic and psychological harms that tone-managing practices produce when subordinate groups are caught in *anger-silencing spirals*.

Tone policing has a prominent epistemic function. The clearest example comes from Audre Lorde's account of a moment during an academic conference when she spoke out of direct and particular anger to a white woman who replied, 'Tell me how you feel but don't say it too harshly or I cannot hear you'. Lorde comments, 'But is it my manner that keeps you from hearing, or the threat of a message that [your] life may change?'[15] Anger is a response to injury; but, for subordinated knowers, it is treated as something to be managed. In general, tone management weakens epistemic credibility by targeting, isolating, and attempting to manage the affective content (the speaker's *manner* of speaking) and the epistemic content (the *message*) in testimony. At its core is the expectation that

[13]   Marilyn Frye, 'A Note On Anger', *The Politics of Reality: Essays in Feminist Theory* (Trumansburg, New York: The Crossing Press, 1983) 84–94.
[14]   Peter Lyman, 'The Politics of Anger: On Silence, Resentment, and Political Speech', *Socialist Review* **11**.3 (1984), 71–2.
[15]   Lorde, 'On the Uses of Anger: Women Responding to Racism', 125.

subordinated knowers, if they want to be heard, must calibrate the timbre of their message, to fall within the audience's comfort zone. The connections between anger and tone management are so predictable that I have come to understand them as anger/knowledge management tactics. In fact, anger's epistemic strength can be measured in direct proportion to the amount of energy used to contain it.[16] But, anger-silencing practices are not just about quieting uncomfortable tones as a parent hushes a child at a movie. There is power in the hush. The hush reasserts dominance: it restores the audience's own epistemic and psychological comfort. There are at least two patterns of managing this angry knowledge.

In cases of *direct angry knowledge management*, tone policing may trigger an exhausting and familiar anger-silencing spiral.[17] Lorde's anger at racial injustices prompts the white woman to make a request for psychological and epistemic comfort. Angry demands for justice are prone to escalation. Suppose that following this exchange that, sensing that she's not been heard, Lorde reasserts her message in a hotter tone. The white woman may understand the amplified tone as further evidence against Lorde's epistemic credibility and more firmly ask Lorde to soften her voice. These exchanges are *anger-silencing spirals*: closed hermeneutical systems in which the speaker suffers a double epistemic injury – neither her testimony nor her anger get uptake, and she is left with a dense, hot, swelling rage in her chest.

Lorde's story illustrates a form of tone policing that focuses *directly* on the audible anger in a speaker's voice, but anger need not be heard to be managed. There is a second, more insidious, form of tone management that happens when an audience *attributes* anger to a speaker's testimony (independently of her tone) simply because the speaker belongs to a group that is culturally characterized as angry. Roxane Gay's description of how race complicates anger gets at the heart of *attributive anger*. She writes,

> I AM an opinionated woman so I am often accused of being angry. This accusation is made because a woman, a black

---

[16] Brittney Cooper, *Eloquent Rage: A Black Feminist Discovers Her Superpower*. (New York: St. Martin's Press, 2018), 167.
[17] This is McKinnon's 'epistemic injustice circle of hell'. See 'Allies Behaving Badly: Gaslighting as Epistemic Injustice', *The Routledge Handbook to Epistemic Injustice*, eds. Ian James Kidd, José Medina, and Gaile Pohlhaus, Jr. (New York: Routledge, 2017), 169, and McKinnon's 'Epistemic Injustice', 240. See also, Sara Ahmed, *Living a Feminist Life* (Durham, North Carolina: Duke University Press, 2017), 38.

woman who is angry, is making trouble. She is daring to be dissatisfied with the *status quo*. She is daring to be heard. When women are angry, we are wanting too much or complaining or wasting time or focusing on the wrong things or we are petty or shrill or strident or unbalanced or crazy or overly emotional. Race complicates anger. Black women are often characterized as angry simply for existing, as if anger is woven into our breath and our skin.[18]

Here, anger is attributed to a speaker even when her tone is well within the listener's comfort zone. Listeners implicitly assign anger to speakers' words based on their social identity. Attributive anger sparks a prescient form of tone policing that I call *tone vigilance*. Tone vigilance prompts an audience either to listen for anger in a speaker's testimony, or to fold a perceived or imagined anger into the testimony because they assume that Black women always speak from an angry place. As if, recalling Gay's words, anger was 'woven into [her] breath and skin'. Attributing anger to marginalized knowers pre-silences them. It triggers an insidious anger-silencing spiral, where reasonable judgments and observations are reduced to the angry nature of a particular group. Sara Ahmed explains,

> The figure of the angry black woman is also a fantasy figure that produces its own effects. Reasonable thoughtful arguments are dismissed as anger (which of course empties anger of its own reason), which makes you angry, such that your response becomes read as confirmation of evidence that you are not only angry, but also unreasonable![19]

When anger is attributed to a speaker based on group membership, the causal relationship between reasonable claims about injustice and the speaker's anger is reversed. It's not that her anger makes the claim unreasonable, it's that the perceived or imagined unreasonableness of the claim is attributed to an angry essence at the core of one's group identity. Ahmed continues,

> [Y]ou might be angry *about* how racism and sexism diminish life choices for women of color. Your anger is a judgement that something is wrong. But in being heard as angry, your speech is read as motivated by anger. Your anger is read as unattributed, as if you

---

[18] Roxane Gay, 'Who Gets to Be Angry?', *The New York Times* (10 Jun, 2016), <https://www.nytimes.com/2016/06/12/opinion/sunday/who-gets-to-be-angry.html>.

[19] Sara Ahmed, *The Promise of Happiness* (Durham, North Carolina: Duke University Press, 2010), 68.

Alison Bailey

are against x because you are angry rather than being angry because you are against x. You become angry at the injustice of being heard as motivated by anger, which makes it harder to separate yourself from the object of anger. You become entangled with what you are angry about because you are angry about how they have entangled you in your anger. In becoming angry about that entanglement, you confirm their commitment to your anger as the truth 'behind' your speech, which is what blocks your anger, stops it getting through.[20]

Tone-managing practices are epistemically and psychologically harmful. Anger-silencing spirals have different consequences for marginalized speakers than they do for dominant hearers. From the perspective of dominators, tone management serves to restore their psychological and epistemic comfort. The white woman's request that Lorde not speak too harshly is a demand to accommodate her unmet psychological need for racial comfort. Tone management is a defence against 'white fragility' – 'a state in which even a minimum amount of racial stress becomes intolerable, triggering a range of defensive moves. These moves include the outward display of emotions such as anger, fear, or guilt, and behaviors such as argumentation, silence, or the desire to flee a stress-inducing situation. These responses, in turn, function to reinstate white racial equilibrium'.[21] The white woman is requesting not to have her epistemic confidence – that is, the sense she has of herself as a good white woman who is knowledgeable about race matters – called into question. It's easier mark Lorde as an angry Black woman, than it is to mark her own white ignorance. It is easier to shut down the conversation than to linger in the uncomfortable silences these conversations create. When white people chose comfort over listening to folks of colour's testimonies, we deny ourselves the opportunity to know something important about the world – a strain of knowledge that is rarely visible to us from where we sit or stand.

However, from the perspective of those silenced, anger-silencing spirals are epistemically and psychologically damaging. Silenced anger faces what José Medina calls a 'wrongful interpretive obstacle'.[22] When anger is misinterpreted it is emptied of knowledge.

[20] Ahmed, *The Promise of Happiness*, 68.
[21] Robin DiAngelo, 'White Fragility', *International Journal of Critical Pedagogy* 3.3 (2011), 54.
[22] José Medina, *The Epistemology of Resistance: Gender and Racial Oppressions, Epistemic Injustice, and Resistant Imaginations* (New York and Oxford: Oxford University Press, 2013), 91.

Instead of being taken as evidence of lived injury, trauma, or harm, the speaker's anger is used to confirm a character flaw or personality disorder. Women's anger is bitchy, crazy, or hysterical rather than civil or righteous. We are too thin skinned. People of colour's rage is uncivil(ized), uppity, or aggressive. They have attitude. These tropes pathologize anger, robbing it of its energy, force, and epistemic content. Our anger is weaponized against us. It is isolated from our testimonies, neutralized, and thrown back at us in limp unrecognizable forms.

Tone management tactics also have a damaging *gaslighting* effect, making speakers feel psychologically insecure and epistemically under-confident. Gaslighting, as Rachel McKinnon explains, 'is when a hearer tells a speaker that the speaker's claim isn't that serious or they're overreacting, or they're being too sensitive, or they're not interpreting events properly. This is used to discount the speaker's testimony'.[23] Gaslighting is part and parcel of most anger-silencing spirals. Telling a woman that she is 'overreacting' or 'being too sensitive' is code for 'you'd better dial it back'. It diffuses angry knowledge by quietly planting seeds of doubt that cause speakers to second-guess the legitimacy of their anger. As Saba Fatima explains, when anger is present, the demands for civility are almost always placed on white women and people of colour. This social pattern leads to paranoia. You begin to doubt your own experience and your own ability to judge that experience. You can never be certain if your emotional reactions are on target. You begin to feel depressed, guilty, or ashamed. You wonder if you have read too much into the situation, or if you are making a big deal out of nothing, or if you are too thin skinned.[24] Here, angry knowers are not simply mistaken about their emotions. Their very ability to judge whether the injuries that their anger signals are real is called into question. She might say to herself, 'I don't know why I'm so angry!' Gaslighting works against the gaslighted because gaslighters are fragile beings who rabidly defend their epistemic home turf. They cannot tolerate interpretations of events that challenge their worldview. So, if their

---

[23] McKinnon, 'Allies Behaving Badly: Gaslighting as Epistemic Injustice', 167.

[24] Saba Fatima, 'Being Brown and Epistemic Insecurity', Hypatia Conference, Villanova University, 29 May 2015. Also, 'On the Edge of Knowing: Microaggression and Epistemic Uncertainty as a Woman of Color', in Kirsti Cole and Holly Hassel (eds.), *Surviving Sexism in Academia: Feminist Strategies for Leadership* (New York: Routledge, 2017), 147–154.

worldview reads women's anger as an irrational or oversensitive response to trivial matters, then all explanations that point to anger as evidence of unjust harm must be extinguished. The disorienting nature of gaslighting neutralizes the knowledge in that anger, trapping angry knowers in a hermeneutically closed system where epistemic traction is rarely possible.

But, the effects tone management has on resistant anger concerns me for another reason. Tone management may prompt speakers to trade our anger for the chance either to be heard or to restore our epistemic confidence. Hoping to be heard, we may consciously soften our voices or swallow our anger half way. Testimonial smothering has an affective dimension, that I call *affective smothering,* a form of self–tone-policing that happens when the speaker recognizes that her audience lacks either the empathy or the affective competence to make sense of her anger as *she* experiences it.[25] Thinking '*they can't understand how this anger feels....*' she swallows her anger half way and repeats herself in a 'more appropriate tone'. I know this feeling intimately. There are times when my own resistant anger has injured my epistemic credibility. In a panic, I circle back to restore my audience's comfort. I soften my anger. Sometimes I apologize and repeat my testimony in honey-toned restatements. But, these retreats come at a cost. The terms of exchange require trading the chance to voice injury and to consider the transformative possibilities of my anger, for the outside chance that restoring my audience's comfort will also restore *my* epistemic credibility. I almost always lose this wager. And, when I do, I become an accomplice in the dominator's anger management project. I assume that my audience's comfort, and not my anger, will restore my epistemic confidence. I convince myself that this is the only way to get epistemic traction. But, I lose ground and my anger is carried forward into the next conversation where there are more wagers to lose. I have, in Martia Golden's words, paralyzed my anger and 'brilliantly shaped it into the soft armor of survival'.[26]

My task in this section has been to make visible the resistant anger that saturates the social practices of silencing. I have argued that *tone*

---

[25] Fatima treats this as testimonial smothering in 'On the Edge of Knowing: Microaggression and Epistemic Uncertainty as a Woman of Color'.

[26] Marita Golden, *Migrations of the Heart* (New York: Anchor Books, 1983), 21. Cited in Patricia Hill Collins, *Black Feminist Thought: Knowledge, Consciousness, and the Politics of Empowerment* (Boston: Unwin Hyman, 1991), 97.

policing and *tone vigilance* are forms of angry knowledge management that injure knowers. Speakers suffer a double epistemic injury – neither their testimony nor their anger get uptake. The next section focuses more intimately on the texture and distinct epistemic features of this resistant anger and sets the stage for my final discussion of anger's transformative power.

4. The Texture and Affective Ancestry of Knowing Resistant Anger

The silences that tone management produces are never empty, still, or mute. Angry tones are not affective embellishments that run alongside knowledge; they are woven tightly into it. Silence is not the voice of submission. Silencing pushes down, but resistant anger pushes back against the normalizing abuse of silencing practices. Resistant anger then, is not a raw unfocused energy. It is a *knowing resistant anger*. 'Knowing' because, in Lorde's words, it 'is loaded with energy and information' and 'resistant' because its vibrancy endures repeated silencing.[27] This anger not an automatic response to silencing; it must be cultivated in the same ways that those working for social justice must cultivate a practical knowledge of how systemic barriers shape their experiences. We must understand the structural origins of our anger. Without an understanding of how oppressed groups' anger is *systemically* silenced, resistant anger feels muddy-headed. So, it's not that some angers have knowledge and others are empty of it, only that anger's knowledge may not yet be intelligible to the subject because anger's resistant possibilities are not yet apparent.

I want to argue that knowing resistant anger is a source of epistemic traction. This requires that I reject the closed hermeneutical framework of the anger-silencing spiral, which is inattentive to the plurality of angry experiences. María Lugones's pluralist account of anger offers a useful vocabulary for making visible the anger that saturates the silences that epistemic injustice repeatedly manufactures. Before making this case, I need to give readers unfamiliar with Lugones's work the basic gist of her pluralist view of the self and explain how this view shapes her account of angry selves.

In 'Playfulness, "World" Traveling, and Loving Perception', Lugones develops a pluralistic feminism, 'one that affirms the

---

[27]   Lorde, 'On the Uses of Anger', 127.

plurality in each of us and among us as richness and as central to feminist ontology and epistemology'.[28] Her pluralist view of the self is revealed through the practice of playful, loving, 'world' travel. The basic idea here is that outsiders to dominant cultures have acquired a flexibility in moving from mainstream constructions of life, where they are constructed as outsiders, to constructions of life where they more or less at home. For example, people of colour must learn to navigate safely white 'worlds' where they feel ill-at-ease and are constructed as outsiders. So, their senses of self are plural because they shift across 'worlds'. Lugones uses the term 'world' in a way that is purposely ambiguous and unfixed. 'Worlds' are purposely incomplete. Worlds are not utopias. They are filled with flesh and blood people. Worlds need not be constructions of a whole society, they may be niches (e.g. a gay bar, a barrio, or a college campus). She is interested in how the shift from one 'world' (e.g. a barrio) to another (e.g. a predominantly white campus) reveals the plurality of self. In some 'worlds' our sense of self is intelligible, in other 'worlds' it is distorted. In the barrio, a Chicana might be at ease, outgoing, funny, or generous. On campus she might be shy, reserved, and cautious. Lugones explains, 'those of us who are "world"-travelers have the distinct experience of being different selves in different "worlds" and of having the capacity to remember other "worlds" and ourselves in them'.[29] She calls this shift from being one self in one 'world' to being another self in another "world" travel'.

Lugones's account of anger reflects her pluralism. If social selves are plural, then angry selves are plural. Our anger is not always intelligible across 'worlds'. In some 'worlds' knowing resistant anger is a clear righteous anger against injustice. In other 'worlds' anger is interpreted as hostile, threatening, or crazy. 'Worlds' have distinct epistemic terrains. So, angry experiences are 'world'-dependent in the sense that 'worlds' shape the *affective textures* of our angry experiences. This means that knowing resistant anger has particular textures and features, which will only be intelligible in particular resistant 'worlds' where its use and value are clear. I'm particularly interested in cultivating an understanding of how different angers *feel* so I can quickly identify those particular angry experiences that

---

[28]   María Lugones, 'Playfulness, "World" Traveling, and Loving Perception', *Pilgrimages/Peregrinajes: Theorizing Coalition against Multiple Oppressions* (Lanham, Maryland: Roman and Littlefield Publishers, 2007), 85.
[29]   Lugones, 'Playfulness, "World" Traveling, and Loving Perception', 86.

offer resources for resisting epistemic injustice. To do this, I need to spell out the specific texture of knowing resistant anger.

In 'Hard-to-Handle Anger', Lugones claims that she can 'make more sense of anger if [she] captures it in its specificity'.[30] Her term, 'hard-to-handle anger' is purposely ambiguous: it contains the plurality of ways angry experiences are 'hard'. If selves are plural, then marginalized knowers are at once oppressed⇔resisting. As Lugones remarks, 'one eye sees that oppressed reality, the other sees the resistant one'.[31] Plurality saturates the hardness of oppressed/silenced⇔resisting/angry subjects' responses to injustice. These are angry pluralist selves. In one sense, hard-to-handle anger has a *hard/heavy* texture that is burdensome, exhausting, laborious, strenuous, and fatiguing.[32] It has a heaviness born of frustration with the exhausting process of directing our anger at dominators in dominant worlds of sense where our anger gets no uptake. For example, when women experience a hard/heavy anger in response to campus sexual violence, the heaviness comes from trying to be heard in worlds of sense shaped by campus rape culture – 'worlds' that construct our anger as unintelligible on the grounds that it is *women's* anger about sexual violence. In these 'worlds' our resistant anger pushes back: it 'has communicative *intent* but it does not always succeed in getting uptake from the oppressor in the official world of sense'.[33] Women's anger about sexual violence can only be hysteria or a delayed reaction to having sex she now regrets. This is, for Lugones, a self-controlled anger 'attentive to the official interpretation of her movements, voice, message, asking for respectability, judging those who have wronged her'.[34]

But, there is a plurality in these angry experiences. They are at once shaped by the one eye that understands oppressed reality and the other eye that pushes back against the oppression from which angry knowers must separate. Hard-to-handle anger also has a *hard/*

---

[30] María Lugones, 'Hard-to-Handle Anger', *Pilgrimages/Peregrinajes: Theorizing Coalition against Multiple Oppressions* (Lanham, Maryland: Roman and Littlefield Publishers, Inc., 2007), 103.

[31] Lugones, 'Playfulness, "World" Traveling, and Loving Perception', 78.

[32] To reduce both the conceptual clutter for those unfamiliar with Lugones's pluralism, and to focus on the textures of anger, I've substituted *hard/heavy* anger for first-order anger and *hard/rebellious* anger for second-order anger. First-order anger sees the oppressed reality and second-order anger resists.

[33] Lugones, 'Hard-to-Handle Anger', 107.

[34] Lugones, 'Hard-to-Handle Anger', 104.

Alison Bailey

rebellious texture that presupposes or establishes the need to speak 'from within separate [non-dominant] worlds of sense. Separate, that is, from worlds of sense that deny intelligibility to the anger'.[35] This anger is hard in the sense that it is messy, disorderly, complex, and difficult to manage. It resists being well-ordered, controlled, disciplined, and tidy. Consider how spaces that affirm women's testimony around sexual violence create resistant 'worlds' where our anger is validated. Women experience a hard/rebellious anger about sexual violence when we seek out or create 'worlds' where our angry experiences are intelligible. I have in mind 'worlds' such as sexual assault survivors' support groups or social media spaces like the #MeToo movement where our safe sound collective anger gets uptake and where rape myths are dim artefacts of 'worlds' where our voices have been silenced.

Following Lugones, I ask that readers hold both anger's hard and rebellious textures in mind. Angry selves have the capacity to remember those 'worlds' where our anger is intelligible and those 'worlds' where it is not. And, as I will argue in the next section, resisting silencing practices requires that, when we are in dominant 'worlds', that we never forget those 'worlds' where our anger at injustice makes perfect sense. So, we must consider questions related to angry selves and the 'worlds' they occupy. We must ask, which self is angry? Is the angry self the subordinate self? Or, the resisting self? Is the subordinate self's anger intelligible in dominate worlds of sense by dominators? Or, is it the subordinate angry self pushing back against dominant worlds of sense in an attempt to be heard? Or, is it the fully resistant angry self, whose anger is fully intelligible in non-dominant worlds of sense? In which 'worlds' is her anger epistemically productive? In which 'worlds' is it neutralized?

My account of knowing resistant anger mirrors Lugones's pluralist view of anger. Knowing resistant anger is a *hard/heavy/rebellious anger* attentive to the epistemic terrains where it is and is not intelligible. It recognizes the hostile 'worlds' that make it heavy, but retains the memory of 'worlds' where its rebelliousness is intelligible. It expands on Lugones's pluralist account by highlighting the epistemic dimensions of anger, acknowledging anger's affective ancestry, and attending to anger's *felt* experiences. So, I will describe this expanded notion of plural angry selves as part of oppressed/silenced⇔resisting/angry communities.

Our angers are never fully our own. They are partially formed by the 'world'-dependent *affective ancestries* of marginalized social

---

[35] Lugones, 'Hard-to-Handle Anger', 104–5.

groups. The anger of the ages is always with us. I believe that some angers are inherited along with the historical traumas of colonized and oppressed peoples and the 'worlds' that gave rise to that ancestral anger. As Lorde observes, 'Every Black woman in America lives her life somewhere along a wide curve of ancient and unexpressed angers'.[36] Members of oppressed/silenced⇔resisting/angry communities have collective memories of their suffering, and that historical trauma and pain shapes the contours of their collective anger. U.S. Black anger's coherent genealogy begins with trafficking African bodies and continues through colonizers' use of enslaved labour, the convict-leasing system, Jim Crow, lynching, the rape of Black women and girls, police violence, incarceration, and the school-to-prison pipeline. I can't help but believe that the memories of past injustices remain alive in these communities today, because these injustices continue under different names. Ta-Nehisi Coates's memoir offers a glimpse of Black ancestral anger. He describes the moment when a white woman came up behind him in a crowded movie theatre and yelled 'Come on!' as she pushed his son out of her way. He writes, 'I turned and spoke to this woman and my words were hot with all of the moment and all of my history'.[37] Anger's abiding historical nature suggests that the differences between and among our lived identities are as affective as they are social and cultural, and that 'various historically coherent groups "feel differently" and navigate the material world on a different emotional register'.[38]

However, hard-to-handle anger's affective ancestry does not mean that its angry energy is oriented exclusively toward the past. Ancestral anger resonates in both backward- and forward-looking ways. Sometimes anger requires that we dwell on the past. Sometimes our anger reorients itself toward the creation and maintenance of new 'worlds'. So, one texture of anger *feels* the oppressed reality and history, and the other *feels* the resistant reality and possible futures. The feminist literature on anger is filled with references to

[36] Audre Lorde, 'Eye to Eye: Black Women, Hatred, and Anger,' *Sister Outsider: Essays and Speeches by Audre Lorde* (Trumansburg, New York: The Crossing Press, 1984), 145.

[37] Ta-Nehisi Coates, *Between the World and Me* (New York: Random House, 2015), 94.

[38] José Estaban Muñoz, 'Feeling Brown: Ethnicity and Affect in Ricardo Bracho's *The Sweetest Hangover* (and other STDs)' *Theatre Journal* **52** (2000), 70.

Alison Bailey

the visionary and transformative dimensions of anger. Lorde's visionary anger is marked by its ability to move people to act in the service of their collective vision.[39] Sara Ahmed acknowledges anger's bi-directional perspective when she remarks that 'anger is not simply defined in relationship to a past, but as opening up the future. In other words, being against something does not end with 'that which one is against'. Anger does not necessarily become 'stuck' on its object, although that object may remain sticky and compelling. Being against something is also being for something, something that has yet to be articulated or is not yet'.[40] Lugones describes anger's transformative power as 'cognitively rich, cut from the same tonality and cloth as metamorphosis'. It's an anger 'driven by the weight of resistance and fully inspiring'.[41] So, these hard/heavy/rebellious angers flicker back and forth. They hold the felt memories of communities of angry selves and their histories along with the transformative visions of future angry resistant communities.

Finally, knowing resistant angry experiences just feel differently. They do *not* feel like the angry experiences you have when you are so angry that you *can't* think straight; that is to say, when your anger moves in unfocused, wasteful, useless, and destructive ways. Unfocused anger moves in ways that diminish its energy, like water moving through the 'shower' or 'mist' settings of a garden hose nozzle. Knowing resistant anger is 'a lucid, clearly focused, and orchestrated anger that is articulated with precision'.[42] It moves with the force and energy of water that flows through the 'jet stream' setting of that garden hose. You are so angry that you *can* see straight. As Lorde explains, 'None of its energy is wasted, for it knows its object and all of its energy is focused on that object in hopes that this anger will be heard and things will change'.[43] It is a 'safe and sound anger', a clear-headed anger with the power to destroy and construct, and to inspire courageous action.[44] Knowing resistant anger is dangerous not because it muddies reason, but because it pushes back against the forces that repeatedly try to rob it of its energy, clarity, and knowledge.

[39]   Lorde, 'The Uses of Anger', 127.
[40]   Ahmed, *The Promise of Happiness,* 175.
[41]   Lugones, 'Hard-to-Handle Anger', 103, 112.
[42]   Lorde, 'The Uses of Anger', 131.
[43]   Lorde, 'The Uses of Anger', 129.
[44]   Frye, 'A Note On Anger', 85.

Readers should now have a sense of knowing resistant anger's plurality, texture, ancestry, and feel. Attention to felt experiences is important. I find it easier to name my anger by attending to how it feels, than thinking about how it fits into a pre-determined taxonomy. I start from the body and work out. This requires attending to which self is angry, in which 'world', the anger's felt texture and its ancestry. My final section explains the ways that knowing resistant anger offers oppressed/silenced⇔resisting/angry groups a resource for resisting epistemic injustice.

5. Knowing Resistant Anger as a Resource against Epistemic Injustice

Feminists have long acknowledged the vital role emotions play in knowledge construction. As Jen McWeeney observes, feminist analyses are grounded in 'the radical idea that *angry experience is a kind of knowing experience*'.[45] This is not news. Resistant epistemic communities have long recognized the transformative energy of anger that the literature on epistemic injustice curiously overlooks.[46] Despite the epistemic wear and tear that hermeneutically closed systems place on disenfranchised knowers, anger-silencing spirals are epistemically rich spaces. The strength of Lugones's pluralism is that it points at once to the ways hard/heavy anger is neutralized and to the ways hard/rebellious anger is a resource that pushes back against dominant 'worlds' of sense. So, where is the knowing resistant anger in epistemic injustice? It's everywhere, but it often escapes our notice because non-pluralist views of anger train knowers to focus exclusively on how anger gets silenced, and not on how anger pushes back. If we shift our attention to the 'world'-breaking hard/rebellious angry experiences (while also keeping hard/heavy anger in mind) we

[45] Jen McWeeney, 'Liberating Anger, Embodying Knowledge: A Comparative Study of María Lugones and Zen Master Hakuin' *Hypatia* **25**.2 (2010), 295.

[46] Consider how Fricker drains anger from her paradigm example of testimonial injustice. She selects the anger-free hotel room conversation between Marge and Herbert in *The Talented Mr. Ripley* rather than the water taxi conversation where Marge's clearly-focused anger is resistant and alive. Anger is also drained from the courtroom testimonial exchanges in her *To Kill a Mockingbird* examples, even though it's clear that Tom Robinson, a Black man, must swallow his anger to be heard, and that Mayella, a young white woman, uses anger to bolster her false rape charge against Tom.

can better understand knowing resistant anger as a transformative creative epistemic resource.

Anger-silencing spirals are epistemically rich spaces. They are as paralyzing as they are transformative. Paralyzing because our anger fails to get uptake, and transformative because this failure obliges us to sit with our anger and in Lorde's words, 'listen to its rhythms'.[47] Sitting mindfully with our anger is transformative because it grounds us, reorients us, prompts us to move, and to seek out alternative epistemic terrains where our anger is intelligible. It brings us 'back to our bodies, to the gut-level, signaling that we are in a situation that is unjust, damaging, cruel, or dangerous'.[48] Lorde's image of anger's rhythm highlights both the meter of our angry tones and the intelligibility of the unjust patterns that repeatedly evoke our anger – the silences that epistemic injustices repeatedly manufacture. Rhythms are patterns. Patterns reveal structures. When we sit with anger's rhythms we are made aware of the epistemically damaging effects practices of silencing have on us. In a recent interview with Access Hollywood, Uma Thurman was asked to comment on the prevalence of the abuse of power and sexual violence in the Hollywood film industry. Speaking slowly and deliberately, through gritted teeth, she responded, 'I don't have a tidy soundbite for you, because I've learned – I'm not a child – and I have learned that when I've spoken in anger I usually regret the way I express myself. So, I've been waiting to feel less angry. And when I'm ready, I'll say what I have to say'.[49] She sat with these rhythms and four months later spoke clearly and directly to the patterns of abuse she endured on and off the Hollywood set.

Here's the general idea. When we shift our attention from the hard/heavy texture of knowing resistant anger toward the hard/resistant texture of our anger its epistemic resources become visible. Knowing resistant anger is transformative because it reorients us. This shift restores our courage and confidence: It prompts us to seek out new epistemic terrains where our anger is alive and intelligible. This intelligibility comes from the epistemic confidence of collectives of oppressed/silenced⇔resisting/angry selves; and, it is an

---

[47] Lorde, 'Uses of Anger', 130.

[48] Alison Jaggar, 'Love and Knowledge: Emotion in Feminist Epistemology', *Inquiry* **32**.2 (1989), 167.

[49] Lindy West, 'Brave Enough to be Angry', *New York Times* (11 Nov 2017), <https://www.nytimes.com/2017/11/08/opinion/anger-women-weinstein-assault.html>.

essential ingredient in the creation and sustenance of resistant communities. This last point requires some unpacking.

For starters, knowing resistant anger reorients knowers by alerting us to the fact that the dominator's interpretations of our anger are not the only means of making sense of that anger. The non-pluralist interpretation of women's anger as 'bitchy' or 'uppity' is simply a privilege-protecting bad epistemic habit. Becoming mindful of anger-silencing patterns creates a space in which to reorient our angry energy toward creating and sustaining 'worlds' where that anger is intelligible. In Medina's words, it offers us 'the lucidity . . . to see things afresh and redirect our perceptual habits, to find a way out of or an alternative to an epistemic blind alley'.[50] Reorienting angry knowledge requires resisting the socialized urges to make our anger heard in hermeneutically closed systems and to resist epistemic bad habits like falling back into making sense of our anger on the dominator's terms. Instead, we must challenge the urge to restore our audience's comfort. Our anger will never be at home in the dominator's anger-silencing spirals. Our anger needs a new home. It must move. But, for anger to move it needs traction, and traction requires that we ground ourselves in a particular kind of angry self – a *knowing resistant angry self*. Returning to Lugones's pluralist view of angry selves we can now ask: which self is angry? The subordinate hard/heavy angry self or the resistant hard/rebellious angry self? On whose epistemic terrain is she angry? Where does her anger get traction? Where does it get silenced?

Knowing resistant anger helps us to move because is a useful instrument of cartography.[51] It helps us to 'see' structure because we continually traverse epistemic terrains where our anger may or may not be intelligible. This is why Uma Thurman waits to tell her story. She knows that she needs to be less angry to be heard in the context of a live television interview. Knowing where, when, and with whom our anger gets traction offers us spatial information about the 'worlds' where we are most vulnerable and the 'worlds' where we are most intelligible. I have a particular image for this practice. Think about how dogs come to know the boundaries of the invisible fences that confine them by repeatedly testing the limits of their movements in any direction. A cartography eventually emerges from this exercise that identifies fissures in the fencing. If there are regions of the unlevel knowing field where injustice robs

---

[50] Medina, *The Epistemology of Resistance*, 45.
[51] Lugones, 'Hard-to-Handle Anger', 107-8. See also Frye, 'A Note On Anger', 94.

anger of its epistemic friction, then we must reorient ourselves, look for fissures, and move toward rougher terrain. We must gather on new ground where our knowing resistant anger is validated and its energy can be redirected productively toward justice-restoring projects. We must seek out new epistemic home terrains where oppressed/silenced⇔resisting/angry selves can gather collectively to restore our epistemic confidence. There we can affirm how practices of silencing are harmful, as if to say 'You *should* be angry! I'm angry too. Together we will pool our anger in a place where it gets uptake, and we will hold firm to its intelligibility even when we are sucked back into anger-silencing spirals. We will keep alive the memory of epistemic terrains where our anger is heard, even when we are on the dominator's terrain. Together, we will not be silenced!'

Next, seeking out or creating resistant epistemic 'worlds' where our anger is intelligible fills our bodies with confidence and courage. On hospitable epistemic terrains, knowing resistant anger can be a creative force for change. From the standpoint of epistemic injustice hard/rebellious anger is an epistemic confidence booster in the sense that it can restore a knower's self-respect. As Frye notes, 'In getting angry one claims that one is in certain way and dimensions respectable. One makes a claim upon respect'.[52] On resistant epistemic home terrains, our anger is heard, it gets traction, and we are made newly aware of our power, agency and self-worth. Anger brings courage. When we are angry enough to be brave we take risks. These acts of resistance are also acts of creation. Consider how those of us who work for social justice continue to weather the anger-silencing spirals we find ourselves in during university diversity committees, city council meetings, or community forums on policing. One occasion stands out for me. I was at a semester-long series of meetings where department chairs were asked to respond to the campus climate report. At some point, I became aware that I was repeating myself. I realized that my claim that there are no safe spaces for students of color on campus was unintelligible to the committee. I gave up and sat with my anger. I listened to its rhythms. In that stillness I realized, *Ohhhhhh! It's not that my argument is incoherent. It's not that I'm not being clear. It's not that I've not given enough evidence. Either they cannot hear what I'm saying, or it makes no sense to them, or they just don't want to hear it.* The committee could not make sense of diversity initiatives outside of the possible ways they could use them to rebrand our campus as welcoming. No traction was possible in that space. Once I realized this I walked out. I no longer yearned to make

[52] Frye, 'A Note On Anger', 90.

myself heard in these spaces or to restore the comfort of my audience. I looked for a new home for my anger. I approached allies after the meeting and asked them, 'Am I right about this? Is this your experience too?' They assured me it was. We shared our angry experiences and from our conversations emerged alternative epistemic communities and projects that focused directly on creating safe spaces where students of colour could be heard.

Knowing resistant anger then, not only restores the collective epistemic confidence of angry selves, it is also an essential ingredient in the creation and sustenance of resistant epistemic communities. It offers us beneficial epistemic friction because we can collectively direct that anger toward change. Projects in feminist epistemology and epistemologies of ignorance have argued that when marginalized knowers encounter hermeneutical sink holes (i.e. anger-silencing spirals) that we would do well to remember that the unlevel knowing field contains alternative interpretive resources and resistant practices.[53] Yet, in academic philosophy, little attention is paid to knowing resistant anger as an alternative resource. This is tragic, because anger is central to the formation and maintenance of resistant communities. Anger has a bonding effect – it provides the affective fuel that brings us together and helps us to form cohesive social networks and organized movements. Anger at injustice unites us because, in our moving, we come to realize that we are not alone in our anger. What first feels like an isolated subordinated anger is really part of a larger collective resistant angry experience. There are terrains where our anger feels at home, where it is supported by coalitions of oppressed/silenced⇔resisting/angry selves. Resistant epistemic communities must treat our collective knowing resistant anger (and its affective ancestry) as an epistemic resource because collaboratively it offers us epistemic traction. For this resource to be effective, however, it must be sustainable; that is, our knowing resistant anger must not exhaust itself. It must maintain the single-pointed 'jet stream' focus on the objects of injustice. We need not be angry all the time, but oppressed/silenced⇔resistant/angry communities need to keep our collective anger hot and oriented towards transformative projects. Our anger must remain alive and accessible, even if it only

---

[53] For examples see Hortense Spillers, 'Mama's Baby, Papa's Maybe: An American Grammar Book', *Diacritics*, **17**.2 (Summer, 1987), 64–81; James C. Scott, *Domination and the Arts of Resistance: Hidden Transcripts* (New Haven: Yale University Press, 1990); María Lugones, *Pilgrimages/Peregrinajes;* Patricia Hill Collins, *Black Feminist Thought;* José Medina, *Epistemologies of Resistance.*

simmers gently below the surface. In Lorde's words, this anger 'expressed and translated into action in the service of our vision and our future is a liberating and strengthening act of clarification, for it is in the painful process of this translation that we identify who are our allies with whom we have grave differences, and who are our genuine enemies'.[54]

Knowing resistant anger then, counters the effects of tone/anger/knowledge management. The purpose of tone policing is to tame, discipline, and extinguish angry knowledge. The purpose of resistant epistemic and political communities is to affirm, nurture, and cultivate that angry knowledge as a resource. Resistant communities are 'worlds' where we practice inoculating our anger against silencing practices. You can't silence anger in an epistemic ecosystem that is designed to keep knowing resistant anger vibrant and visible. The trick here is to keep the communal memory and feeling of knowing resistant anger fresh within us when we find ourselves trapped in anger-silencing spirals. Resistant communities keep anger hot by maintaining cultures where tone management and other silencing practices are ineffective. In this way, they can collectively take action based on their knowledge of epistemic injustice. It is difficult to silence anger in communities that come together around injustices that are transparent to them. Think about how resistant movements in the United States, such as Black Lives Matter, Standing Rock Sioux water protectors, or national student walk-outs in response to gun violence have made their knowing resistant anger of police violence, water rights, and the impact of gun violence available to their communities to the point where that knowledge is so widespread and obvious that it has become woven into the very fabric of their epistemic home terrain. As if to say: We've had enough! We can't be silenced! This stops NOW! Don't you dare tone manage us and spin our stories! There is no doubt that the collective anger of these communities is justified and real.

The purpose of this discussion has been to excavate the resistant uses of anger that circulate in anger-silencing spirals and to suggest that Lugones's pluralist account of anger offers a way of making knowing resistant anger visible as an epistemic resource. On a closing note, I want to circle back to the concern I raised in the introduction. I'm worried that accounts of epistemic injustice that fail to recognize anger's plurality and power will continue the work of

---

[54]   Lorde, 'Uses of Anger', 127.

silencing, dismissing, and erasing angry knowledge as a resource for resisting epistemic injustice. I worry that we have failed to heed Kristie Dotson's cautionary tale that 'when addressing and identifying forms of epistemic oppression one needs to endeavor not to perpetuate epistemic oppression'.[55] The failure to engage knowing resistant anger is not a simple oversight. As Gaile Pohlhaus's work suggests, ignoring knowing resistant anger's transformative power is itself an act of wilful hermeneutical ignorance that occurs 'when dominantly situated knowers refuse to acknowledge epistemic tools [e.g. Lorde's transformative anger and Lugones's pluralism] developed from the experienced world of those situated marginally'.[56] I fear that such oversights leave too many of us to wallow in *epistemic despair*: a condition that happens when epistemic communities swallow their anger, surrender to silence, and lose hope of ever being heard. Epistemic despair drains off knowers' resistant energies and consigns us to a world where epistemic traction is a matter of chance.

Illinois State University
baileya@ilstu.edu

---

[55] Kristie Doston, 'A Cautionary Tale: On Limiting Epistemic Oppression', *Frontiers: A Journal of Women's Studies* **33**.1 (2012), 24.
[56] Pohlhaus, 'Relational Knowing and Epistemic Injustice: Toward a Theory of Willful Hermeneutical Ignorance', *Hypatia* **27**.4 (2012), 715.

Just Say 'No': Obligations to Voice Disagreement

CASEY REBECCA JOHNSON

Abstract

It is uncontroversial that we sometimes have moral obligations to voice our disagreements, when, for example, the stakes are high and a wrong course of action will be pursued. But might we sometimes also have epistemic obligations to voice disagreements? In this paper, I will argue that we sometimes do. In other words, sometimes, to be behaving as we ought, qua epistemic agents, we must not only disagree with an interlocutor who has voiced some disagreed-with content but must also testify to this disagreement. This is surprising given that norms on testimony are generally taken to be permissive, and epistemic obligations are usually taken to be negative. In this paper I will discuss some occasions in which epistemic obligations to testify may arise, and I will attempt to investigate the nature of these obligations. I'll briefly discuss the relationship between epistemic and moral norms. I'll offer an account of what it takes to discharge epistemic obligations to testify. Finally, I'll look at some accounts of epistemic obligation that might explain these obligations.

1. Disagreeing and Voicing Disagreement

In 1994, Richard Herrnstein and Charles Murray published *The Bell Curve*. In it, the authors notoriously argued that the difference in performance on IQ tests across races is due to genetics rather than socialization. They argued that difference between African American average IQ scores and white American scores is caused, at least in part, by genetic differences. They further argued that this difference in genetics also explains differences in income, job success, and criminality, among other things.[1] These claims, according to Herrnstein and Murray, were the results of years of work in behavioural genetics.

The Bell Curve was met with wide public protest. There were (and continue to be) sit-ins and calls for Murray to resign his various academic posts (Herrnstein died soon after publication). Some behavioural geneticists, particularly those interested in animal behavioural genetics, dismissed the work as well. Geneticist David

---

[1] Richard J. Herrnstein and Charles Murray, *The Bell Curve: Intelligence and Class Structure in American Life* (New York: Simon and Schuster, 2010).

doi:10.1017/S1358246118000577   ©The Royal Institute of Philosophy and the contributors 2018
Royal Institute of Philosophy Supplement **84** 2018   117

Botstein, for example, called the text, 'so stupid that it is not rebuttable'.[2]

However, the academic reaction was not entirely negative. In the 1995 keynote address to the Behavioral Genetics Association, Glayde Whitney, professor of behavioural genetics, suggested that Murray and Herrnstein's work be pursued – that *The Bell Curve* opened many lines of important research. Indeed, many geneticists interested in intelligence voiced their support of the book, going so far as to call it an important contribution. An editorial in *The Wall Street Journal*, signed by fifty-two geneticists defended Herrnstein and Murray against accusations that their data and analysis were problematic.[3]

Despite signing this editorial, many of these same geneticists thought that the science of the book was deeply flawed. Subsequent interviews with signatories to that editorial revealed that they never thought that the relationship between genetic correlates for intelligence and race were informative or even possibly informative. These scientists, then, disagreed with the findings of *The Bell Curve*. They just didn't say so.

It seems to me that these disagreeing scientists failed to meet their obligations. The interviews were anonymous, so we'll call two of the scientists Lucy and Ethel. Lucy and Ethel failed in a couple of ways. First, Lucy and Ethel participated in the publication of an editorial that said, or perhaps implied, something they did not believe. To some extent, they lied or misled the readers of that editorial.[4] Second, Lucy and Ethel ought to have said something about what they in fact believed. Intuitively, Lucy and Ethel should have *publicly testified* that they disagreed with the findings in *The Bell Curve*.

Lucy and Ethel probably had some practical reasons not to voice their disagreement: the political climate was uncertain, Murray, Whitney and other proponents of the book were powerful, and the field of behavioural genetics was new. To fight within the field might have cast doubt on the whole discipline. Further, they may

---

[2] Jon Beckwith and Franklin Huang, 'Should we make a fuss? A case for social responsibility in science.' *Nature biotechnology* **23**.12 (2005), 1479–1480.

[3] Aaron Panofsky, *Misbehaving Science: Controversy and the Development of Behavior Genetics* (Chicago, IL: University of Chicago Press, 2014).

[4] Jennifer M. Saul, *Lying, Misleading, and What is Said: An Exploration in Philosophy of Language and in Ethics* (Oxford: Oxford University Press, 2012).

have had principled reasons to protect scientists from intimidation and protest – it is reasonable to think that scientific progress depends on a high degree of academic freedom, and that that freedom is only protected if scientists can publish their results regardless of public outcry.

These reasons, however, don't seem to override the sense that Lucy and Ethel ought to have voiced their disagreements with their findings. We can imagine a graduate student in Lucy's lab being confused or misled by *The Bell Curve*. This grad student might go on to pursue a faulty plan of study. Lucy could, plausibly, have prevented this by telling her graduate student that she disagreed with the findings. We can imagine Ethel's African-American neighbour coming to believe that she will, as a matter of genetic predisposition, be unable to retain her job or keep her children out of prison. If Ethel had testified that she disagreed with Murray and Herrnstein's findings, she could have helped assuage these fears. These obligations seem to over-ride the practical considerations against testifying.

So, there were good reasons for Lucy and Ethel to testify that they disagreed with the findings of *The Bell Curve*. They had, I think, an obligation to do so.[5] Further, I think they had an *epistemic* obligation to do so. That is, Lucy and Ethel, by failing to testify that they disagreed, were failing to behave as they epistemically ought. And this is the case whether or not they *believed* as they epistemically ought.[6] I will defend this claim in this paper.

In the next section I will briefly discuss epistemic obligations in general. In section three, I'll demonstrate that our obligations to voice disagreement are plausibly epistemic, even if they are sometimes also moral. Then, in section four, I'll offer a hypothesis of what it takes to discharge obligations to voice disagreements. Finally, in section five, I'll consider four accounts of the source of these obligations. These accounts are not competitors – however, by highlighting multiple possible accounts I will attempt to make the best possible case for the claim that we have a prima facie epistemic obligation to voice disagreements.

---

[5]   Here I'm moving between 'having x-type reasons to φ' and 'having x-type obligations to φ'. I recognize that these are importantly different in some literatures. What I mean, in this context, is that having an obligation to φ means that failing to φ constitutes a failing to do what one ought.

[6]   That is, their epistemic mistake cannot be explained in terms of mistakenly forming beliefs.

Casey Rebecca Johnson

2. Epistemic Obligations

The discussion of epistemic obligations in the philosophical literature is largely concerned with the formation of beliefs. Usually these obligations are negative – they are obligations to refrain from certain epistemic actions.[7] For example, we ought not believe that p if our evidence rules p out. We ought (perhaps) not to remain as confident in our belief q if our epistemic peer disagrees. Positive epistemic norms are often considered to be permissions rather than obligations. Given a set of evidence E, you *may* believe that p. So, epistemic obligations to testify to disagreement, if indeed we have them, have gone largely unnoticed in the literature.

It is not plausible that we have an ultima facie obligation to testify when we disagree, even if a case can be made for some kind of obligation to do so. If I voice all of my beliefs whenever they happen to be in disagreement with content already expressed,[8] I'd likely be violating other sorts of norms. Testifying to all my disagreements would be weird, rude, and exhausting. I probably have no all-things-considered obligation to voice my disagreement with a stranger I overhear on the bus, for example. Considerations of politeness and practicality will override what obligation I do have. I can imagine a case (say, of overt harmful racism or verbal abuse) in which my obligation is not overridden in such a context, but these cases are in the minority. I'll return to this in more detail below, but for now let me note the following: the obligation that I'll be defending is a prima facie duty to voice disagreements – one that is more or less easily overridden in various contexts.

How might the features of a context affect the strength of an obligation? Considerations of manners, morals, practicality, and propriety are stronger in some contexts than in others. At a dinner party

---

[7]   Mark T. Nelson, 'We Have No Positive Epistemic Duties.' *Mind* **119**.473 (2010), 83–102; Phil Goggans, 'Epistemic obligations and doxastic voluntarism', *Analysis* **51**.2 (1991), 102–105. Notable exceptions are Matthew Chrisman's middle road between doxastic involuntarism and epistemic deontology, Edward Hinchman's paper on intra- vs. inter-personal epistemic obligations, and Matthew Sample's work on the epistemic obligations of scientists. See Matthew Chrisman, 'Ought to Believe', *Journal of Philosophy* **105**.7 (2008), 346–370; Edward Hinchman, 'Reflection, Disagreement, and Context', *American Philosophical Quarterly* **49**.2 (2012), 95; Matthew Sample, 'Stanford's Unconceived Alternatives from the Perspective of Epistemic Obligations', *Philosophy of Science* **82**.5 (2015), 856–866.

[8]   Or presupposed, or implied, etc. See section 5 for more on this.

hosted by my spouse's boss, practical and conversational considerations will probably outweigh many of my obligations to voice my disagreements. If, however, I can do so at little cost to manners or propriety, or if the subject of disagreement is particularly important, my obligation may be mitigated but not outweighed.

Put a slightly different way, sometimes obligations are (or at least appear to be) in conflict. In some contexts, my obligation to protect someone's feelings, to advocate for myself, or to reach some desirable conclusion might conflict with my obligation to voice my disagreement. If I'm not terribly confident in the belief I'd be voicing, my obligation is easier to override. If I have a high degree of credence, and the stakes and conflicts are comparatively low, my obligation is stronger than if I barely count as believing the proposition and expressing it would be rude. In cases like this, the conflicting obligations must be weighed against one another to determine what ultima facie obligations I have. Figuring out my ultima facie obligation may be complicated, and will certainly depend on the details of my situation.

These conflicting obligations, however, press us to address a further question: are the obligations to testify merely moral obligations to do something epistemic? Or are we *epistemically* obligated to voice (at least some of) our disagreements? We'll turn to that in the next section.

3. Distinguishing Epistemic and Moral Obligations

We might coherently hold that Lucy and Ethel have an obligation to voice their disagreement and yet deny that this obligation is particularly epistemic. Perhaps it seems that Lucy and Ethel have a *moral* obligation, and it is merely incidental that the action they are obligated to perform has an epistemic flavour. The fact that they're obligated to testify does not, by itself, demonstrate that they have an epistemic obligation.[9] The subject matter, and the consequences of *The Bell Curve* make the case for a moral obligation easy – the book contributed to and appeared to justify the continuation of the systematic subordination and disenfranchisement of African Americans, and those racialized as black. This is seriously immoral, so Lucy and Ethel quite plausibly have a moral obligation to stop it if they can. But I don't think this accounts for all the obligations they face.

---

[9]   After all, the obligation to feed the hungry isn't plausibly a culinary obligation.

Casey Rebecca Johnson

To bolster the case for epistemic obligations to voice disagreement it would help to have an example that prompts the intuition that there is an obligation to testify, but where there are no (or no major) moral stakes.[10] So, imagine that you're having lunch with your friend Stella, the mechanic. You mention that you're planning to replace your brake pads to fix the squealing sound your car makes. Stella thinks that this is a mistake. She does not believe that replacing brake pads will fix squealing. Nonetheless, she does not say anything to you about her disagreement. She remains quiet, or makes non-committal noises until the subject changes.

It is plausible that in a case like this Stella has an obligation to tell you she disagrees with you. And yet, this does not seem like a case with major moral stakes. This suggests that Stella's obligation, if indeed she has one, is epistemic.

On the other hand, while this case is not of *moral* import, perhaps we take it to have too much *prudential* import to cleanly demonstrate that Stella's obligation is epistemic. I don't find this convincing, myself. Perhaps you prudentially ought to get more information before you make your purchase, and perhaps you prudentially ought to ask Stella for her help, rather than merely assert your plans to her. Whatever *you* should prudentially do, it doesn't seem that *Stella* has prudential obligations. However, let's grant, for the sake of argument, that Stella's case is still too fraught to demonstrate that there is an epistemic obligation here.

So, we need an example in which there are neither major moral *nor* prudential stakes, and yet there is an epistemic obligation. So, imagine that Carla, a historian of ancient art, is giving a presentation to her research group. She is a well-respected, emeritus scholar, speaking to other well-respected emerita faculty. As a small aside of her presentation she makes the claim that Babylonian architecture influenced Assyrian ceramic art. Carla's colleague, Theresa, disagrees. Theresa believes that Babylonian architecture did not influence Assyrian ceramic art. Nonetheless, she remains silent, even through the question and answer portion of the presentation. She does not voice her disagreement.

Here we have a case with no major moral or prudential stakes. Carla and Theresa will, in all likelihood, face no practical consequences as a result of this (lack of) conversation. Carla may independently decide

---

[10]   If all cases have moral stakes (to some extent), then all we need is for there to be a mismatch between the level or gravity of the moral stakes and the strength of the obligation. So a case with low-grade moral stakes but strong obligations will work.

that that part of the presentation lacks evidentiary support and leave it out in future work. Or she may bolster it with footnotes and further claims. Theresa might do some investigating of her own, or she may recall that she never cared much about Assyrian ceramics anyway. At any rate, it is unlikely that correcting this aside has great prudential import. So, if Theresa has an obligation to voice her disagreement, and neither prudential nor moral stakes can account for this obligation, then the obligation is probably epistemic.

Perhaps it seems more plausible that Theresa, like Stella, has an obligation *in so far as she is an expert.* That is, expertise might confer special obligations, and this explains why we don't feel that Theresa does as she ought when she fails to testify. While I'm not inclined toward this explanation of Theresa's and Stella's obligations because I don't think that the obligations they have are particular to experts, I don't think it is entirely off the mark. Expertise plausibly affects the *strength* of one's obligation to testify. But notice, even if this explains the strength of their obligation, this does not mean that the obligation to voice disagreement is not epistemic. After all, expertise is an *epistemic* category. If Theresa's expertise generates her obligation to testify, then this is just an example of the kind of obligation I'm getting at. An obligation due to expertise just is an epistemic obligation.

Of course, we may doubt that stories or examples like these help us cleanly distinguish epistemic obligations from other kinds of obligations. It may be that our intuitions about Stella, Theresa, and the rest are insufficiently fine-grained to help us in such an analysis. I think there is something to this concern. Indeed, I think that there is probably not much to be gained from drawing too sharp of a line between kinds of obligations. And I take myself to be in fairly good company on this score: Miranda Fricker, in her 2007 text, argues for a similar point with respect to her idea of testimonial justice.[11] Fricker argues that there are so-called hybrid virtues – virtues that are both epistemic and moral. When we are concerned with truth, the virtue's epistemic side is more apparent, and when we're concerned with ethics, the virtue is apparently moral. The hybrid virtue doesn't bother Fricker, so perhaps hybrid obligations need not bother us.

If we agree with Fricker that the line between the moral and the epistemic is not as thick or sharp as it might appear, then there is good reason to think that we need not distinguish our moral from our epistemic duties too cleanly. At least Fricker's conception of a hybrid virtue opens the conceptual space for a similarly hybrid

---

[11]   Miranda Fricker, *Epistemic Injustice: Power and the Ethics of Knowing* (Oxford: Oxford University Press, 2007).

Casey Rebecca Johnson

obligation. All I want to claim, here, is that the obligation to testify to disagreement is an epistemic obligation, even if it is also a moral one.

4. Discharging the Obligation

Let's grant, for now, that we have a defeasible epistemic obligation to voice our disagreements. When these obligations aren't overridden, how are we to discharge them? What, in other words, must a speaker like Theresa do to meet her obligation (assuming it isn't overridden)? While the details of this are likely to depend on the situation, in this section I'll hypothesize about the generalities.

In general terms, to discharge one's obligation to voice disagreement with proposition p requires that one add to the conversational scoreboard some content that appears to be incompatible with p. I'll spend the rest of this section explaining and (to some extent) defending this hypothesis.

According to this requirement, an agent like Theresa must put forward some content in order to discharge her obligation. Putting content forward is the correct level of specificity for this requirement. While I'm calling this an obligation to *voice* disagreement, the agent need not literally use her voice. Signs, signals, notes, and gestures are all possible methods of discharging one's obligation. We might imagine Carla taking a poll to see which of her audience members disagreed with her. If she did this, then Theresa's raised hand would surely discharge her obligation. We can also imagine making a face or hand movement to express disagreement. Demanding verbal expression, in some cases, is asking too much. On the other hand, one must put forward some content or other. Theresa disagreed with Carla's claim about Babylonian architecture, and her speech action should (to some extent) convey that.

Still, it doesn't seem like the only way for Theresa to discharge her obligation is to say 'Babylonian architecture didn't influence Assyrian ceramic art', or 'I disagree about the influence on Assyrian ceramic art'. Though these responses might be sufficient, they are not clearly necessary. Theresa could, instead, say, 'I think you should check into your sources on Babylonian architecture', or 'Some of the inferences about influences seemed off to me'. It is too specific to require speakers to voice *not p* when they disagree with an expression of p, or that they make explicit that they are disagreeing[12].

---

[12] In addition to being unnecessary in some cases, this kind of direct rebuttal is probably not effective in many cases. Direct rebuttals may prompt

Just Say 'No': Obligations to Voice Disagreement

Surely, though, Theresa can't express just any content. There are many utterances Theresa could make that would *not* discharge her obligation. It won't discharge her obligation to ask, 'Do you think that Babylonian architecture influenced Assyrian art?' in most cases (though asking 'Do you *really* think that...' might). If she says, 'I read that Babylonian architecture was terrible' she probably doesn't do the job either. What she expresses must be (or appear to be) incompatible with the objectionable content to some extent.

Also, if Theresa tells her students, or her partner, or her barista some content that is incompatible with Carla's aside, she also does not seem to have discharged her obligation. If she does this, Theresa has added her belief to a conversation, but not to the same conversation that inspired her disagreement. One way to put this is that Theresa's contribution is made to a new or different conversational scoreboard.[13] So, this part of the requirement means that the content must be put on to roughly the same conversational scoreboard as the objectionable content.

There are, however, pragmatic concerns about voicing objectionable content, given facts about social subordination and privilege: It can be pragmatically difficult, especially for members of socially subordinated social groups, to voice disagreement with content, particularly content expressed by those in positions of privilege. This can be because of the ways in which members of these social groups are socialized, or because of the ways in which speech acts by members of these groups are perceived. But it would be a knock against the hypothesis if it placed unfair burdens on agents who already experience systematically unfair social and epistemic situations. If Lucy, for example, is a person of colour, it might be more pragmatically difficult for her to voice her disagreement, especially if she were obligated to voice her disagreement to Charles Murray or some other powerful white scientist.

I think there are two ways to go in light of this concern. First, it may be that Lucy can discharge her obligation by voicing her disagreement to *some but not all* of the participants in the original conversation. If she can tell some other scientists, some known allies, or even members of her own lab that she disagrees, that plausibly discharges her obligation. Second, it may well be that Lucy's obligation

---

defensiveness rather than uptake or reasonable conversation. However, efficacy may or may not be at issue, as we'll see below.

[13] David Lewis, 'Scorekeeping in a Language Game', *Journal of Philosophical Logic* **8** (1979), 339–359.

to voice disagreement is outweighed by the practical considerations in this case. There will certainly be contexts in which voicing disagreement is too risky, given unequal social powers and privileges. There are probably contexts in which one or the other of these options will be appropriate for disagreeing agents.

There's a further concern, here. Returning to our art history example, surely Theresa isn't obligated to express her disagreement with *every* potentially objectionable proposition. Many utterances could be understood to mean, presuppose, suggest or implicate something objectionable. This is because what is said when someone utters some content, is, famously, vexed.[14] Theresa's obligations to voice disagreement don't extend to all possible content that might be expressed or implicated.

An example will help us here. Imagine that Theresa and her friend Roger have a running feud over ancient art such that any mention of Assyria in a conversation with Roger would be objectionable to Theresa because of the implications that content would have in that context. If Roger is not at Carla's lecture, then these implications plausibly will not arise. In a case like this, Theresa need not voice her objection just because the content would be objectionable in some other context.

The most natural and precise way to address this concern and to specify which objectionable contents warrant voiced disagreement is to turn, again, to the conversational scoreboard, or to what Stalnaker calls the *common ground*. The common ground of a conversation is, according to Stalnaker, the background information of that conversation – what the conversers take, or act as if they take for granted.[15] For a proposition p to be on the common ground is for the conversers to presuppose that p and to presuppose that their conversational partners also presuppose that p.

When Carla says that Babylonian architecture influenced Assyrian ceramic art, she attempts to add that content to the common ground. Because of the meaning of the parts of this sentence, the presupposition that Babylonian architecture preceded or

---

[14] Elisabeth, Camp, 'Contextualism, metaphor, and what is said', *Mind and Language* **21**.3 (2006), 280–309; Recanati, François, 'What is said.' *Synthese* **128**.1–2 (2001), 75–91, Jennifer M. Saul,. 'Speaker Meaning, What is Said, and What is Implicated.' *Noûs* **36**.2 (2002), 228–248; Saul, *Lying, Misleading, and What is Said;* H. P. Grice, 'Meaning', *Philosophical Review* **66**.3 (1957), 377–388.

[15] Robert Stalnaker, 'Common ground', *Linguistics and Philosophy* **25**.5 (2002), 701–721.

was concurrent with the development of Assyrian art is also put forward for inclusion in the common ground. Perhaps so too is the presupposition that an artist in Assyria was aware of Babylonian architecture. I'd like to suggest any content that is in the common ground or that a converser has attempted to add to the common ground is a candidate for objectionable content. Hearers who disagree with this content, then, would be at least *prima facie* obligated to voice that disagreement. This means that the content that would be generated in a similar conversation with Roger is *not* on the common ground in the conversation with Carla. This is because Carla would not take those propositions to be added to the common ground, and Theresa would not expect her to. So, Theresa need not make her opinions about Babylonian architecture known generally – she need not make known all possible disagreements, but the obligation to voice disagreements ranges over objectionable content that is part of, or is put forward to be part of the common ground.

It should be noted that conversational scoreboards, like conversations, are messy and their boundaries are vague.[16] There might be cases in which Theresa could discharge her obligation by voicing her disagreement to an audience whose membership was not identical to Carla's. If, for example, some of the faculty leave Carla's talk before the Q and A, Theresa is not obligated to track them down and tell them about Assyrian art – the conversation and the conversational scoreboard intuitively survives the loss of those members. On the other hand, if there is no overlap in audiences then presumably Theresa's obligation is not discharged. Many cases, however, will be in between these extremes.

It would also be asking too much of Theresa that she *convince* Carla, or anyone else, to agree with her about Babylonian architecture. If Carla and her cohort are intransigent, surely that doesn't reflect on Theresa's epistemic behaviour. Further support for this point comes from the fact that we sometimes disagree with people who aren't in a position to be convinced. Herrnstein, for example, died soon after the publication of *The Bell Curve*. So, convincing *him* by voicing disagreement is too much to ask.

It is more plausible that sometimes intelligibility by one's interlocutors or reasonable exchange with them is required. If Theresa voices her disagreement to her English-speaking colleagues in Danish, she's not discharged her obligation. And, plausibly, if she yells 'Nuh-uh!' and then runs out of the room, her obligation goes

---

[16] Perhaps we ought to understand academia (or science or genetics) as a single long extended conversation.

unfulfilled. As we'll see in the next section, though, the details of this will depend on the source of the obligation.

And, finally, according to my hypothesis, the content that Theresa expresses must *appear to be* incompatible with the objectionable content. I hedge on requiring incompatibility because incompatibility is not always obvious. Sometimes we can be surprised by what is compatible with what, and it is too much to ask that Theresa be sure of the logical consequences of the content she disagrees with and the content she uses to express that disagreement. It may be enough (in many contexts) that the content she expresses (if true) makes the objectionable content less likely. The degree of incompatibility required will vary from context to context, determined by the details of the conversation and beliefs of the participants. If Theresa and Carla share a false presupposition that p and q are incompatible, and Carla has expressed that p, Theresa can discharge her obligation by expressing that q. This suggests that the appearance of incompatibility is sufficient.

So, for these reasons, I suggest that for an agent to discharge her obligation to voice disagreement with proposition p requires that that agent add to the conversational scoreboard some content that (at least) appears to be incompatible with p.[17] This might seem unsatisfyingly vague, but as above, there are going to be considerations that are specific or internal to particular conversations that will bear on the details of when contents count as disagreeing, and so when people expressing those contents have discharged their obligations. Further complicating matters is the fact that here, as in the discussion of convincing interlocutors, the particular details of the obligation may depend on the source thereof. That is, the different sources will determine different kinds of obligations, obligations that arise in different contexts, and obligations with different requirements. In the next section, I'll look at the most plausible candidate sources.

5. The Source of the Obligation

If we grant that there is a prima facie epistemic obligation to testify as to our disagreements, the next natural question is this: what generates

---

[17] As mentioned above, an agent need not voice her disagreement in a way that registers that disagreement with every participant. It might well be that a particular agent can voice her disagreement with something a previous speaker has said in a way that the speaker himself does not recognize. If other participants in the conversation do recognize this, she might well have discharged her obligation.

this obligation? There are at least four plausible ways we might go about answering this question. One way (following Fricker) is to understand our obligation as self-regarding – to see it as a way to build the epistemic skills necessary for epistemic well-being. Another way (following Catherine Elgin) is to see it as an obligation incurred in virtue of participating in inquiry. A third way (following Margaret Gilbert) is to understand the obligation as part of a commitment to joint action. A fourth source of the obligation is to take a lesson from Mill seriously – namely that beliefs and actions cannot be justified without being discussed and submitted to scrutiny. While these four views are more or less compatible (that is, some combination of the four could be true/generating the obligation), I'll treat them each separately for clarity.

Fricker offers a theory of epistemic justice and injustice.[18] In so doing, she describes a variety of ways in which an agent might be better or worse off epistemically. One component of epistemic well-being is that agents are able to testify and to have their testimony taken seriously – they are able to participate in the epistemic economy. This is part of why, when an agent's testimony isn't taken seriously due to identity prejudices, that agent is the victim of epistemic injustice. One of the dangers of epistemic injustice is that the victims thereof lose confidence and internalize the credibility deficits they suffer in the eyes of their prejudiced interlocutors. This makes them worse off, epistemically. Voicing disagreement, in certain contexts, could help agents avoid some of these pitfalls. Recall the example of Stella the auto mechanic. Auto mechanics is a male-dominated field. It seems likely that, in many cases, women's testimony hasn't been properly attended to in conversations about auto mechanics. Their testimony has either been pre-empted, or hasn't been given its due epistemic weight. We can imagine that Stella has experience with this. Say that Stella doesn't voice her disagreement about your brakes because she lacks confidence. Voicing her disagreement could be instrumental in overcoming this lack. And, if this is the case, then agents like Stella have an obligation to themselves to testify that they disagree.

So, perhaps the epistemic obligation to voice disagreement is self-regarding, and grounded in the conditions for epistemic thriving. This yields a fairly far-reaching obligation – all agents whose epistemic well-being could be improved by voicing their disagreements are obligated to do so. And many agents are in this position.

---

[18]   Fricker, *Epistemic Injustice*.

Casey Rebecca Johnson

To see how considerations of epistemic flourishing generate an obligation to voice disagreement, let's return to the case with which we began: Lucy and Ethel and *The Bell Curve*. Recall that one component of epistemic well-being is participation in the epistemic economy. One way for Lucy and Ethel to do this is to publish editorials. However, if they're not sincere in their contributions to the economy, it's not clear that they're flourishing epistemically. And, if they're not adding their sincere beliefs to the conversation, it is not clear that they're contributing to the epistemic (rather than, say conversational or rhetorical) economy. A sincere contribution, especially when objectionable content is being considered, is a better way to contribute.

Another component of epistemic well-being is epistemic justice. Suppose that Lucy is a member of a socially subordinated group (this is plausible if she is a woman in the sciences), and that part of her social identity involves being subject to a credibility deficit. If this is the case, and if voicing her disagreement is one way for her to participate in the epistemic economy, then she has a defeasible obligation to do so. And if Fred is not a member of a socially subordinated group, then for him, this self-regarding obligation does not arise (at least in this case), as he does not need to voice his disagreement to overcome an unfair perceived credibility deficit.

Of course, this depends on a contingent generalization about psychology: the claim that voicing disagreement develops one's ability to participate in the epistemic economy and to overcome perceived credibility deficits. It seems like a plausible claim to me, but psychological work would have to be done to confirm it.

Another worry, here, is that sometimes voicing disagreement could epistemically harm someone. If I am teaching a class and a student expresses some objectionable content, I might epistemically harm them if I voice my disagreement, especially if that student already faces some identity prejudice involving credibility deficits (like stereotype threat, or imposter syndrome). Don't I have an epistemic obligation, then *not* to voice my disagreement?

I think not. There is a difference between an obligation to stay quiet and an obligation to be kind, polite, or pedagogically responsible. In this case, while I might have a good reason to be careful about *how* to voice my disagreement, the obligation to voice it remains. And in most cases our obligations to keep quiet won't be epistemic, but rather will stem from the overriding of our epistemic obligation to voice disagreement by moral or prudential considerations.

So, an account like Fricker's generates an epistemic obligation to voice disagreement that agents have insofar as voicing their disagreements helps them develop epistemically, participate in the epistemic economy, and avoid the harmful effects of negative identity prejudices. However, if the obligation indeed comes (solely) from this source, the obligation is contingent on the psychological facts of the agents involved. That is, if Stella's confidence won't be improved by voicing her disagreements, then she is not obligated to do so. This might be a palatable result, but we might plausibly want something that is not dependent on agent psychology in this way.

The second possible explanation for the obligation is inspired by the work of Catherine Elgin. Elgin argues that, 'Science requires collaboration. [And] that collaboration requires trust'.[19] Science requires collaboration and trust, she argues, for the same reason it requires models, inference, and idealizations: the subject matter is too complicated, and our findings are too fallible for any scientist to make much progress on her own. She must be able to trust her fellow scientists to let her know when she's in error, or going astray. In other words, she needs to be able to trust her fellow scientists to voice their disagreements with her findings or her methods. And she needs to be able to rely on their collaborative contributions.

Elgin's argument extends beyond the natural sciences. She argues that pursuits like arts and auto mechanics make similar requirements on those who pursue them.[20] Perhaps participation in these pursuits, then, generates the epistemic duty to voice disagreements: collaboration and trust are unlikely if agents keep disagreements to themselves. Carla would probably not value presenting to her peers if they did not make a habit of voicing their disagreements. And in his work on *The Bell Curve*, Panofksy argues that concealed disagreements contributed to the collapse of behavioural genetics as (what he calls) a well-behaved science.[21] Agents who pursue collaborative inquiry, then, are obligated to voice disagreements because of the basic requirements of that pursuit.

One kind of trust involves believing that people are sincere in their utterances. When trustworthy people assert, they believe the content asserted. When they ask questions, they're not sure about and are interested in the answers. This is similar to the kind of trust described by Hinchman and Moran in their interpersonal accounts of

[19]   Catherine Z. Elgin, 'Science, ethics and education', *Theory and Research in Education* **9**.3 (2011), 251–263, at 252.
[20]   Catherine Z. Elgin, 'Understanding: Art and Science', *Midwest Studies In Philosophy* **16**.1 (1991), 196–208.
[21]   Panofsky. *Misbehaving Science*.

assertion.[22] This minimal trust is not the kind of trust that Elgin has in mind – it would not be sufficient for science to function. Science requires a more substantial kind of trust.

Science, and inquiry more generally, requires substantive trust because the subject matter is too broad and the literature too vast for any one scientist (or even team) to read and assess it all. A scientist can't reproduce all of the experiments on which their work is based and still have time to do innovative and creative work. Thus they have to trust the process that reviews and publishes scientific findings. This trust requires that, when people disagree with findings or methods, those disagreements are voiced. For the scientific process to be reliable and to proceed, scientist are required to voice their disagreements – the process generates an obligation to do so. And, as inquiry is an epistemic pursuit, so too is the obligation it generates.

Similarly, collaboration generates a requirement to voice disagreement. Indeed, it is hard to see how someone is collaborating at all if they don't make their disagreements known. Perhaps collaboration alone won't generate Stella's obligation to voice her disagreement in the brakes case (unless conversation counts as a science-like inquiry), but surely it would be sufficient to generate obligations for Theresa and for Lucy and Ethel.

Unlike in the case of the Fricker-style account above, here the inter-personal efficacy of the testimony matters. Because the voicing of disagreement is instrumental to the functioning of science, it matters that it contributes to that function, at least enough of the time. And for that to be the case the disagreement must alter the conversational scoreboard in some way.

It might be objected that Theresa and Carla, as colleagues, have only a very slight acquaintance, while Lucy and Ethel have none at all with Murray and Herrnstein. What kind of trusting relationship should we expect (and require agents to honour) between strangers and mere acquaintances?

The kind of trust in question, and the kind that Elgin has in mind, is not the kind of personal trust that develops between intimates. Nor is it an unrestricted trust that extends to all parts of the agents' conducts. Instead it is an impersonal trust, which is entirely independent of the familiarity or the relationship between the person who is trusted and the person who is trusting. It is a kind of trust that is

[22]   Edward Hinchman, 'Telling as inviting to trust', *Philosophy and Phenomenological Research* **70**.3 (2005), 562–587; Richard Moran, 'Getting Told and Being Believed,' *Philosophers' Imprint* **5**.5 (2005), 1–29.

more than the minimal trust described by Hinchman and Moran, but less than the kind of trust required to make people deeply connected and intimate. It is the kind of trust one would have of a tool or method a scientists has used with good results. Any scientist should, according to Elgin, be trustworthy and (at least to some degree) trusting in this way. To be otherwise is to commit scientific misconduct and would be wildly inefficient.

So, Elgin's account generates an epistemic obligation to voice disagreement when participating in science or other inquiry-based practices (broadly construed). This obligation is generated by the basic requirements of the practices themselves. These practices require collaboration and trust, each of which is only possible in communities in which disagreements are voiced. This means that, according to Elgin's account, the epistemic obligations only arise in those conversations that take place in communities that require these features. Perhaps this is reassuringly narrow – perhaps this focus is a benefit – but this source certainly generates an obligation for fewer agents than that which is generated by Fricker's account.

Third, perhaps our epistemic obligation to voice disagreements is generated by a joint commitment – here we're following Margaret Gilbert.[23] My reconstruction of Elgin, above, claimed that mere participation in a sphere of inquiry generates obligations for participants. It might seem strong, however, that mere participation in the same pursuit generates obligations for agents to voice their disagreements. We might think that obligations like these are more or less operative given certain commitments agents have made (or perhaps they're only operative when commitments have been made). The intuition might be that I am not obligated to do anything regarding someone else's expressed position unless I have some kind of commitment to them or for which they are relevant. Gilbert's account of joint action offers an understanding of our obligations to voice disagreement that is based on commitments.[24] According to Gilbert, when agents make joint commitments, the individuals are committed to doing something *together* – not merely at the same time, but *as members the same group*. These commitments generate obligations for the agents involved.[25]

[23] I am grateful to Nathan Sheff and Graham Hubbs for helpful discussions of the Gilbert-inspired source.
[24] Margaret Gilbert, 'Rationality in Collective Action', *Philosophy of the Social Sciences* **36**.1 (2006), 3–17.
[25] This does not mean, of course, that joint commitments always go smoothly. Sometimes, she says, 'discussion among the parties may be

To see how this source generates an obligation to voice disagreements, it will be helpful to look at one of Gilbert's central examples. She illustrates what it is to jointly commit to some activity by contrasting taking a walk *beside* another person and taking a walk *with* another person. When you and I are taking our lunchtime walks, and our paths overlap for a ways, we're walking besides one another. If I change my mind and go home early, or take a different route, I've done nothing wrong and owe you no explanation, because our overlapping paths don't generate any obligations for me (except, perhaps, staying out of your way or being polite). If, however, we're walking *together*, the situation and my obligations are different. If I invite you to take a walk with me, I must explain or excuse myself before changing destinations, or quitting and going home. Our joint commitment has generated obligations for me (and for you too). While there are many more details to Gilbert's analysis, this difference is symptomatic of a joint-commitment.

Agents who have jointly committed to some activity have obligations that are specific to that activity. In the case of you and I walking together, I have the obligation (among others) to match my pace to yours, or to ask you to slow down. You have the obligation to wait for me while I stop to tie my shoe, etc. And other activities will generate other activity-specific commitments. If we're jointly committed to organizing a conference, then we have conference-organization-specific obligations. And if we're jointly committed to some science or area of inquiry, that will generate some obligations specific to that activity.

It is easy to see how Teresa and Carla are jointly committed to an area of inquiry. Part of what explains Carla's talk is that she is seeking input on her inquiry into art history. The function of the practice of giving academic talks to one's colleagues is, at least in many departments, to get feedback on one's work and ideas. Teresa, by attending the talk, is committed to working on that with Carla. This is what makes academic talks different from traditional plays or performances. The oboist playing a concert at the conservatory is not (or at least not obviously) committed to any joint activity with her audience. A fellow expert in the oboist's audience might have feedback (and notice, if she doesn't offer this feedback there's the sense that she's failed to do as she ought), but the oboist doesn't

---

called for in order that individual efforts are effective'. And that discussion, presumably, would sometimes involve voicing disagreements. See Gilbert, 'Rationality in collective action', 8

give a performance in order to get constructive criticism from her audience members. Teresa and Carla, on the other hand, are jointly committed to scholarship. This generates some commitments and some obligations for them.

Does a joint commitment to inquiry generate an obligation to voice disagreement? I think it does, for at least two reasons. For one, as Elgin points out, inquiry is an activity that benefits from (perhaps even requires) honest voicing of disagreements. Second, voicing disagreement is the sort of behaviour that could help jointly-committed agents come through on their joint commitments to inquiry. Another example of joint commitment will help us to see why.

Say that Jamie and Jean decide to buy a house together. They jointly commit to paying the mortgage. This generates all kinds of mortgage-paying-specific commitments for each of them, and neither can decide to stop paying into their shared account without telling the other. Imagine, however, that Jamie has recently started going to the local casino. Jamie hasn't yet failed to pay into the shared account, but Jean is concerned. Does Jean, in light of the joint commitment to pay the mortgage, have an obligation to express her concern to Jamie? It seems plausible that she does. It seems especially plausible given Michael Bratman's account of shared cooperative activities. According to Bratman, one of the features of a shared cooperative activity (like paying a mortgage or studying some area) is a commitment to mutual support.[26] A commitment to mutual support requires that jointly committed agents are each committed to supporting the efforts of the other to play her role in the joint activity[27]. So, if Jean takes Jamie to need support to avoid gambling, then Jean should tell Jamie that she's worried or otherwise convince her to save her money.

Similarly, if Theresa and Carla are jointly committed to art history, they are also (if Bratman is right) committed to mutually supporting one another in the aims of that activity. Given their disagreement, Theresa may take Carla to be pursuing a sub-optimal line of inquiry or resting on false premises in her paper. If she does, then their joint commitment to art history and the commitment to mutual support that that joint commitment requires generates an obligation for Teresa: she must point out (what she takes to be) Carla's

[26] Michael Bratman, 'Shared Cooperative Activity', *The Philosophical Review* **101**.2 (1992), 327–341.
[27] Bratman and Gilbert don't fully agree about the nature of shared intentionality, but nothing in Gilbert precludes the use of the commitment to mutual support, here.

error as part of supporting Carla in her efforts to discover art-historical truths.

So, perhaps we can understand the obligation to voice disagreement as part of and as generated by the joint commitments undertaken by the obligated agents. This would significantly limit the number of such obligations we have – Theresa and Carla are jointly committed to scholarship, but you and your mechanic friend Stella haven't clearly undertaken such a commitment. So, Theresa is obligated to voice her disagreement, according to an account like this, while Stella is not. Whether this limit is a feature or a flaw I leave to future discussion.

Finally, the obligation to voice disagreement might be due to the nature of doxastic justification itself. John Stewart Mill argued that for an agent to be justified in a belief that belief must be subjected to scrutiny and discussion.[28] Mill argues for this in the context of advocating against prohibitions on free speech however, his reasons have as much to do with epistemic considerations as with political or moral ones. He says,

> Complete liberty of contradicting and disproving our opinion is the very condition which justifies us in assuming its truth for the purposes of action; and on no other terms can a being with human faculties have any rational assurance of being right... it has been [the wise person's] practice to listen to all that could be said against him; to profit by as much of it as was just, and to expound to himself, and on upon occasion to others, the fallacy of what was fallacious.[29]

So, Mill is explicit that wise agents subject their beliefs to scrutiny and discussion. They must not only subject their own beliefs to scrutiny, but must (at least on occasion) voice their disagreements with what they take to be fallacious. And this is for practical and political and moral reasons, but also because such behaviour is a necessary condition of doxastic justification[30].

If Mill is right about our fallibility and the nature of doxastic justification in light of that fallibility, then voicing our disagreement contributes to doxastic justification. And, contributing to doxastic

---

[28] John Stuart Mill, *On Liberty* (London: Longmans, Green, Reader, and Dyer, 1869).

[29] Mill, *On Liberty*, 37–39.

[30] For further discussion of this, see Casey Rebecca Johnson, 'For the Sake of Argument: The Nature and Extent of Our Obligation to Voice Disagreement' in *Voicing Dissent* (London: Routledge, 2018), 105–116

justification is contributing to an epistemic good. We are, then, epistemically obligated to voice our disagreement insofar as we are epistemically obligated to contribute to epistemic goods. And this seems like a plausible understanding of epistemic obligation.

6. Conclusion

In the above I've argued that agents have a *prima facie* epistemic obligation to voice their disagreements with content that other agents have added (or attempted to add) to the conversational score board. I've also sketched four different sources that that obligation could have – that is, belief in any of the four background theories should motivate belief in the epistemic obligation to voice disagreement in at least some cases. It is also important to note that the accounts from Fricker, Elgin, Gilbert, and Mill could work in combination. The accounts are not in conflict and could be complementary parts of a more complicated theory of our epistemic obligations to testify. Such a theory is beyond the scope of the current paper, but I hope to have made a good case for exploring these options and developing such a theory.

The crucial thing, for our purposes, is that each of these sources of the obligation can explain why Ethel and Lucy have an obligation to voice their disagreement with parts of *The Bell Curve*, albeit obligations of different strengths. If epistemic well-being generates the epistemic obligation, then Lucy and Ethel have self-regarding obligations to voice their disagreements. If they already have sufficient skills at doing so, perhaps their obligations are easily overridden. If participation in science generates the epistemic obligation, then Lucy and Ethel are obligated to voice their disagreement precisely because they are geneticists. For trust and collaboration to exist in the field, they must voice their disagreements with Murray and Herrnstein. If joint commitment drives the obligation to voice disagreements, then, to the extent that Lucy and Ethel are committed to the joint enterprise of science, they are obligated. This might help explain why a former scientist, or retired professor might not be obligated to voice her disagreements. Lucy and Ethel, though, seem to be invested in the joint project, to at least some extent. If Mill is to be believed, then Lucy and Ethel are obligated to voice their disagreement because of the nature of doxastic justification. And so, all four sources of the epistemic obligation can explain why Lucy and Ethel failed to behave as they epistemically ought.

Casey Rebecca Johnson

If this is right, then we have four plausible and potentially complementary explanations for the intuition with which we began. Agents who object to content that is put on the conversational scoreboard have an epistemic obligation to voice their disagreement with that content. This is a prima facie obligation and can be overridden by other considerations, but it also explains why we sometimes ought to voice our disagreements even when doing so is, to some extent, improper or impractical. This obligation warrants further examination, and certainly more details of its source are due, but for now, it is clear that we have at least one positive epistemic obligation – the obligation to voice our disagreements.

University of Idaho
crjohnson@uidaho.edu

Empathy and Testimonial Trust

OLIVIA BAILEY

Abstract

Our collective enthusiasm for empathy reflects a sense that it is deeply valuable. I show that empathy bears a complex and surprisingly problematic relation to another social epistemic phenomenon that we have reason to value, namely testimonial trust. My discussion focuses on empathy with and trust in people who are members of one or more oppressed groups. Empathy for oppressed people can be a powerful tool for engendering a certain form of testimonial trust, because there is a tight connection between empathy and a (limited) approval of another's outlook. I then argue that the qualities of empathy that make it such a powerful tool for bridging differences and building trust also have a problematic upshot: they make it the case that reliance on empathy will sometimes have a distorting effect upon the ways we extend testimonial trust.

1. Introduction

In the ongoing public debates about oppression and privilege, one common refrain is that empathy is conspicuously and dangerously missing from the outlook of the powerful and well-off. There is, it is claimed, 'a crisis of empathy' amongst white Americans, a 'crisis of empathy' concerning reproductive rights, a 'crisis of empathy' that has corrupted European attitudes toward refugees.[1] Sometimes, declarations like these really amount to calls for loving care. 'Empathy' has many uses, one of which is as a synonym for compassion. But sometimes, the declarations involve a call for empathy in the sense that I will be concerned with here, a form of emotionally-charged imaginative perspective taking. So, for instance, we find Hillary Clinton saying in the aftermath of the Dallas shootings on July 7, 2016: 'We need to try as best we can to walk in one another's

---

[1]   Andrea Grimes, 'White Women, Let's Get Our Shit Together', *Rewire* (5 Nov, 2014), <https://rewire.news/article/2014/11/05/white-women-lets-get-shit-together/>; Leslie Watson Malachi, '40 Years After Roe, My Personal Fight for Justice', *The Huffington Post* (22 Jan, 2013). <http://www.huffingtonpost.com/leslie-watson-malachi/40-years-after-roe-my-per_b_ 2526408.html>; RS21, 'In or Out, We Must Show Solidarity with Migrants and Refugees', *RS21* (15 June, 2016), <https://rs21.org.uk/2016/06/15/in-or-out-we-must-show-solidarity-with-migrants-and-refugees/>.

doi:10.1017/S1358246118000589   © The Royal Institute of Philosophy and the contributors 2018

Royal Institute of Philosophy Supplement **84** 2018

shoes, to imagine what it would feel like if people followed us around stores or locked their car doors when we walked past'.[2]

Philosophers have recently voiced various concerns about empathy – that it is impossible to distribute fairly, that it underwrites political passivity, or that it encourages 'colonizing' others' suffering.[3] I want to highlight a beneficial feature of empathy that has so far gone un- noticed, and then introduce a new reason to be wary of our collective enthusiasm for empathy that is intimately tied to that beneficial feature. Both the beneficial feature and the reason to be wary are found in the relationship between empathy and another phenomenon of epistemological interest: testimonial trust. Empathy can provide important support for testimonial trust, because it can provide a basis for the attribution of epistemic competence needed for trust in testimony. This is its beneficial feature. But the qualities of empathy that make it such a powerful tool for bridging differences and building trust also have a problematic upshot: they make it the case that reliance on empathy will sometimes inhibit the extension of epistemically warranted and urgently needed testimonial trust. Taken together, these two facets of empathy's relation to testimonial trust place those who aim to cultivate appropriate testimonial trust in a bind. They can allow their empathetic efforts to guide their trust, and risk distorting their sense of which testimony is trustworthy, or they can try to prevent their empathetic efforts from guiding their trust, and thereby discard a particularly powerful basis for trust.

I will concentrate in particular on empathy with and trust in people who are members of one or more oppressed groups.[4] There is a

***

[2]   Quoted in Abby Phillip, 'Clinton: "We know that there is something wrong in our country"', *The Washington Post* (8 July, 2017), <https:// www.washingtonpost.com/news/post-politics/wp/2016/07/08/after-deeply- troubling-dallas-killings-clinton-calls-for-more-respect/?noredirect=on &utm_term=.53539fb14353>.

[3]   For worries about fair distribution, see Jesse Prinz, 'Against Empathy', *The Southern Journal of Philosophy* **49** (2011), 214–233 and Paul Bloom, *Against Empathy: The Case for Rational Compassion* (New York: HarperCollins, 2016). For worries about passivity and coloniza- tion, see Morgan Boler, 'The Risks of Empathy: Interrogating Multiculturalism's Gaze', *Cultural Studies* **11** (1997), 253–273 and Carolyn Pedwell, *Affective Relations: The Transnational Politics of Empathy* (New York: Palgrave Macmillan, 2014).

[4]   I will use the term 'oppressed' as shorthand for 'oppressed, subju- gated, discriminated against, or otherwise systematically disadvantaged'. One can simultaneously be a member of one or more oppressed groups and one or more privileged groups.

well-documented gap between the levels of testimonial trust and empathy people who are privileged along some dimension tend to extend on the one hand to people who are likewise privileged, and on the other to those who are relatively oppressed along the same dimension.[5] Therefore, the situation of people who are oppressed has been a locus of philosophical attention for both those interested in the value of testimonial trust and those interested in the value of empathy.

2. Trust

Let me begin by describing the nature and value of testimonial trust. Testifying is a particular way of presenting a proposition as true. When one testifies, one extends an offer to one's audience. The (intended) recipients of one's testimony are invited to believe in the truth of the proposition on a particular basis. Here are two ways of identifying that basis, which I take to be interchangeable: when one testifies that p, one invites one's audience to trust one that p, or to take one's word for it that p.

Accepting the testifier's invitation involves taking oneself to be relieved of one's usual epistemic responsibility to review the evidence before making up one's mind about whether p.[6] It also involves abstaining from reviewing the evidence for the purpose of making up one's mind about whether p. A policy of 'trusting but verifying' is self-undermining: when one trusts in testimony, one hands over

---

[5]   The last decade has seen a wave of philosophical interest in the ways that stereotypes about members of oppressed groups shape attributions of credibility. For particularly influential work in this area, see Lorraine Code, *Ecological Thinking: The Politics of Epistemic Location* (Oxford: Oxford University Press, 2006), Miranda Fricker, *Epistemic Injustice: Power and the Ethics of Knowing* (Oxford: Oxford University Press, 2007), and Charles Mills, 'White Ignorance', in Shannon Sullivan and Nancy Tuana (eds.), *Race and Epistemologies of Ignorance* (Albany: State University of New York Press, 2007), 11–38. For evidence of cross-group empathy 'gaps', see Sophie Trawalter, Kelly M. Hoffman, and Adam Waytz, 'Racial Bias in Perceptions of Others' Pain', *PLOS ONE* **7** (2012), and Robert Eres and Pascal Molenberghs, 'The Influence of Group Membership on the Neural Correlates Involved in Empathy', *Frontiers in Human Neuroscience* **7** (2013).

[6]   One way this observation has been framed is that in accepting testimony, one accepts the testifier's *assurance* that p. See e.g. Richard Moran, 'Getting Told and Being Believed', *Philosophers' Imprint* **5** (2005), 1–29.

Olivia Bailey

responsibility for judging the sufficiency of the evidence to the testifier, and one cannot wrest it back without ceasing to trust. Finally, when one trusts testimony that p, one commits to dismissing or discounting at least some evidence that $\sim p$. Absolute trust in testimony that p would involve a commitment to believing that p in the face of any and all counterevidence. One can count as trusting testimony that p even if one would be willing to abandon one's belief that p in the face of *some* indications that $\sim p$, but if I am willing to abandon or downgrade my confidence that p in the face of even weak counterevidence, then I can only be said to trust in an etiolated sense.

One cannot trust another's testimony unless one is willing to attribute two qualities to the testifier. The truster must attribute to the testifier a sufficient degree of honesty and also a sufficient degree of epistemic competence. Epistemic competence encompasses a number of different proficiencies, most centrally the abilities to recognize, gather, and properly evaluate evidence. This second trust-enabling condition is the one we will focus on here, because it bears a particularly significant relation to empathy.

Testimonial trust can be based on evidence. If I believe a testifier T wholly or partly on the basis of evidence that he is epistemically competent and honest, then my belief can count as an instance of testimonial trust.[7] But testimonial trust that p must be distinguished from a different sort of evidentially-based belief that p, one which we can call 'belief occasioned by testimony'. Such belief arises out of testimony in the sense that the testifier's communication is at least partially causally responsible for the audience's coming to believe that p. Unlike testimonial trust, however, this belief is not based in evidence of the epistemic competence or honesty of the testifier. For example, if T's testimony that p inspires me to reflect on whether p, but I judge that p based on my own intuitions about the matter, and not because I trust T, then my belief that p is an instance of belief occasioned by T's testimony but not an instance of trust in T's testimony.

I am going to concentrate on testimony about features of circumstances encountered experientially, because (as we will see) trust about this kind of testimony bears the most obviously fraught relationship to empathy. We might think of testimony about experience

---

[7]   I say 'can' because simply (1) being aware of T's testimony and (2) believing that p on the basis that T, an epistemically competent and honest agent, has testified that p is not strictly sufficient for testimonial trust. It must also be the case that I have accepted an invitation issued by T to believe T that p. I set aside, here, questions about belief based on overheard testimony.

as testimony about 'what it's like for' the experiencer. The locution 'what it's like for', though, risks obscuring the difference between two forms of experientially-based testimony. On the one hand, there is testimony like 'I felt threatened by the man's attentions', or 'I experienced the stare as hostile'. On the surface, at least, those statements merely amount to testimony about the presence of a psychological state within the testifier. On the other hand, there is experientially-based testimony like 'The man's attentions are threatening', or 'That stare is hostile'. This latter kind of testimony is about the qualities of things in the world outside the subject, but it is (at least in the kind of cases I have in mind) testimony born of an experience of the world. When I register eyes on me, and shudder at the cold nature of the gaze, I perceive a hostile stare, and I can report it as such. This is the type of testimony that interests me. Of the two kinds of experientially-based testimony, it is also the one that is harder to trust. It is one thing to believe that a person who reports a threatening encounter *feels* threatened, and it is another to believe her that there actually is something threatening about her situation. The former attitude does not require that we accept that the testifier is a competent detector of threat, the latter does.

3. Empathy: What It Is, and How It Supports Testimonial Trust

With this picture of testimonial trust in hand, we can now turn to the question of the role that empathy can play in supporting it. It is criterial for empathy in the sense that interests me that it involve using one's imagination to 'transport' oneself, and more particularly that it involve considering the other's situation as though one were occupying the other's position.

Empathy that by definition involves perspective taking is sometimes called 'cognitive empathy'.[8] This is a potentially misleading term, especially since it is sometimes implied that empathy of this sort has nothing to do with feeling. Empathy as I understand it

---

[8]   Those who draw a distinction between 'cognitive empathy' and empathy that involves feeling include Antti Kauppinen, 'Empathy, Emotion Regulation, and Moral Judgment', in Heidi Maibom (ed.), *Empathy and Morality* (New York and Oxford: Oxford University Press, 2014), 97–121, and Martin Hoffman, 'Empathy, Justice, and the Law', in Amy Coplan and Peter Goldie (eds.), *Empathy: Philosophical and Psychological Perspectives* (Oxford: Oxford University Press, 2011), 230–254.

does draw upon the empathizer's emotional resources. A rough and ready way of thinking about emotions' role in empathy is to conceive of the empathizer as encountering the other's situation through an appropriate emotional lens. When we try to empathetically imagine how things are for a recent widower, for instance, we attempt to look at his situation through the lens of grief. It does not matter for my purposes here whether we ought to describe the empathizer's emotional experience as one of really feeling, or as feeling-in-imagination, or as pseudo-feeling. What matters is that empathy in my sense is not bloodless or coldly cognitive.

To see how empathy supports trust, we can return to one of the earliest descriptions of empathy's operation: Adam Smith's *The Theory of Moral Sentiments*. According to Smith, empathy (which he calls 'sympathy') provides the unique means by which we judge the propriety of others' attitudes.[9]

> When the original passions of the person principally concerned are in perfect concord with the sympathetic emotions of the spectator, they necessarily appear to this last just and proper, and suitable to their objects; and, on the contrary, when, upon bringing the case home to himself, he finds that they do not coincide with what he feels, they necessarily appear to him unjust and improper, and unsuitable to the causes which excite them. To approve of the passions of another, therefore, as suitable to their objects, is the same thing as to observe that we entirely sympathize with them; and not to approve of them as such, is the same thing as to observe that we do not entirely sympathize with them.[10]

According to Smith, after we come to know (through testimony or observation) how another person emotionally registers their circumstances, we assess their emotional apprehension of their situation by trying to imaginatively enter into their position, such that we imaginatively duplicate their experience. If (and only if) we succeed in matching our imagined emotional response to the situation to the testifier's own reported response, we approve of the other's attitude as a fitting one. Our own empathetic emotion furnishes our standard of assessment. I am now going to argue that while this Smith's account needs to be qualified, the core insight is correct:

[9] Smith consistently uses 'sympathy' to refer to emotionally-charged imaginative perspective taking.

[10] Adam Smith, *The Theory of Moral Sentiments*, D. D. Raphael and A. L. Macfie (eds.) (Indianapolis: Liberty Classics, 1982), 16.

there is a deep connection between empathy and approval. I'll then make it clear how this connection underlies empathy's positive contribution to testimonial trust.

Commentators have been sceptical of this proposal of Smith's for a number of reasons. Some have protested there are surely other ways of judging others' emotional reactions to be appropriate, ones that have nothing to do with empathy.[11] I will not deal with that objection here. Rather, I will be concerned with the kind of worries expressed in Thomas Reid's commentary on *The Theory of Moral Sentiments*: 'When, [Smith] says, I judge your resentment by my resentment, your love by my love & so on, this is a way of speaking altogether new–this should be confined solely to our judging powers… to say that my resentment is the faculty by which I judge of your resentment is incommutable to all of our ideas of Resentment; we may as well say, I judge of my hunger by your hunger'.[12]

There are two possible ways of understanding Reid's complaint. His objection might be that our hunger response is simply an impulse that assails us, one that cannot even get things wrong or right. Far from being a power of judgment, the thought might go, the sense of hunger does not even offer a representation of the world that could in turn be the object of judgment. Reid may be recommending that we think of instances of emotion, whether empathetic or normal, in the same way: as mere sensations that do not represent the world at all.

In response to this first reading of the complaint, we can note that while some forms of hunger may shade into emotional experience, the physical sensation of an empty belly is importantly different from emotion, because emotions present the world as being a certain way. Suppose I am angry at some slight. What does that involve? There are the familiar bodily symptoms: a pounding heart, sweaty palms, etc. There are also the tendencies to act and to express myself in particular ways: to speak harshly, to refuse attempts at reconciliation. Importantly, these actions, symptoms, and expressions are not arbitrary. The many physiological and behavioural dispositions associated with the emotion are unified by their connection to my recognition of certain features of the situation as inviting or demanding my ire. Emotions focus our attention on some features of

---

[11] A prime example is Prinz, 'Against empathy'.

[12] From the 'Lecture 100th', March 1870. Transcription from Elmer Duncan and Robert Baird, 'Thomas Reid's Criticisms of Adam Smith's Theory of the Moral Sentiments', *Journal of the History of Ideas* **38** (1977), 517.

our situation, push others into the background, and present certain objects or events as calling out for particular kinds of treatment. So, I attend to the intolerable smugness of the offender's smirk, the outrageousness of their audacity. The relative triviality of the situation and the good qualities of the offender recede into the background. It is helpful to think of emotions as being, at heart, ways of seeing in virtue of which things take on a particular evaluative sheen. Since emotions present situations as laden with evaluative properties, they (unlike hunger sensations) can represent reality.

Even if that point is granted, though, one might suspect that the fact that we are able to imaginatively match another's emotional representation of her circumstances is itself evaluatively neutral: it is still equally open to us to accept her representation as accurate or reject it as illusory. And this is the other thought we might draw out of the hunger analogy. Whether or not our sense of hunger issues representations, one might insist, it is not itself a judging faculty. The fact that we are hungry for some delicious cake does not entail that we judge our desire for the cake to be appropriate; that judgment must be issued by a distinct faculty, whose verdicts are not in any way constrained by our hunger. Similarly, the fact that we experience an emotional presentation of the world does not at all constrain our judgment about the presentation's propriety.

To see what that suspicion misses, consider how our non-empathetic emotional experiences relate to approval. It is certainly true that we can have an emotional response without fully endorsing it. We might register the prospect of crossing the chasm as utterly terrifying, but still think that all in all we oughtn't really be afraid. Or we might continue to resent a friend for missing our party, even though we judge that she had a reasonable excuse. But this does not mean that there is no significant connection between having an emotional experience and approving of it.

Two observations will bring out the nature of this connection. First, although it is true that there is a gap between having an emotional response to some phenomenon and fully endorsing that response, we are in general powerfully inclined to treat our emotionally-coloured perceptions of the world as accurate. Confidence in our own emotional representations is our default attitude. If this latter claim is surprising, it is only because we have a tendency, when thinking about emotions in the abstract, to focus on the cases in which they differ most sharply from more 'rational', 'objective' mental states. So, we call to mind burning rage or acute, all-consuming terror. But it is misleading to think of these as paradigmatic emotional experiences. Our ordinary experience of the world is valenced – things show up as boring, enticing, regrettable, and so on, and we are accordingly attracted or repulsed by these appearances. That is, ordinary experience is emotional, and we usually take those experiences at face value.

It is possible for us to shy away from our own emotional evaluative representations: I might suspend my acceptance of an emotional representation of the party as delightful until I've had an opportunity to reassess whether the party meets standards for delightfulness that I can wholeheartedly endorse. But we do not typically downgrade our confidence in emotional representations until we have done this kind of reflective work. And this is just as well: if we were to refuse to accept what is right before our eyes, emotionally speaking, we would have an awful lot of trouble making our way through the world.[13]

Second, although we undoubtedly do sometimes depart from this default, it is very difficult for us to sustain an emotional representation without regarding it as to some degree appropriate. To bring out the point: imagine that I am at first angry with my friend for spilling my secret, but after reflection I conclude that her passing the secret on was not a genuine betrayal. Importantly, I don't just *try* to convince myself of this. I genuinely judge that there is nothing in what she did that calls out for my ire. Can I remain angry with my friend? Certainly the residual 'heat' of anger may be retained; I can still feel pumped up with adrenaline. Still, if I wholeheartedly believe that there is no offense in any way worthy of ire, it will be difficult, if not impossible, for me to continue to really represent her conduct as outrageous. And, as I've already suggested, such representations are a critically important part of emotions. Without them, emotions dissolve, leaving behind mere sensations.

Now let us apply these observations about the connection between emotion and approval to empathy. Suppose an acquaintance tells me that her colleagues' admiration of her 'beautiful accent' is irritating, and I regard her testimony as honest. If I succeed in imaginatively seconding her exasperation, and am confident that this is what I have done, then it will be very difficult if not impossible for me to believe that her irritation is entirely uncalled-for. And what is more, if I have what I've suggested is the normal attitude concerning my emotional experience, if I take my sense of the irksome to be accurately attuned, my empathy with my acquaintance's frustration will

---

[13] Damasio's studies of planning and decisional deficiencies in emotionally impaired subjects support this claim. See Antonio Damasio, *Descartes' Error: Emotion, Rationality and the Human Brain* (New York: Penguin Books, 1994).

incline me to think that she is totally right about her colleagues' compliments.

This all means that Smith's claim about the connection between empathy and approval is not grossly overstated. He held that 'to approve of the passions of another, therefore, as suitable to their objects, is the same thing as to observe that we entirely sympathize with them'. I suggest we amend that to: when we empathize with the passions of another, and recognize that this is what we are doing, we are in general powerfully inclined to regard those passions as fully reflective of the evaluative properties her situation really manifests, and it is extremely difficult if not impossible to dismiss them as wholly inappropriate.

What are the implications of this observation for testimonial trust? First, I will briefly articulate the primary implication, and then I will point to a complication that requires us to render that initial articulation more precise.

We can express the primary implication in terms of our case, above. When I empathize with my acquaintance, imaginatively seconding her irritation at her colleagues' comments, I will be practically bound to conclude that there is something right in my acquaintance's judgment, and I may also be inclined to conclude that her judgment is wholly correct. These conclusions about her judgment, taken separately or together, provide a reason to believe that my acquaintance is appropriately sensitive to irritating phenomena. And, since appropriate sensitivity is part of being epistemically competent, I thereby secure a reason to attribute epistemic competence to my acquaintance. The attribution of epistemic competence constitutes one of testimonial trust's enabling conditions. So, my empathetic effort will furnish a basis for trust in my acquaintance's testimony.

It is important to note that a successful empathetic effort does not provide support for trust in *all* of the testifier's testimony. In particular, if T testifies that p, and I conclude on the basis my empathetic effort that T is right that p, my conclusion does not provide a basis for my trust in T that p. It fails to do so simply because my undertaking the relevant empathetic effort *precludes* my trusting T that p. When my acquaintance testifies that her colleagues' admiration is irritating, and I succeed in empathetically working myself into her position such that I apprehend the irritating quality of the admiration, I thereby secure a reason to believe that the admiration is irritating, namely that I have 'seen' it for myself. Notice, though, that my empathetic assessment of the testimony involves considering how the other's situation appears to me. In doing so, I am reviewing the evidence that the admiration is irritating and on that basis making up my mind about whether the admiration is irritating. When I empathize with my acquaintance, I am verifying the truth of her testimony, and as I explained earlier, it is not possible to 'trust but verify'.

Still, my empathetic engagement with my acquaintance's judgment about her colleague's admiration can provide a basis for my trust in her testimony about other cases and even other evaluative properties. My conclusion that my acquaintance is right about her colleague's admiration provides evidence for the conclusion that she is appropriately sensitive to irritating phenomena, and that attribution of competence constitutes a basis for trust in her other testimony about what is irritating. Furthermore, insofar as I think that accurate emotional attunement in one domain is positively correlated with accurate attunement in other domains, the conclusion that she is right about the admiration gives me reason to attribute to her broader emotional sensitivity to evaluative properties. That broader attribution of competence in turn provides a basis for wider-ranging trust in testimony about what is threatening, heartening, offensive, and so on.

Empathy has the power to dramatically reshape one's willingness to trust others' testimony. Suppose my acquaintance's testimony about the irritating nature of her colleagues' remarks surprises me. It doesn't fit with my general understanding of what kind of things are irritating. The colleagues are highlighting one of my acquaintance's positive traits, and being admired for a positive trait is usually a good thing. In this case, it would be natural for me to initially suspect that my acquaintance is just touchy, and the thought of her as touchy will incline me to discount her testimony about what is troublesome or offensive. But if I take the time to imaginatively place myself in her position, and feel the stirrings of annoyance in myself, matters will look very different. Her irritation will no longer look unaccountable. The possibility of dismissing her testimony as the erroneous upshot of an excessively querulous outlook will recede from view. And next time she mentions that some apparently benign treatment actually isn't, I will be more inclined to take her word seriously.

4. Trust without Empathy

So far, the picture of the relation between empathy and trust that I've been developing is generally rosy. Empathy provides a means of redeploying our approval of our own emotional perceptions to support attributions of epistemic competence to others. In so doing, it helps to

Olivia Bailey

clear away a barrier to testimonial trust. We might therefore think that if we want to promote trust in oppressed people's testimony, we ought to lean heavily on empathy. However, a policy of relying on empathy to support testimonial trust is more epistemically and morally problematic that it initially seems. To begin to bring the relevant difficulties to light, let me now introduce a few reports from members of oppressed groups about how they want their testimony to be taken.

From Mx Nillin (a nonbinary person): 'I know that all of this [my experience of my gender] is very hard for many cisgender, and even many binary trans people, to understand. But the truth is that I don't need you to understand....You don't have to get it. Just respect that I know my body and gender better than you do'.[14]

From an anonymous African American, writing on behalf of the collective Real Talk: 'Don't question our experiences. You'll never understand them because you don't walk through the world with black or brown skin. Just sit there and listen'.[15]

From Kirsty Major (a woman): 'If a woman is saying you are being sexist, you definitely have to listen, because you've never lived life as a woman and don't know what it is like to face sexism every single waking hour of your life...If you still can't see it or understand it, at least acknowledge that the other person did'.[16]

I'm not interested in whether these particular requests are totally fair or wise. Rather, I highlight them because they can be read as expressing a demand for testimonial trust that is not based on empathy. Nillin's remark can be understood in two different ways, depending upon the tone with which it is read. It could be understood as a declaration that efforts to really feel what it's like for Nillin are supererogatory: nice, but not required. Shift the stresses, though ('You don't *have* to *get* it') and it is readily understood instead as communicating exasperation with others' apparent need to 'see' the other's point of view for themselves before placing their confidence in Nillin's testimony about their experience. The latter two remarks

[14] Mx Nillin, 'Bathrooms and Being Non-Binary', *Mx Nillin* (26 Apr, 2016), <http://mxnillin.com/bathrooms-and-being-non-binary/>.
[15] Anonymous/Real Talk: WOC and Allies, 'White People, Stop Asking Us to Educate You About Racism', *Medium* (27 May, 2017), <https://medium.com/@realtalkwocandallies/white-people-stop-asking-us-to-educate-you-about-racism-69273d39d828>.
[16] Kirsty Major, 'If You're a Man Who Calls Himself a Feminist, You Need to Actually Act Like One', *The Independent* (1 Apr, 2017), <https://www.in dependent.co.uk/voices/sexism-men-woke-misogynists-feminism-male-feminists-what-to-do-a7660841.html>.

similarly recommend deferring to testimony *rather* than pursuing an understanding 'from the inside' of oppressed others' points of view. They also communicate frustration with the emphasis their addressees place on 'getting' how women and racial minorities see things. All three claims can be understood as expressing a sense that others' need to see things from the testifier's point of view, their reluctance to move on to trusting before doing so, is actually symptomatic of a distressing distortion in their patterns of trust.

I will now turn to two tasks. First, I'll show it can be morally important and epistemically responsible to trust others' testimony even when one finds one cannot empathize with their evaluative outlooks. Second, I'll suggest that in relying on empathy to help us sustain and extend our testimonial trust, we make it harder for ourselves to trust under this kind of condition.

As we saw in the previous section, empathy works to enhance our confidence in others' epistemic competence because when we manage to (imaginatively) work our way into experiencing things as others do, our own confidence in the accuracy of our emotional representations inclines us to regard their attitudes as appropriate. An important consequence of this dynamic is that the more alien we find the other's purported perspective, the less support empathy can provide for trust. Is it important, good, needful that we trust the other's testimony even when we find we cannot enter into the other's position, despite our best efforts to do so? To answer that question with a full-throated affirmation, I take it that we need to establish both that it could be epistemically responsible to trust in the face of failure to empathetically match the others' emotional response and that it could be morally and/or practically valuable to trust in this way. If trust in the face of empathetic failure were morally important but epistemically irresponsible, or epistemically responsible but not particularly morally valuable, we would have reason to doubt whether we ever ought to trust testimony under these conditions, all things considered.

Let us begin with the question of epistemic responsibility: would a willingness to so trust necessarily compromise our status as appropriately cautious believers? There is reason to believe that, far from being reckless, this kind of trust could be a critical corrective to distortions in the attribution of competency that would arise from making trust highly dependent upon empathic success. Our success or failure to empathetically match another's emotional perception is often not a good guide to the propriety of others' emotional expressions, because our ability to empathize is subject to two kinds of impairments that have nothing to do with the accuracy of the point of view that serves as our empathetic target. Interestingly, these impairments will end up making themselves felt particularly strongly in cases where a privileged person is asked to empathize with the perspective of an oppressed person.

First, our imaginative abilities are affected by numerous idiosyncrasies that have a real effect on what we can empathize with, and how. These features are undoubtedly helpful in some respects. Still, they can warp our empathetic abilities, such that the outcome of our empathetic efforts becomes a poor test for whether testimonial trust is warranted. I will offer just a couple of examples here. For one thing, imaginatively engaging with painful experiences is normally itself a painful activity. Imaginatively attending to experiences of rejection and humiliation as though from the perspective of the one demeaned involves intense focus on a bad experience, and that kind of focus may prompt dismay and dread in the empathizer. These are emotions we would rather avoid. All things considered, then, we will be more resistant to empathy with painful experiences than delightful ones, even if there is just as much to approve of in the perspective of the suffering person as there is in the joyful one. Our perspective-taking abilities also vary substantially depending upon whether the target of our empathy is part of the social 'in-group' with which we primarily identify.[17] Human beings struggle to imaginatively adopt the points of view of individuals who are not part of their social circles, even in the absence of a good reason to think that social outsiders have less coherent or accurate perspectives on the world. These two features of our imagination give us some reason to think that facts about what we are able to empathize with are not perfect guides to facts about whose perspectives are most worthy of our approval. More particularly, they also give us reason to think that suffering individuals who are part of one or more oppressed groups will receive especially little empathy from the relatively privileged (which means that empathy-based trust in their testimony on the part of the relatively privileged will correspondingly be in short supply).

Aside from problems related to limitations on our imaginative abilities, there are also reasons to worry about the reliability of would-be empathizers' sensitivity to (certain kinds of) evaluative facts. In cases where our failure to empathize is the result of such insensitivity, it

---

[17] See Martin Hoffman, *Empathy and Moral Development: Implications for Caring and Justice* (Cambridge: Cambridge University Press, 2001), 197–219.

would be a mistake to allow the verdicts of our empathetic efforts to shape our testimonial trust.

Some rare individuals suffer from a complete inability to experience anything as frightening: to them, snakes, heights, and knives look exciting rather than terrifying. A person with this kind of impairment, like the real-life 'fearless woman' known in the psychology literature as S.M., will not be able to empathize with other's reported experiences of threats as frightening.[18] However, it does seem rational for S.M. to trust that others are right when they say that it is frightening to be faced with, say, a gun-wielding stranger: she knows that her abnormal way of looking at the world involves insensitivity to a quality that, were she able to track it, would help her to avoid the dangerous situations she has fallen into over the years. Now, if insensitivity to evaluative facts were confined to unusual cases like S.M.'s, this wouldn't give us much of a reason to think we really need trust not based on empathy. But is such insensitivity limited to cases of brain trauma? Or is it a much more common phenomenon?

Members of oppressed groups often claim that the prospect of real empathy with their position on the part of the relatively privileged is not just difficult but impossible. So, we find David, a homeless person, asserting, 'You [well-off people] can't understand what it's like to be homeless,' and Terrell Jermaine Starr, a black racial justice activist, claiming that when it comes to 'a white supremacist system that oppresses us and excludes us in every area of American life – economic, educational, social and political – [e]ven the most empathic white person is just not going to know what that's like'.[19] These sorts of remarks seem to express the thought that occupying a position of privilege is something like being in S.M.'s situation. But it is unclear exactly what we should do with these claims, particularly since what is at issue is the question of when it is epistemically responsible to accept testimony.

Social epistemologists remain deeply divided over whether minorities and members of oppressed groups have unique access to some

---

[18] S.M.'s case is described in a number of articles, including Justin Feinstein et al., 'The Human Amygdala and the Induction and Experience of Fear', *Current Biology* **21** (2001), 34–38.

[19] 'David' cited in Michael Hoinski, 'Close to Homeless', *Texas Observer* (29 Jan, 2010), <https://www.texasobserver.org/close-to-homeless/>; Terrell Jermaine Starr, 'Dear White People: Here are 5 Reasons Why You Can't Really Feel Black Pain', *Alternet* (4 Dec, 2014), <http://www.alter net.org/dear-white-people-here-are-5-reasons-why-you-cant-really-feel-black-pain>.

sorts of knowledge.[20] I can't hope to adequately address the matter in a programmatic way here. I will suggest, though, that privilege can foster a kind of insensitivity to certain qualities, in analogy to the case of the fearless woman.

Consider, for example, perception of the threat of sexual violence. Men generally do not have a fine-tuned awareness of the threatening nature of casual street harassment.[21] In fact, some men report thinking of their shouted sexual comments and wolf-whistles as not only non-threatening but a boon for their targets: claims that women experience these things as frightening are sometimes met with rejoinders from the harassers that they themselves would enjoy being the target of such attentions, and cannot see them as hostile.[22] And yet: empirical evidence does point to the existence of a robust connection between the tendency to objectify women (of which street harassment is an expression) and the tendency to engage in sexual violence.[23] If there is such a connection, that gives us good reason to believe that women are, in general, sensitive to a real feature of the world that (many) men are much less well attuned to, even when these men attempt to see things from women's point of view.

More generally, it stands to reason that people who are oppressed will be more sensitive than others to those evaluative features of the world that matter to navigating the dangers imposed on them by systems of oppression. Women's safety depends upon a keen ability to detect hostility or threat of a sexual nature in a way that men's safety generally does not. This observation is actually enshrined in some courts' determinations concerning sexual harassment. When

[20] For a collection of the variety of positions on offer, see Sandra Harding (ed.), *The Feminist Standpoint Theory Reader: Intellectual and Political Controversies* (New York: Routledge, 2004).

[21] Casual street harassment centrally includes: graphic, unsolicited commentary on the target's body, demands or invitations to engage in sexual activity, wolf-whistling, following the target down the street.

[22] An interview with a street harasser who articulates this view is available in Ira Glass and Eleanor Gordon-Smith, 'Hollaback Girl', in 'Once More, With Feeling', *This American Life* **603** (WBEZ Chicago, 2 Dec, 2016), <https://www.thisamericanlife.org/603/once-more-with-feeling/act-one>.

[23] See e.g. Eduardo Vasquez et al., 'The Sexual Objectification of Girls and Aggression Towards Them in Gang and Non-gang Affiliated Youth', *Psychology, Crime & Law* **23** (2017), 459–471, and Sarah Gervais, David DiLillo, and Dennis McChargue, 'Understanding the Link Between Men's Alcohol Use and Sexual Violence Perpetration: The Mediating Role of Sexual Objectification', *Psychology of Violence* **3** (2014), 1–44.

it comes to determining whether a work environment is hostile, for instance, the Ninth Circuit asks not whether any reasonable person would judge the environment to be hostile, but whether a reasonable woman would judge it to be so.[24]

The problems of imagination and sensitivity just surveyed give us strong reason to think that trust even in the face of empathic failure is sometimes epistemically warranted. Let me now turn to the question of such trust's practical or moral value for its would-be recipients, in light of what we have already seen of the value of testimonial trust more generally. Trust under these conditions could be practically valuable in part because it may sometimes be necessary for the uptake of important facts. Some conditions that people urgently need others to believe them about may not be possible objects of trust for those who stick strictly to trust based on empathy. The case of testimony about street harassment discussed above is, I think, one example of a situation where this value could be manifest.

But such trust isn't valuable just because it makes the transmission of important information possible. It also has a significant symbolic or communicative function. The risk inherent in trust makes the expression of it a powerful way of displaying and affirming one's belief in the testifier's competence and honesty. Still, not all trust has equal communicative power. Trust that is based (albeit indirectly) on one's confidence in one's own imaginative and discriminatory abilities (as trust based on empathetic effort is) comes comparatively cheap: it doesn't involve acknowledging the possibility that the testifier's competence might outstrip one's own. Conversely, if I trust you even though I find that your way of seeing is not empathetically accessible to me, my trust evinces a serious epistemic humility: it amounts to an admission that 1) I take my imaginative abilities to be so flawed as to deliver a seriously distorted picture of your circumstances, 2) I take my sensitivity to (some kind of) evaluative fact to be inferior to yours, or 3) both. For people who are systematically distrusted, an acknowledgement that their discriminatory abilities may outpace the truster's represents a dramatic departure from the status quo, one that is all the more significant because in trusting thusly, the truster makes himself epistemically reliant on the abilities of the one trusted.

---

[24] From *Ellison v. Brady*, 924 F.2d 872 (9th Cir. 1991): 'We adopt the perspective of a reasonable woman primarily because we believe that a sex-blind reasonable person standard tends to be male-biased and tends to systematically ignore the experiences of women'.

I've claimed that empathy does not actually provide support for trust under some circumstances where trust would be both epistemically responsible and practically or morally valuable. At this point, it might seem tempting to conclude that we still have no reason to think that empathy's relationship with testimonial trust is *ambivalent*: empathy does not play a role in supporting all the testimonial trust one might reasonably demand, but it does nothing to undercut testimonial trust. The problem with this conclusion is that empathy's powerful ability to provide support for the trust it *can* sustain derives in large measure from the fact that when we 'get' some outlook empathetically, we are strongly inclined to regard it as correct. Conversely, when we attempt to empathize, and find we cannot, we are liable to be similarly strongly inclined to think that there can't be anything to what the testifier tells us. Claims that we can't empathize often have a judgmental dimension. Think about what is conveyed when we say: 'I will never understand why he would want that', or 'You say it's worthwhile, but I just can't see it'. Or take this example from a Chicago Tribune Op-Ed: 'So I will never get this sexting craze. I can't empathize with a teenage girl seeking acceptance by sharing photos of her breasts'.[25] The literal claim being made is just that the author is not able to make sense of teenage girls' sexting habits. But the heavy implication is that there is *no sense to be gotten*.

There is a defeasible but non-accidental connection between our trying and failing to empathize with another's attitude and our disapproving of it. A truly epistemically humble person might well think: whether or not I can imaginatively get myself to a version of the other's attitude has no bearing on whether her attitude is correct, because I myself am (for instance) emotionally and/or imaginatively stunted in some respects. Still, this kind of humility is hard to maintain. It is importantly different from, and more difficult than, deference to testimony about evaluative facts in cases where one has not even attempted to adopt the other's perspective. We may be relatively content, sometimes, to skip the empathizing and let others put in the work when it comes to determining whether something is beautiful, or just, or unsettling. However, once we do try to look at things from the other's point of view, marshalling our emotional sensitivities and applying them to the task of figuring out whether the other is right about how things are, the *import* of the choice to trust shifts.

[25] Mitch Albom, 'When Sexting Becomes a Crime', *Chicago Tribune* (20 Oct, 2014), <http://www.chicagotribune.com/news/opinion/commentary/ct-sexting-jennifer-lawrence-pornography-pedophili-20141020-story.html>.

Suppose we fail to 'get' the other's way of understanding things, despite our best efforts. In that case, trusting the other's testimony means accepting that one is flawed in (at least) one of two ways. First, one might opt to trust in cases like these because one accepts that one's perspective-taking capacities are in some respects deficient. Accepting that condition is no easy thing, because we heavily depend upon this imaginative ability for our everyday understanding of other people. It is a crucial item in our mental tool kit. The ability to take on other perspectives is crucial to our identity as social beings who experience our fellows not as mysterious 'black boxes', but rather as creatures with sensible, if not totally rational, preferences and projects.

The admission that other's perspectives may (sometimes, in some respects) be beyond our imaginative ken is, of course, not strictly incompatible with a conception of ourselves as social beings of this kind. However, it does pose some threat to it. And the grosser the imaginative deficit we have to admit, the greater the threat. For instance, it will be particularly difficult to accept that our imagination is not up to the task of supporting a trustworthy verdict about others' attitudes in cases where it seems like we are not taxing our imagination very much. When the other person is not separated from us by obscuring expanses of time or space, and when their circumstances are clearly described (conditions that will frequently apply in cases of contemporary testimony about oppression), we cannot hide behind the defence that too much is being asked of our imaginations.

The concession in the face of empathetic effort and failure that one's imaginative abilities are in some respects inadequate may be paired with a second admission that is perhaps still more difficult. We have already discussed the strength of our inclination to go along with our own emotional representations of the world. The flip side of that inclination, which makes empathy such a powerful enabler of trust, is that it is extremely difficult to accept that one's emotional sensitivities are misaligned. Most of us, most of the time, are practically bound to think of ourselves as well-equipped to see whether a death is worth mourning, whether a habit is irritating, whether a joke is funny…and also whether an encounter is demeaning or threatening. Accepting that we are in some respects like S.M., that our emotional attunement to the world is dull or distorted (even if just with respect to a relatively narrow set of properties or circumstances) is a difficult prospect for reasons that largely parallel those in play in the case of acknowledging imaginative deficiencies.

Some people might seem to be cavalier about their own emotional failings. Certain forms of masculine ideology, for instance, practically make a virtue of insensitivity to the more 'tender' evaluative properties, such as the delicate, the adorable, and the kind. But there are forms of emotional sensitivity to evaluative properties that tend to lie near the heart of our self-conceptions, even for those who would not like to be called 'sensitive' or 'emotional'. It would not be that unusual for a person to readily admit insensitivity to what is tactful, and easily opt to simply trust others' testimony about this property. But accepting that one is not a fully reliable detector of what is cruel, for instance, is a much trickier proposition. An inability to see the cruel for what it is, even in a limited set of cases, cannot be written off as a harmless character quirk. The vast majority of people, I think, would agree that their good sense of what is needlessly hurtful is important to them as people who try to navigate life without being vicious to others.

The same kind of caveat I made in the case of conceding imaginative fault is relevant here. I can admit that my sense of the hurtful is significantly flawed in some respects without thinking that I am totally at sea when it comes to distinguishing what is wounding from what is harmless fun. I might maintain that my sense of this distinction is generally fine, except when it comes to a narrow band of experiences. But especially in cases where others perceive a policy, attitude, or behaviour as a clear-cut and central instance of malignity (as is often the case when we are dealing with testimony about oppression) the admission that one can't 'get' it is a costly one.

When one trusts another's testimony even after finding one cannot empathize with the other, it will not always be clear which of the admissions described above one is making. They tend to interact with and shade into one another; our abilities to accurately imagine the relevant background conditions may be shaped by our emotional sensitivities, and our emotional sensitivities may be influenced by our patterns of imaginative perspective-taking. Return to the cat-calling case. Consider the man who can't hear his comments about a stranger's body as hostile, despite his empathetic efforts. If he is nevertheless going to trust a woman's testimony about the issue, an admission like this might be appropriate: I'm having trouble finding my way to her perspective because my social position has both freed me from needing to cultivate sensitivity to the threat of sexual violence and given me permission not to hone that sensitivity through a practice of empathy with women's experiences.

Rather paradoxically, the more confidence we have in the accuracy of our own emotional perceptions, the more support empathy yields for one form of trust, but greater confidence in this accuracy will also tend to diminish our ability to trust in others' testimony when we find ourselves unable to empathize with them. That latter form of trust is most easily fostered by a policy of humility about our own perceptual and imaginative abilities. When Nillin and Major, whose remarks I cited above, express exasperation at others' apparent need to empathize in order to believe testimony about experience, part of what they seem to be targeting is a tendency for people to be too taken in by how they imagine things would look to them. At the same time, though, a policy of distrust in the deliverances of empathic efforts on the part of the relatively privileged would not only be very difficult to sustain, but would also deprive people who are in some respect(s) oppressed of an important source of confidence in their word.

5. Conclusion

The uneasy relation between empathy and testimonial trust that I have aimed to draw out in this paper has practical implications for members of privileged groups who aim to correct their practice of testimonial trust and for activists facing questions about what kind of attitudes to encourage in people privileged along one or more dimensions. The way forward is not to try to sever the connection between empathy and testimonial trust. Such an effort is very unlikely to be successful, and if it were to achieve its end, a significant basis for urgently needed testimonial trust would be lost. On the other hand, when it comes to the end of trusting well, in a way that is both epistemically responsible and appropriately responsive to the needs of testifiers, the privileged ought not simply obey calls to have faith in empathy. Clinton might be right that we all need to try to walk in others' shoes, but doing so incautiously is liable to lead to an incorrect apportioning of testimonial trust.

For those who want to reform practices of extending or withholding testimonial trust, especially when it comes to trust across significant differences in privilege, a better option is to draw attention to the respects in which imaginative abilities and emotional sensitivities are limited. Working to keep those limitations firmly in view promises to be helpful in two respects. First, it can help would-be trusters to develop a more refined sense of when the deliverances of their empathetic efforts are likely to yield the right verdicts about trustworthiness, and when they are not. Second, an awareness of these deficiencies can spur efforts to improve one's imaginative abilities and emotional sensitivities, such that one's empathetic efforts become a more reliable guide to testimonial trustworthiness. Some of empathy's typical limitations may be more easily mitigated than

Olivia Bailey

others. Still, with enough practice and resolve one may, for instance, overcome some of the natural preference to empathize with pleasure over pain, or develop a finer sensitivity to the outrageous and the cruel.[26]

Tulane University
obailey@tulane.edu

---

[26] Earlier versions of this article were presented at the Harvard Workshop in Moral and Political Theory and the Penn-Rutgers-Princeton Social Epistemology Workshop. I thank the participants in those workshops, as well as the attendees, presenters, and organizers of the Royal Institute of Philosophy Conference.

Ambivalence About Forgiveness

MIRANDA FRICKER

Abstract

Our ideas about forgiveness seem to oscillate between idealization and scepticism. How should we make sense of this apparent conflict? This paper argues that we should learn something from each, seeing these views as representing opposing moments in a perennial and well-grounded moral ambivalence towards forgiveness. Once we are correctly positioned, we shall see an aspect of forgiveness that recommends precisely this ambivalence. For what will come into view will be certain key psychological mechanisms of moral-epistemic influence – other-addressed and self-addressed mechanisms of moral social construction – that enable forgiveness to function well when it is well-functioning, but which are also *intrinsically prone* to deterioration into one or another form of bad faith. Thus forgiveness is revealed as necessarily containing seeds of its own corruption, showing ambivalence to be a generically appropriate attitude. Moreover, it is emphasized that where forgiver and forgiven are relating to one another in the context of asymmetries of social power, the practice of forgiveness is likely to be further compromised, notably increasing the risk of negative influence on the moral-epistemic states of either the forgiver or the forgiven, or both.

…We will only shout with joy, and keep saying, 'It's all over! It's all over!' Listen to me, Nora. You don't seem to realise that it is all over. What is this? – such a cold, set face! My poor little Nora, I quite understand; you don't feel as if you could believe that I have forgiven you. But it is true, Nora, I swear it; I have forgiven you everything. (Torvald Helmer to his wife Nora, in *A Doll's House* by Henrik Ibsen.)

Our interpersonal practices of forgiveness are fragile and peculiarly prone to deformation of various kinds. Given this fragility, it is not surprising that in philosophy, as in moral thinking generally, we are somewhat prone to mixed attitudes towards forgiveness, being inclined now to idealize it as essential to moral life, and now to mistrust it as involving an inherently dishonest subterfuge. On the one hand we find philosophical accounts that carefully specify ideal forms of forgiveness as a strictly reasoned interpersonal moral justice or (in an alternative ideal) as a special magnanimity of a gracious heart;[1] yet on

---

[1] For the first ideal, see for example Charles Griswold's paradigm of forgiveness in his *Forgiveness: A Philosophical Exploration* (New York: Cambridge University Press, 2007); for the second, see for example Glen

doi:10.1017/S1358246118000590

the other hand there are also significant contemporary exponents of a Nietzschean pessimistic view that denigrates the whole business as a dishonest subterfuge, as one or another form of veiled, possibly self-deceived, interpersonal attack. In this latter connection, witness Martha Nussbaum's recent unqualified excoriation:

> [T]he forgiveness process itself is violent toward the self. Forgiveness is an elusive and usually quite temporary prize held out at the end of a traumatic and profoundly intrusive process of self-denigration. To engage in it with another person (playing, in effect, the role of the confessor) intrudes into that person's inner world in a way that is both controlling and potentially prurient, and does potential violence to the other person's self.[2]

In short, it seems that when it comes to forgiveness we move between admiration and suspicion. What should we make of this conflict? It could of course simply be a matter of one side being plain wrong, or of both sides talking past each other. However, I suspect that these views are best construed as opposing moments in a perennial moral *ambivalence* about forgiveness – an ambivalence that is well grounded. At any rate, I aim to locate a philosophical angle on forgiveness that brings into plain view what is right about each of these opposing perspectives. Once we are correctly positioned, we shall see an aspect of interpersonal forgiveness – considered as a change of heart that is normally though not necessarily communicated to the wrongdoer – which precisely recommends just such an attitude of ambivalence. For what will come into view will be certain key psychological mechanisms of moral influence – both other-addressed and self-addressed – that enable forgiveness to function well when it is well-functioning, but which are also *intrinsically prone* to deterioration into one or another form of bad faith. In particular I hope to highlight that under circumstances of inequality forgiveness can all too easily descend into moral domination – a moral-epistemic wrong whereby one party has undue moral-epistemic influence over the other, steering them into seeing the situation according to the dominator's one-sided moral perspective. A dominating forgiver, moreover, will often do this in a manner that is peculiarly

---

Pettigrove's notion of 'grace' in his *Forgiveness and Love* (Oxford: Oxford University Press, 2012).

[2] Martha C. Nussbaum, *Anger and Forgiveness: Resentment, Generosity, Justice* (Oxford: Oxford University Press, 2016), 72–3.

hard to recognize at the time, because it is in the very nature of forgiving someone that the emotional effort tends to suppress both parties' awareness of the power dynamic, as we shall see – the mechanisms of moral influence on which I shall be focussing are such as to cover their own tracks. To anticipate, the key psychological mechanism in question will emerge as an interpersonal *social constructive* power that is exerted (actively or passively; sometimes knowingly sometimes not; sometimes verbally, sometimes not) by the forgiver who communicates forgiveness to the wrongdoer. Granted that the forgiver is generally responding from a place of moral wounding, the social constructive powers operating as part of the communicative process of forgiveness have a tendency for deterioration, even corruption, so that it becomes compromised, and sometimes badly deformed. If we add into this interpersonal picture a social background such that people are responding to one another's moral claims in the context of unequal social power (like Nora and Torvald, the nineteenth-century bourgeois husband and wife protagonists of Ibsen's famous play), then this significantly increases the risk that the forgiveness expressed (whether verbally or in some other way) will result in moral-epistemic domination. Power inequalities tend to magnify the risks of degeneration that I shall be depicting as already intrinsic to our practices of interpersonal forgiveness. I shall pay some attention to this example by way of illustration as things progress, but my core argument will not depend on issues of the contingent social inequalities between forgiver and forgiven, for my main claim will be a more functional one about some characteristic features *intrinsic* to central forms of forgiveness itself: that the reason why a certain ambivalence towards forgiveness is permanently in order is that the very business of forgiving is intrinsically susceptible to deterioration into manipulative and/or self-deceived forms. While forgiveness plays a profoundly important role in moral life, and remains not only psychologically possible but perhaps all the more precious for its vulnerabilities; still an important fact about the key aspects of forgiveness I shall be bringing under scrutiny here is that they constitute respects in which the relevant kinds of forgiveness necessarily contain the seeds of their own corruption.

Social Constructive Powers Operating in Blame: A 'Proleptic Mechanism'

In order to bring into view the particular psychological mechanism internal to communicated forgiveness that is chiefly relevant to our

Miranda Fricker

purpose, I must first introduce the mechanism by way of its incarnation within blame. Communicating moral blame to a wrongdoer – understood as a matter of letting her know that you find moral fault with her, thereby effectively urging her, at least provisionally, to see matters more from your point of view – can serve as a fundamental means through which we either shore up existing shared moral understandings, or productively generate new ones. I believe that blame of this kind is crucial to how we maintain and grow shared moral consciousness.[3] But whatever one may think about this idea in relation to how best to theorize blame in general, all may accept that some such communicative practice of blame is capable of reaffirming existing shared moral meanings. This role can hardly be far from the surface of any communicated blame: I wrong you, and you communicate blame to me for it, thereby (at the very least) reminding me of any shared values I have transgressed. That communicated blame is at least sometimes capable of achieving this will not be controversial.

What is less obvious is that communicated blame can involve a mechanism of social construction that belongs to the genus *causal social construction*: in treating X as if it (already) has feature F, one can thereby cause X to come to have feature F (at least to some degree). This is a broad phenomenon, and often discussed in connection with negative cases. Self-fulfilling stereotypes function this way, for instance. If, for example, a portion of the population is treated as if they are financially irresponsible (perhaps the usual terms of bank loans and credit cards are not made available to them), then they are liable to start acting in ways characteristic of the financially irresponsible.[4] The causal power may operate in a way that is mediated attitudinally, or else it may operate more superficially and directly

---

[3] Elsewhere I argue for this view in relation to what I call Communicative Blame – blame communicated in a manner suitable to elicit remorseful moral understanding on the part of the wrongdoer. See Fricker, 'What's the Point of Blame? A Paradigm Based Explanation', *Noûs* **50**.1 (2014), 165–183.

[4] See Peter P. Swire, 'Equality of Opportunity and Investment in Creditworthiness', *University of Pennsylvania Law Review*, **143**.5 (1995), 1533–1559: 'a person may reasonably decide not to bother participating in a lending market that seems discriminatory. And, if a person is in fact approved for a loan in such a market, greater incentives exist to take the money and run, or at least not to strive so valiantly to pay on time' (1534–5). I thank Boudewijn de Bruin for directing me to this work. For a virtue-based account of the broader issues, see de Bruin *Ethics and the Global Financial Crisis: Why Incompetence is Worse than Greed* (Cambridge: Cambridge University Press, 2015).

on behaviour, without any psychological mediation. Thus group members may respond to their financial exclusion with an attitude of defiant short-termism ('Let's just spend it while we've got it – the whole system's stacked against us anyway'); or they may have no such change of attitude, but simply be forced by circumstance into unfavourable practical options such as borrowing from loan sharks whose escalating interest rates make the loans impossible to re-pay, sending the borrowers into a spiral of debt. Either way, whether psychologically mediated or not, what we see in the behaviour is the effect of the self-fulfilling prophecy that is causal social construction. One way or the other the group is caused to go in for financially irresponsible behaviour – behaviour that infuriatingly provides an apparent retrospective justification for the original belief and treatment. Such scenarios are obviously highly negative for the group in question. More happily, however, there can also be positive self-fulfilling prophecies. In some circumstances, if you treat another person (not yet trustworthy) as if she were already trustworthy, then she may thereby be caused to become trustworthy. Indeed some have persuasively argued this is a general feature of trusting another person: other things equal, the fact that one has placed one's trust in them, thereby creating common knowledge that one is depending on them, gives the trusted party an added reason and motive to live up to that trust.[5] When this happens, a morally useful piece of causal social construction has taken place interpersonally.

Such interpersonal operations of causal social construction can occur in other areas of ethical life too. Following Bernard Williams' lead, I have elsewhere argued that communicated blame can effect just this kind of morally useful interpersonal social construction.[6] In Williams's exposition we encounter the idea that blame's expression can sometimes have a salutary effect even on a relatively hard-case culprit by way of a 'proleptic mechanism'. And I have argued that we should recognize this mechanism as a fundamental means

[5]   See Richard Holton, 'Deciding to Trust, Coming to Believe', *Australasian Journal of Philosophy* **72** (1994), 63–76; Paul Faulkner 'Norms of Trust', in A. Haddock, A. Millar, and D. Pritchard (eds.) *Social Epistemology* (Oxford: Oxford University Press, 2010); and Karen Jones 'Trust as an Affective Attitude', *Ethics* **107**.1 (1996), 4–25.
[6]   See Fricker, 'What's the Point of Blame? A Paradigm Based Explanation'; and Bernard Williams, 'Internal Reasons and The Obscurity of Blame', in *Making Sense of Humanity and other philosophical papers 1982–1993* (Cambridge: Cambridge University Press, 1995).

by which we actively generate new shared moral understandings. When a proleptic mechanism functions within blame, the blamer treats the wrongdoer *as if* he already recognizes a reason (which he does not yet recognize), thereby causing him to come to recognize it.[7] Of course, this proleptic mechanism will only work given the wrongdoer has sufficient basic respect for the blamer to be moved by his admonishments; but so long as that more basic respect is in place, then we see that the proleptic blamer is (possibly unwittingly) exercising a power of *interpersonal moral social construction.* Communicated blame operating proleptically, then, involves an exertion of moral influence that can work to bring the wrongdoer's moral understanding into alignment with that of the wronged party. It is of course contingent how well this works in any given instance, but it surely must work much of the time, for otherwise it is hard to imagine how a genuinely shared moral culture could develop and stabilize itself interpersonally – without its powers to change people, blame communicated to those who do not already share the relevant values would have merely expressive or cathartic value at best.[8] Of

[7]   See Williams 'Internal Reasons and The Obscurity of Blame', 40–43. Williams does not use the term 'recognize' of course, which is a term of art on my part. In relation to practical reasons Williams generally used the verb 'have', since his commitment to the doctrine of internal reasons pictures reasons as relativized to a semi-idealized set of motivational states in the agent (her 'S'). From this it follows that the proper description of any case in which a proleptic mechanism has any real work to do must be given in terms of the wrongdoer actually *lacking* a reason the blamer might however cause him to *acquire.* (In Williams's idiom, the bad thing about really bad people is that they really lack moral reasons.) No doubt proleptic mechanisms can cause some other things in this general vicinity: realizing I have a reason I didn't know I had, for instance, because the requisite motive was either already in my motivational set but concealed from me, or because it should have been there but, owing to an error of fact or reasoning on my part, wasn't.

[8]   Benjamin Bagley discusses these issues in a way that envisions blame's proleptic action as a matter of retrospectively rendering determinate some patch of the culprit's normative psychology presumed to have previously been less than fully determinate. (See Benjamin Bagley, 'Properly Proleptic Blame', *Ethics* **127** (2017): 852–882. While I would agree that increasing psychological determinacy is indeed one *modus operandi* of prolepsis, and an important one to emphasize, still I do not regard it as the only one. In my view (and I believe in Williams's conception) being blamed is one kind of experience that stands a chance of *changing* one's outlook or sensibility, adding or subtracting an item in one's S, or shifting the order of priority among existing items so as to produce new sound deliberative routes and

course communicated blame is not the only resource for this purpose, but still without the spontaneous moral reactions of those we wrong, how would we learn the first-order moral significances of our actions in their vivid human colour? It is an important feature of well-functioning blame of this kind ('Communicative Blame' as I call it)[9] that it is not morally dogmatic. The attempt to get the person who has wronged you to see things more from your point of view is the natural means of getting them *to acknowledge the moral significance of what they've done.* But the proper practice of this kind of blame carries no arrogant or narcissistic presumption on the part of the wronged party that her interpretation is unassailable – she is only human and may be over-reacting, or unaware of other aspects of the situation that put a different gloss on things. So the kind of blame appropriate to the morally constructive task will be communicated in a manner that is open to dialogue with the wrongdoer, on pain of moral dogmatism or manipulation. Victoria McGeer has discussed this issue in terms of a potential worry about blame's 'regulatory' role, and she proposes a helpful test in this regard:

> To be respectful of you qua believer is to be respectful of you qua reasoning agent. But in order to be respectful of you in this way, it does not matter that I explicitly aim at getting you to change your beliefs; what matters is that I choose a means whereby your own rational faculties are the proximate cause of the change in your beliefs. That is to say I must offer you argument and/or evidence in favor of p... One significant and important test of this fact is that you not only have the power to withhold your belief, but you have the power to challenge my arguments and my evidence, thereby exposing me to the very same process and possibilities to which I expose you – specifically the possibility of changing *my* mind as to the truth of p in light of your argumentative response.[10]

Provided we can allow that an argumentatively inexplicit moral-emotional exchange can count as the relevant sort of 'argument' or 'evidence' that is required here, so that for instance your telling me (or

---

thus new reasons for the agent. New experiences sometimes change us; new morally relevant experiences sometimes change us morally.

[9] Fricker, 'What's the Point of Blame? A Paradigm Based Explanation'.

[10] Victoria McGeer, 'Civilizing Blame', in D. Justin Coates and Neil A. Tognazzini (eds.), *Blame: Its Nature and Norms* (Oxford: Oxford University Press, 2013), 179.

perhaps merely showing me) that I hurt and offended you when I made some thoughtless quip is enough to count as your moral argument, and my feeling sorry and ashamed when I see how my stupid remark has upset you can count as sufficient for my own rational faculties being the proximate cause of the change in my beliefs, then McGeer's proposed test strikes me as exactly right.[11] It makes precise what is achieved in the more general condition of blame's being open to dialogue and potential push-back on the part of the blamed party.

So far so good: blame communicated with a view to getting the wrongdoer to appreciate the moral significance of what she's done need not be disrespectful, dogmatic, or bullying. But still, what of its pitfalls? It is generally fairly close to the surface of any communicated blame that it is prone to deteriorated formations: excessive anger, retributive impulse, high-handedness, moralism, *ressentiment*, and so forth. We are on the whole only too aware of these risks in everyday moral interaction; hence the popular suspicion of blame as a moral response. However, the present focus is not on the merits or demerits of this or that kind of blame, but rather on blame's sheer capacity to operate proleptically by way of an interpersonal psychological mechanism whose generic form I have suggested we should recognize as that of causal social construction, and the inherent riskiness that this introduces – riskiness as regards the likelihood that any given blamer, coming from a place of moral wounding, will step over the mark and be less open to dialogue than they should be. Proleptic blame, in virtue of its ambition to *change* the other party, is a highly valuable moral response to wrongdoing; and yet the very power in which its special value inheres runs a special risk that the wounded party may bully the wrongdoer into a one-sided view of the putative wrong done, and thus effect a moment of moral-epistemic domination.

This proleptic mode of blame and its attendant risk indicates where we should look for our desired angle on forgiveness: Might forgiveness sometimes involve a proleptic mechanism too? If it does, or inasmuch as it does, then I think we may locate the position from which to view forgiveness so that the two conflicting perspectives on it – now

---

[11] Insisting on more explicitly articulate moral argumentation would seem intellectualist, and not in the spirit of McGeer's general Strawsonian approach; so I take myself, I hope correctly, to be presenting McGeer's self-same view when I stretch the notions of 'argumentation', 'evidence' and own 'proximal reasons' to encompass the rational sensitivities that are expressed in an exchange of spontaneous moral reactive attitudes and feelings.

admiration, even idealization; now mistrust, even cynicism – are resolved into one complex image of an essential human response to wrongdoing whose second-personal communication normally involves, consciously or not, an operation of moral influence on the other party. Ambivalence will prove to be in order because, as with most exercises of power, however benignly intended or plain unwitting, there is a built-in risk of tipping over into morally problematic forms such as moral-epistemic domination. Let me now explore the different proleptic moments in our practices of forgiving, so that we may be led to some answers about what forms of bad faith are perpetually in the offing when we forgive.

Proleptic Moral Powers Implicit in Forgiveness

Now we have introduced the idea of a significant power of other-directed moral-social construction that can operate in communicated blame, we have a lens that will help us discern similar proleptic moments secreted in the structures forgiveness. What might these be? Let us scrutinize what I take to be the two main kinds of forgiveness, both of which essentially involve an attitudinal change towards the wrongdoer that may or may not be communicated. First, a 'conditional' kind according to which the forgiveness is earned or justified through remorse and/or apology on the culprit's part;[12] and an essentially 'unconditional', or 'elective' kind where the forgiveness is precisely un-earned or 'unmerited', its distinctive moral value consisting largely in this fact.[13] I trust I can take these two broad types as understood and recognizable from everyday life as well as from the philosophical literature that details their possible contours. At any rate,

---

[12] For some recent views of this kind see Griswold, *Forgiveness: A Philosophical Exploration*; Pamela Hieronymi, 'Articulating an Uncompromising Forgiveness', *Philosophy and Phenomenological Research*, **62**.3 (2001), 529–555; Jeffrie Murphy in Jean Hampton and Jeffrie Murphy, *Forgiveness and Mercy* (Cambridge University Press, 1998); Christopher Bennett, 'Personal and Redemptive Forgiveness', *European Journal of Philosophy* **11**.2 (2003), 127–144; among many others.

[13] For some recent views of this kind see Pettigrove, *Forgiveness and Love* (Oxford: Oxford University Press, 2012); Lucy Allais 'Wiping the Slate Clean: The Heart of Forgiveness', *Philosophy and Public Affairs* **36**.1 (2008), 33-68; and 'Elective Forgiveness', *International Journal of Philosophical Studies* **21**.5 (2013), 637–653; and Eve Garrard and David McNaughton, 'In Defence of Unconditional Forgiveness', *Proceedings of the Aristotelian Society*, **103**.1 (2004), 39–60.

for a theoretically minimal working model of the first kind – the earned kind of forgiveness that waits for (something approximating) remorseful apology – let us rely on P. F. Strawson's characterization of the 'reactive attitude and feeling' of forgiveness. He characterises it as essentially involving the forgiver's *forswearing* of (what I shall neutrally gloss as) blame-feelings towards the wrongdoer once the wrongdoer has offered a *repudiation* of the wrong done:

> To ask to be forgiven is in part to acknowledge that the attitude displayed in our actions was such as might properly be resented and in part to repudiate that attitude for the future...; and *to forgive is to accept the repudiation and to forswear the resentment.*[14]

This kind of forgiveness, let us notice in passing, might be seen to carry a risk that the demanding attitude it waits on becomes excessive or controlling ('Let's hear that repudiation loud and clear – tell me just how wicked you've been!'). This is the corruption that Nussbaum rightly draws critical attention to. It has nothing to do with proleptic mechanisms, but rather the tendency for conditional forgiveness to become blame-ridden, so that the forgiveness invisibly straightens into another stick to beat the wrongdoer with. Later we shall see that this tendency to become blame-ridden is in fact a risk that adheres to *any* kind of forgiveness that is spoken, but for the time being let us note that the particular form of corruption that Nussbaum highlights is less a corruption of the forgiveness itself but rather of the *blame* that is its condition and precursor. For as soon as the proper business of forgiving – namely the forswearing of blame-feeling – is under way, the intrusive excess that Nussbaum characterizes as potentially involving a kind of psychological violence is by definition already over. But even if we allow that the blamer's demand is also part and parcel of the forgiver's stance, which perhaps it is, still I see no reason to agree with her blanket view that all kinds of forgiveness require the fulfilment of demands that are intrusive or moralistic, let alone psychologically violent. There is no reason to lose faith in the possibility of gentler, generous, and non-excessively demanding forms of conditional forgiveness; though we certainly do well to heed her warning about the risks.

This much I find to be somewhat on the surface of our practices and not concealed – largely for the reason just mentioned, namely that the corruptions of conditional forgiveness as regards what it

---

[14] P. F. Strawson, 'Freedom and Resentment', in *Freedom and Resentment and Other Essays* (London: Methuen, 1974), 6 (italics added).

does to the wrongdoer are really corruptions internal to the communicated blame that precedes it, and we are generally alive to the likely corruptions of blame. What is more opaque, I believe, is how the second kind of forgiveness – an unconditional kind of forgiveness I shall call Gifted Forgiveness[15] – may itself be prone to deterioration into forms of moral dogmatism and manipulation. It looks rather unlikely on the surface, because the whole point about any unconditional forgiveness is that its distinctive feature is its *non-demandingness* towards the culprit. The gifting forgiver demands no repudiation of the wrong. Rather he abstains from the normal entitlements of the wounded party in relation to a wrongdoer, and forgives anyway, even though the normal conditions of forgiveness are not satisfied. For this reason some aptly describe this kind of forgiveness as involving an 'unmerited' act of grace.[16] So if the gifting forgiver just lets the culprit go free in this way, without moral demand, then it seems obscure how such a practice would have any features that render it intrinsically prone to descend into any kind of moral-epistemic bullying. But I believe our newly acquired awareness of the subtle operation of proleptic mechanisms in moral relations promises to shine some light on this relative obscurity.

In Gifted Forgiveness the distinctive feature, as we have just remarked, is that the wronged party forgives *for free*; that is, without demanding any prior repudiation of the wrong. Thus Gifted Forgiveness is given as an arrestingly generous, because normatively transgressive, moral gratuity. Now, what we have not yet observed about this phenomenon is that this norm-busting moral gratuity tends to induce a certain effect in the forgiven party: the gift-forgiven wrongdoer, in recognizing the transgressively generous nature of the gift, may be jolted after the fact into the humility that ushers in remorseful recognition of her wrongdoing. Gifted Forgiveness, exploiting as it does a background common knowledge that some sort of repudiation is the normal condition on appropriate forgiveness, is structured perfectly to exert a power of moral-social construction: if we look carefully we can discern that the structure of this interpersonal moral exchange is the already familiar one of *prolepsis*. In this case the proleptic mechanism is as follows: the gifting forgiver effectively treats the wrongdoer *as if she already* satisfied the normal

---

[15] See Miranda Fricker, 'Forgiveness: An Ordered Pluralism', *Australian Philosophical Review* (forthcoming).
[16] Glen Pettigrove, *Forgiveness and Love* (Oxford: Oxford University Press, 2012), chapter 7.

condition on appropriate forgiveness, thereby causing her (if the mechanism achieves its end) to fulfil that very condition after all.

The *gift* in Gifted Forgiveness is not merely the commitment to direct no (further) blame-feelings towards the wrongdoer for what they have done, though that is surely part of it. Rather the gift more importantly includes a commitment to a morally optimistic perception of the wrongdoer, as someone who 'knows better' or 'knows better *really*', and who is therefore capable of repudiating the wrong they have done and perhaps acting differently in the future. Proleptic forgiveness directly addresses itself to the wrongdoer's better nature. Moreover the gifting forgiver's cart-before-horse forswearing of blame-feeling affirms the possibility, perhaps the hope, that the wrongdoer's better nature may soon *actually* come to the fore, somewhat precipitated by the very fact of having been forgiven in this normatively transgressive, un-earned manner. I trust this underlines the fact that the kind of power exercised by the gifting forgiver (whether he knows it or not, intends it or not) is indeed a power of *causal moral-social construction*: in treating the wrongdoer as if they already fulfilled the condition of conditional forgiveness he causes them to fulfil it (if they do) after the fact. Here we discern the generally morally progressive proleptic mechanism detected in the very structure of Gifted Forgiveness.

Before we move on to the ways in which this mechanism creates a risk of deterioration into moral domination, let me emphasize two points regarding what is meant by the idea of the proleptic mechanism being 'built in' to the practice. First, a practice having a proleptic power built into its structure does not entail that it always, or even ordinarily, achieves its point. The aim built into the structure of solo card games of 'solitaire' or 'patience' is to get all the suits to work out in sequence; but that only actually happens about half the time, if that. Or consider another ethical practice, briefly mentioned earlier: trusting someone to do something. One's trust will certainly not always have the effect that the practice aims at, but still the rationale of the practice depends on the idea that it is well designed to have the effect, other things equal. So it is, I am suggesting, with Gifted Forgiveness. Just like trusting someone to do something, gift forgiving will *tend*, other things equal, to bring about a certain morally desirable psychological effect. There are limits to the analogy of course. I would not wish to insist, for instance, that the act of Gifted Forgiveness provides the wrongdoer with an added moral reason to repudiate her wrongs (though it surely might in some contexts); but certainly the analogy holds in that the act of Gifted Forgiving, like the act of trusting, is apt to move the forgiven party in the morally desirable direction. It is not guaranteed – far from it – but the practice is culturally evolved to tend towards this effect. Indeed, as Glen Pettigrove has argued, there is some empirical evidence for a fairly high estimation of the 'transformative power' of this kind of forgiveness (which he conceives as involving an act of grace, understood as an act of unmerited favour).[17]

The second point concerns the forgiver's moral motivations. Also like trust, while Gifted Forgiveness may be practised entirely non-strategically and guilelessly as regards the proleptic power it contains, still there need be nothing manipulative or ungenerous, let alone bullying, about a clear-eyed forgiver who did engage in the practice in full consciousness of its implicit rationale, or even who employed it as a deliberate moral strategy. Such a clear-eyed gift forgiver might simply see that gifting the forgiveness is the best-bet response in a case where anything else is only going to entrench moral hostilities. Forgiveness can be somewhat strategic without thereby being manipulative, for having a moral strategy in how to deal with a difficult situation – for instance one in which someone has wronged you but is only likely to get more hostile if you confront them about it – is manifestly an instance of moral wisdom. A good deal of our moral lives is a matter of coping with each other's moral limitations, including our own, so the everyday strategies – ethical common sense, one might say – about how best to handle this or that situation of wrongdoing, hurt feelings, on-going vulnerabilities and resistances is part and parcel of wise moral response. The bottom line, as with blame, is that provided the Gifted Forgiveness prompts the wrongdoer to an appropriate remorseful moral understanding of which a proximal cause is her own moral sensibility (which might simply be a matter of her coming to feel truly sorry as a result of the blamer's bringing her to a more realistic and vivid perception of the hurt she'd caused him), then there need be nothing manipulative or ungenerous about the proleptic purpose.

This completes the case for the claim that Gifted Forgiveness inherently operates a proleptic mechanism, whether actively employed by a savvy forgiver whose pity for the wrongdoer contains the knowledge that nothing else can help him now but the gratuitous generosity of the person wronged, or merely passively operative through a forgiver who is entirely focussed on a personal ethical ideal of a wilfully open heart. As ever, the particular moral-cultural formation of Gifted Forgiveness is highly contingent, capable of manifesting itself in a religious form, or in a secular one; perhaps a formation that is primarily

---

[17] Pettigrove, *Forgiveness and Love*, 126, and see also 140 nn. 57, 58.

focussed on the moral health of the forgiver, or alternatively on that of the wrongdoer, or of course both. Either way, this kind of communicated Gifted Forgiveness is invested with a power of *causal moral-epistemic social construction* that is apt to prompt the wrongdoer to repudiate her bad action after the fact. I have argued that this prompting depends upon the wrongdoer being moved by the norm-busting generosity displayed by the forgiver who does not demand repudiation up front but rather forgives as a matter of moral gratuity; and I have argued that it need not be manipulative, even when it is part of a self-conscious moral strategy. However, with the potency of this psychological dynamic put before us, I hope we are now better positioned to see how this kind of forgiveness is nonetheless intrinsically susceptible to deterioration into something that *is* manipulative, and potentially a form of moral-epistemic domination.

Corruptions of Proleptic Powers

Let us start with the obvious point that Gifted Forgiveness is a special kind of gift giving. The general comparison is instructive, for the giving of gifts needs to be done in the right spirit. Quite what the right spirit requires will vary from context to context. But, for example, in contexts where there is a general background presumption of reciprocation other things equal, giving something in the right spirit will depend on achieving a certain delicate balance between simple generosity (it's for *them*) and a perfectly proper background awareness that this sort of thing is generally reciprocal (maybe if they never gave you a present in return, you might stop bothering to get them one – that'd be fair enough; and anyway it might be socially ill-judged, even mildly coercive, to persist). The giving of birthday presents can be like this in a given circle of friends. But too much motivational focus on the prospect of receiving something in return instrumentalizes generosity, and your gift is rendered a travesty. In other contexts, the expectation of like-for-like reciprocation may not be at issue, but rather some other kind of obliquely expected goal that is lodged in the rationale of the practice. In Gifted Forgiveness the relevant expectation will concern the forgiven party's potential prompting into a repudiation of her bad action. Here the 'right spirit' requires maintaining a balance between forgiving out of generosity but in the context of a (perhaps not-so-background) awareness that this may prompt a change in the wrongdoer. As regards the aim of successfully pricking the conscience of the wrongdoer, quite how much motivational prominence can be tolerated in a given context without spoiling the proper spirit of moral generosity will surely vary with the situation and relationship. (There are some contexts in which the only non-spoiling answer to the question 'Why did you forgive me?' would be 'Because you're my friend'. Others in which it would be perfectly fine to say 'Because I could see that nothing else was going to get us anywhere'.[18]) However we can say that in any given case, too much motivational emphasis on the aim of changing the wrongdoer risks over-instrumentalizing the forgiveness and thereby spoiling the spirit of moral generosity of which, at its best, it is the open-hearted expression: too much trying to change others descends into manipulation and even an attempt at moral-epistemic domination. The spirit of even the savviest, most influence-aware gifting forgiver is not one of pulling the strings of puppet wrongdoers. And relatedly, as in the case of communicated blame, the well-functioning practice of communicated Gifted Forgiving gives no shelter to moral dogmatism. Rather it remains open to dialogue and pushback from the wrongdoer. So the balance of generosity and attempted moral influence that is inherent in any Gifted Forgiving is a delicate one. Maintaining the right spirit involves resisting two closely related deteriorations: the over-instrumentalization that would cast one's forgiveness too much as a mere means of securing the desired moral response from the wrongdoer; and the closedness to dialogue that amounts to moral dogmatism as regards the content of the moral-epistemic perspective one hopes to bring them to take up. The attitude behind well-functioning Gifted Forgiving might often be one of hopefulness (that the wrongdoer will come around), and even moral confidence about one's interpretation of events; yet, as in the case of communicative blaming, that confidence is partly earned through a continued *openness to dialogue* (as regards the moral content of the claim of wrongdoing), and a willingness to revise one's interpretation of events where countervailing responses are forthcoming.[19]

These balanced attitudes are difficult to maintain interpersonally at the best of times. If we add to this the fact that the forgiver will always be coming from a place of some moral wounding, then we see all the more clearly how easily the proleptic power implicit in Gifted Forgiveness can descend into attempted moral domination. Let us imagine a situation in which the Gifting Forgiver is forgiving a

[18]   I thank David Enoch for a helpful discussion of these issues.
[19]   Here, as earlier, I am indebted to McGeer's discussion of the 'regulation' worry in relation to blame (McGeer, 'Civilizing Blame').

genuine wrong done in a context of social equality. Perhaps we can imagine two friends, whose relationship is not characterized by any notable inequalities of social power, where one has betrayed the other in some way, and the wronged party aims to forgive her friend even though Friend (let us call her) does not seem to be fully acknowledging what she has done, and indeed there is some question in the mind of the forgiver as to whether Friend is in some denial about its moral seriousness. In a situation like this, the forgiver may hope that Friend, in being gift forgiven, might be prompted to acknowledge the full significance of the betrayal. So far so all right. And yet it is not difficult to see how this could easily descend into something less well-balanced and more controlling, as our forgiver might be frustrated by what she sees as Friend's under-estimation of the wrong, and repeatedly communicates her magnanimous gesture of forgiveness as a means to prompt Friend into some sort of moral realization that matches the forgiver's perception of things. What begins as a legitimate hopeful effort of moral influence can all too easily intensify, when insufficiently dialogically open, into an excessive emphasis on the goal of prompting a preconceived desired change in the moral-epistemic states of the wrongdoer. Where there is interpersonal moral dogmatism there is manipulation, and in some cases to a degree that merits description as moral-epistemic domination.

This is especially so if we take seriously the possibility that Friend, considered by the hurt party to be under-estimating the moral seriousness of her conduct, may not be so much in denial as in a state of some genuine disagreement about the moral significance of her behaviour. The moral meanings of our actions are often contested and up for negotiation. ('I admit that what I did was pretty thoughtless, but to say it was a "betrayal of our friendship" is melodramatic... But now I don't even have the chance to discuss it, because apparently I am "already forgiven".') How does our supposedly generously fast-tracked forgiveness look now that we see it in this light? Its would-be generous one-sidedness seems to have deteriorated into a technique of silencing the other party and imposing a one-sided moral interpretation. Here the wrongdoer is paying a price for the very absence of moral demand – demand for upfront repudiation and therefore the opportunity for dialogue – that the practice frames as an act of generosity towards her. In such a case, the Gifted Forgiveness may be entirely well-intentioned and yet it is facilitating an inadvertent act of moral-epistemic domination. (We can easily imagine cases that are less well-intentioned and less inadvertent too of course.) The ever-present risk in the great one-sided emotional efforts of the Gifting

Forgiver is that she simply by-passes the opportunity for moral dialogue and contestation that communicated blame is likely to openly
inspire.[20] Thus we see how Gifted Forgiveness can be employed,
whether innocently or strategically, to pre-empt dialogue and thereby
to impose the hurt party's moral interpretation in a way that renders it
somewhat immune to challenge. The purported wrongdoer who
might have gladly taken up an opportunity to challenge the forgiver's
moral-epistemic perspective is effectively pre-empted, wrong-footed,
perhaps altogether silenced.

Interestingly this kind of moral-epistemic domination through
pre-emptive Gift Forgiving can occur even in cases where the Gifted
Forgiveness is not communicated to them. Imagine someone with
something of a martyr complex privately Gift Forgiving another
who they feel has wronged them; yet where the best interpretation of
their magnanimous one-sided and secret gift is that they are thereby
protecting themselves from any dialogue that might challenge the
idea that they have been wronged. The purported wrongdoer in this
scenario may not even be aware that she is regarded as having done
something wrong, and yet she is already forgiven for it – the nature
of her alleged moral crime thus self-servingly fixed in the psychology
of the forgiver.

Even between two subjects of roughly equal social power and
status, this much flows all too naturally from the very nature of
Gifted Forgiveness as a one-sided fast-tracked form of forgiveness
that speeds past the usual stage of communicated blame and the dialogue it invites. Add into this cocktail a twist of social inequality
between the two parties, and things are likely to deteriorate further.
In situations of greater social power on the part of the forgiver, his
communication of Gifted Forgiveness will wield *undue moral-
epistemic influence* on the alleged wrongdoer because, let's imagine,
we are in bourgeois circles in a nineteenth-century Norwegian town
and the forgiver is the 'husband' who is master in his home and the
wrongdoer his 'wife'. In Torvald and Nora's case, as quoted in my
epigraph, he is forgiving her for something authentically culpable –
she committed a significant crime (fraud) that exposed them to blackmail. Happily the blackmail threat swiftly abated, though not before
Torvald had been decidedly foul to Nora so that the scales fell from
her eyes as regards the meaning of their marriage and of her
imposed infantilized existence. As the master of the house, Torvald
exercises an unduly inflated authority in general, and this looks
ready to spill over into their moral exchange. For much of the play

---

[20] I thank Antony Duff and Christel Fricke for discussion of this point.

Miranda Fricker

one might find both Torvald and Nora pretty insufferable, but even if
they had both already been feminists of their time there would be
limits to how far they could expunge the patriarchy from their relationship, for it is delivered in the gendered identities they are lum-
bered with, and in the institution of marriage that rigidifies and
incentivizes them. (One recalls John Stuart Mill's statement in
which he repudiated the 'odious powers' conferred on him in marry-
ing Harriet Taylor and lamented the impossibility of legally divesting
himself of them.) Even when the parties dissent, the social statuses in
which one is operating still tend to insinuate themselves through the
passive operation of identity power.[21] Despite best efforts, the very relationships we stand in can unbalance the everyday forms of moral influence that would otherwise (in a situation of equality) be more
straightforward and candid. Even if you are critically aware of those
unequal social statuses, still the forgiveness that may flow between
you and another is likely to be compromised in some measure.
Perhaps you presume too easily that if someone does not repudiate
their action then they are surely in denial, or plain wrong; or perhaps
you presume too much as regards the credentials of your moral interpretations, and wind up imposing them on others who are not enabled
to challenge you effectively. At any rate, the point is simply that whatever risk of descent into moral manipulation already inheres in the proleptic mechanism as wielded by someone who has been morally
wounded, it is likely to become heightened if for reasons of social
power the forgiver exercises an asymmetrical moral authority.

Let us stay with Torvald and Nora for a moment longer to see what
else we may observe regarding this subject of Gifted Forgiveness's
deterioration into a tool of moral-epistemic domination when operating in a context of unequal power. Here we find them at the moment
when Torvald has discovered they are released from the threat of
blackmail to which Nora's crime had exposed them:

> Torvald: ...We will only shout with joy, and keep saying, 'It's all
> over! It's all over!' Listen to me, Nora. You don't seem to realise
> that it is all over. What is this? – such a cold, set face! My poor
> little Nora, I quite understand; you don't feel as if you could
> believe that I have forgiven you. But it is true, Nora, I swear it; I
> have forgiven you everything. I know that what you did, you did
> out of love for me.

---

[21] I set out the idea of 'identity power' in chapter 1 of *Epistemic
Injustice: Power and the Ethics of Knowing* (Oxford: Oxford University
Press, 2007).

Nora: That is true.

Torvald: You have loved me as a wife ought to love her husband. Only you had not sufficient knowledge to judge of the means you used. But do you suppose you are any the less dear to me, because you don't understand how to act on your own responsibility? No, no; only lean on me; I will advise you and direct you. I should not be a man if this womanly helplessness did not just give you a double attractiveness in my eyes. You must not think anymore about the hard things I said in my first moment of consternation, when I thought everything was going to overwhelm me. I have forgiven you, Nora; I swear to you I have forgiven you.

Something that is very noticeable here is that Torvald is operating with a rigid presumption that he knows exactly what has gone on morally, showing zero interest in anything Nora might have to say on the subject. He prattles on, presuming she has nothing to contribute besides perhaps contrition and gratitude. Torvald's spontaneous forgiveness (I don't say it's exactly Gifted Forgiveness – he may or may not be presuming she is remorseful as he pays so little heed to the idea of her as a moral agent) pre-empts the possibility of achieving any genuinely shared moral understanding of what has gone on between him and his wife. Instead he is only interested in his own understanding, and just assumes Nora will see things his way. That is what he is used to doing in every other area of their life, and so it is presumed here. Of course we know that Nora ultimately refuses all this, and the only way she can communicate it is by leaving with the famous final door slam. What is somewhat on display in this passage, I would suggest, is the closedness to dialogue that we have identified as signifying moral-epistemic domination. *Chez* Torvald and Nora this stems largely from the social institutions of gender and marriage, and the way in which he has all along constructed her as barely responsible or able to think for herself – a performance of gender ideology in which she has so far actively colluded. These contemporary kinds of unequal social identity positions – 'husband' who is master and protector, 'wife' who is obedient and protected – play directly into the hands of the intrinsic tendencies for corruption already identified in the very psychological mechanisms of Gifted Forgiving. Those intrinsic tendencies chart twin patterns of deterioration: what may start as a candid attempt at respectful moral influence descends into manipulation, even moral-epistemic domination; and what starts with a generous sparing of the wrongdoer from the travails of condemnation deteriorates into the silencing of potential moral contestation.

Miranda Fricker

Other Intrinsic Tendencies Toward Deteriorated Forgiving – Blame's Return

I have so far been focusing exclusively on the likely corruptions that come from something special to Gifted Forgiveness, namely the *other-directed* proleptic mechanism that is internal to it. I would like in this last section to broaden our purview a little and look for other tendencies towards deterioration that may be either essential or at least normal features of forgiveness in general – that is, conditional forgiveness as well as the central kind of unconditional forgiveness that is Gifted Forgiving. The first point I shall discuss was briefly flagged at the outset in relation to all communicated forgiving and does not depend on any prolepsis. Instead it stems from an observation about the power of *presupposition* – specifically here its power to render expressions of forgiveness surreptitiously blame-ridden. The second point will return us to proleptic mechanisms, but not of the familiar *other-directed* kind, but rather to a kind that is intriguingly *self-directed* – a moment of reflexive causal moral-social construction that is often involved in the forswearing of blame-feelings, whether expressed or kept private.

First, the power of presupposition. Forgiveness in general presupposes that the person to be forgiven is *blameworthy*. Though possibly not an absolutely universal rule, it would be a rare scenario in which one would be in a position to forgive someone who was not at fault and so blameworthy for their actions.[22] So the presupposition of blameworthiness is generally apt – part of the generic logic of forgiveness. But presuppositions can be unruly – noisier than they are intended or pretended to be, and insidiously influential. Rae Langton discusses the introduction of presuppositions into conversational contexts in terms of 'back-door testimony'.[23] Her particular interest is in how back-door testimony of an objectionable kind – it might be prejudiced

---

[22] Espen Gamlund has argued that we can make sense of forgiving someone even for a wrong that was wholly excused (see Gamlund 'Forgiveness Without Blame' in Christel Fricke (ed.), *The Ethics of Forgiveness* (London: Routledge, 2011). And Nicolas Cornell has argued that one can forgive someone pre-emptively, before they perpetrate the wrongdoing (Cornell, 'The Possibility of Pre-emptive Forgiving', *Philosophical Review* **126**.2 (2017), 241–272).

[23] Rae Langton, 'Blocking as Counter-Speech', in Daniel Harris, Daniel Fogal, and Matt Moss (eds.), *New Work on Speech Acts*, (Oxford: Oxford University Press, forthcoming). Langton draws explicitly on David Lewis's notion of 'rules of accommodation' in 'Scorekeeping in a Language Game', *Journal of Philosophical Logic* **8** (1979): 339–359.

speech, for instance – can be 'blocked'; and how if it isn't blocked then it winds up effectively 'accommodated'. Accommodation keeps the presupposition in play as something all parties to the conversation have at least passively allowed in. Back-door testimony takes a significant effort of conversational disruption to block, for one has to first make the presupposition explicit and then challenge it. This amounts to stopping the conversational action ('Cut!') and forcing something into shot whose presence was intended to be only obliquely sensed off-screen. Such challenges are not always easy; though they certainly can be made, as Langton illustrates:

Attempts to block can be...mundane, like this light-hearted and high-decibel exchange I witnessed in 1990, at a Melbourne football game:

St. Kilda supporter to sluggish player: 'Get on with it, Laurie, you great girl!'

Alert bystander: 'Hey, what's wrong with a girl?'

St. Kilda supporter: 'It's got no balls, that's what's wrong with it!'[24]

Langton analyses this 'great girl' speech act as doing at least two things – implicitly *testifying* that girls aren't up to much when it comes to football; and implicitly *legitimating* broader *norms* that give men a dominant role. And of course the bystander 'blocks' these things by challenging the presupposition. Langton goes on to present a mode of blocking that functions by explicitating and challenging the presupposition, thereby de-authorizing the speaker so that his/her speech act misfires. Unlike Langton's 'great girl' example, in which the objectionable nature of the presupposition is that it is false or at least condescending to women, so that de-authorizing it is an appropriate aim; in the case of forgiveness my point is not at all that there is anything wrong with the content of the presupposition. There isn't: forgiveness generally presupposes blameworthiness. My point is rather that the presupposition, and the implicit assertion of blameworthiness that it entails, can all too easily degenerate – especially given that the would-be forgiver is emerging from a moral wounding – into serving as a vehicle for back-door blaming. Under the surreptitious influence of the back-door assertion of blameworthiness, an initial attempt at forgiving can unfortunately deteriorate into a mere reassertion of the fact that they did wrong. Blame smuggles itself back on set, concealed in a cloak of forgiveness. Thus we can see how the presupposition of blameworthiness entails

---

that when one communicates forgiveness one thereby implicitly expresses the view that the person is blameworthy. This is an aspect of forgiveness that calls for an active repression of the blaming attitude to keep it off-screen where it now belongs, if indeed you really are forswearing the blame-feelings it inspires. This brings me to the second point – the point about what is typically involved in any forgiver's internal self-disciplinary effort to forswear his blame-feelings.

Now that we are sensitized to the operation of proleptic mechanisms we can look away from other-directed forms of causal social construction and turn our gaze inward to the first-personal aspect of forgiveness. What one does in forgiving, if I may continue to use Strawson's characterization (which I think is indeed apt for forgiveness in general) is *forswear* blame-feelings towards the wrongdoer for what she's done. That is, we commit to drastically reducing such feelings, and if possible relinquishing them altogether. So how do we achieve this? Sometimes it will be easy and spontaneous – the wrongdoer repudiates her action and we instantly feel the indignation, annoyance, or hurt simply evaporate without effort. In such cases, forgiveness comes upon one passively in the form of spontaneous relief from the burdens of blame-feeling. Sometimes, however, it is not at all easy and spontaneous. Often, and certainly in the case of more serious wrongdoing, or repeated wrongdoing that makes blame-feeing linger and grow from one occasion to the next like an intensifying allergic reaction, it is a serious job of work to follow through on the forswearing. What does a forgiver do who finds that his blame-feelings do not melt away swiftly but instead call for an enduring effort of forswearing? The answer is that he will typically, and quite properly, have recourse to a common behavioural technique: he will behave *as if* the blame-feelings have already subsided more than they have, largely as a means of causing them to further subside. That is to say he'll try to act normal as a means of helping him bring his emotions into line. Our earlier discussions of other-directed prolepsis equips us now to recognize this technique of emotional self-discipline as one of *self-directed prolepsis*: the forgiver behaves *as if* he already had feature F and, if successful, he thereby comes to have feature F.[25] Forswearing, when it is not easy and instead requires on-going

---

[25] This is very close to Agnes Callard's idea of self-addressed proleptic reasons that take the form of 'self-management reasons' (Callard, 'Proleptic Reasons', in Russ Shafer-Landau (ed.), *Oxford Studies in Metaethics* **2** (2016); and also somewhat to David Velleman's idea that sometimes in order to embrace an ideal we must pretend to it (Velleman, 'Motivation

emotional and attitudinal self-discipline, employs a strategy of reflexive causal moral-social construction. If you like, one *performs* a completed forgiveness on the outside in order to progress the requisite inward change of heart.[26]

This is on the whole a sound technique. But we can see how it too carries an inherent risk of descent into self-deception. Why? Because if I behave as if I have already relinquished blame-feeling towards another party, I am precisely *not attending* to the blame-feelings that do in fact persist. Non-attention to such residual feelings is part of the self-constructive technique. I need to ignore them in order that they may subside further, staying determinedly out of touch with those feelings *pro tem*, in order to push ahead with the business of forswearing them which involves some successful relinquishing of them.[27] This methodological denial is a proleptic technique we often rely on, and rightly so. But of course this very technique makes it likely that in the event that I cannot in fact rid myself of those significant blame-feelings towards the wrongdoer, then I am not well placed to see it. Indeed I may be the last to know, for the reason I cannot see it is that I'm too busy doing just what I was meant to be doing if only the technique had worked – looking the other way, and generally carrying on as if the blame-feelings were already in the past. So long as well-functioning forswearing of blame-feeling calls upon the would-be forgiver to actively ignore and cultivate a methodological denial about her continued blame-feelings, then it is obvious that the signature pitfall of this core aspect of any effortful forgiveness is self-deception; possibly accompanied by deception of others too, notably the wrongdoer, not to mention a likely pattern passive-aggressive reactions to them. What starts out as a sensible transitional technique – perhaps even an

---

by Ideal', *Philosophical Explorations* **5**.2 (2002): 89–103). But in the case I am describing here, the forgiver already embraces the reason and motive to forgive; she is simply trying to get her continuing or residual blame-feelings to catch up.

[26]   For the related idea that the justification of a speech act of forgiveness may precede the requisite change of heart, see Kathryn Norlock, *Forgiveness From A Feminist Perspective* (Lanham: Rowman & Littlefield, 2009).

[27]   Charles Griswold suggests that a success condition of forswearing is that one has had at least a little success already at actually relinquishing the blame-feelings, and this seems right, on pain of the commitment being empty – forswearing is more than lip-service. See Griswold, *Forgiveness: A Philosophical Exploration.*

Miranda Fricker

essential one – slows all too easily into a drawn-out performance of bad faith.

Conclusion

I started with the observation that our attitudes towards forgiveness seem to be conflicted, exhibiting a certain habit of idealization on the one hand, and a pessimistic scepticism on the other. I have argued, however, that the lesson we should take from these conflicting attitudes is that forgiveness rightly inspires ambivalence – an ambivalence that is grounded in deep interpersonal and intrapersonal features of what is often involved in forgiving someone. Firstly, Gifted Forgiveness involves an operation of proleptic moral influence – an *other-directed* social constructive power that is intrinsically prone to deterioration into manipulation, even moral-epistemic domination, especially under conditions of inequality. Second, I drew attention to the generic fact that blameworthiness is presupposed to forgiveness, so that any communication of forgiveness inevitably invokes the fact of blameworthiness, with the result that the forgiver may easily find herself inadvertently communicating not only forgiveness but also, and perhaps chiefly, *back-door blame*. And, finally, I turned our gaze inwards to the first-personal effort of forswearing blame-feelings that constitutes the emotional core of all forgiveness, and I observed that wherever the forswearing requires some effort it will tend to call upon another kind of prolepsis: a *self-directed* form of moral-social construction. This mechanism depends upon a certain methodological denial about one's persisting blame-feelings, and so renders the would-be forgiver notably vulnerable to self-deception as regards her level of success.

These three different kinds of deterioration in our quite genuine efforts to forgive tend towards one or another form of bad faith. Moreover they attend our efforts of forgiveness owing to intrinsic features of the practice, rather than accidental aspects of the social environment. In particular, I have hoped to make plain that the *other-directed* prolepsis operating within Gifted Forgiveness, and the *self-directed* prolepsis often involved in the effort of *forswearing* blame-feelings quite generally, together reveal the social constructive powers so often at work in forgiving. An increased awareness of power's integral role in these responses, and the specific psychological mechanisms by which it is exercised, may help us to watch out for its degenerative tendencies. It also indicates a philosophical conception of forgiveness as often involving delicately balanced moral powers to be exercised in relation to self and other – a conception that avoids both idealization and scepticism, and instead, learning something from each, stabilizes in a tender ambivalence.[28]

The Graduate Center, CUNY
mfricker@gc.cuny.edu

[28] Earlier versions of this paper were given in a number of places including Sheffield, Oslo, Jerusalem, Tel Aviv, Princeton, Vanderbilt, NYU, The Graduate Center CUNY, and The Society for Applied Philosophy Annual Conference 2018. I am grateful to the many people who were present on these occasions for helpful discussion. I also thank the editors and an anonymous reviewer for helpful comments.

The Epistemology of Terrorism and Radicalisation

QUASSIM CASSAM

Abstract

This paper outlines and criticises two models of terrorism, the Rational Agent Model (RAM) and the Radicalisation Model (RAD). A different and more plausible conception of the turn to violence is proposed. The proposed account is Moderate Epistemic Particularism (MEP), an approach partly inspired by Karl Jaspers' distinction between explanation and understanding. On this account there are multiple idiosyncratic pathways to cognitive and behavioural radicalisation, and the actions and motivations of terrorists can only be understood (rather than explained) by engaging with their subjectivity in a way that depends on a degree of empathy. Scepticism is expressed about attempts to model radicalisation and predict political violence. This scepticism is based on reflections concerning the nature of complex particulars. The implications of MEP for counterterrorism are briefly discussed.

1.

Not long before Mohammad Sidique Khan killed himself and five other people by detonating a bomb at London's Edgware Road tube station on 7 July 2005 he recorded a so-called 'martyrdom' video in which he explained and justified his action in the following terms:

> Your democratically elected government perpetrates atrocities against my people all over the world. And your support of them makes you directly responsible, just as I am directly responsible for protecting and avenging my Muslim brothers and sisters. Until we feel security, you will be our targets.... We are at war and I am a soldier.[1]

---

[1] 'London bomber: Text in Full', *BBC News* (1 Sep 2005), <http://news.bbc.co.uk/1/hi/uk/4206800.stm>. There is more about Khan and his background in: Shiv Malik, 'My Brother the Bomber', *Prospect Magazine* (30 June 2007), <https://www.prospectmagazine.co.uk/magazine/my-brother-the-bomber-mohammad-sidique-khan>.

doi:10.1017/S1358246118000607   © The Royal Institute of Philosophy and the contributors 2018
Royal Institute of Philosophy Supplement **84** 2018

Quassim Cassam

A question that is often asked is: what leads a person to turn to political violence?[2] It has been suggested that we still don't know the answer to this question but if the person in question is Mohammad Sidique Khan then it might seem that we need look no further than his own words for a perfectly straightforward answer: he turned to violence because he had certain political objectives and believed his action would help him achieve those objectives.[3] This explanation is in line with what might be called the Rational Agent Model (or RAM, as I will call it) of terrorism. RAM says that terrorism is the work of rational agents employing violent means to pursue political objectives. It is, or can be, what Martha Crenshaw describes as 'a collectively rational strategic choice',[4] involving 'logical processes that can be discovered and explained'.[5]

RAM has not, on the whole, been accepted by Western governments or the majority of terrorism experts. As Richard Jackson notes, 'with only a handful of notable exceptions, little effort has been made by terrorism experts and officials to try and understand terrorist motivations by listening to their own words and messages, and seriously engaging with their subjectivity'.[6] There may be several reasons for this: the assumption that it isn't possible to engage with the subjectivity of people like Mohammad Sidique Khan, the conviction that their words offer little genuine insight into their deeds, or the worry that accepting that terrorists are rational agents comes perilously close to accepting that their murderous acts might, at least in principle, be justifiable. The model to which most Western governments have subscribed in recent years is not RAM

[2] This is the question with which Marc Sageman begins his seminal paper 'The Stagnation in Terrorism Research', *Terrorism and Political Violence* **26** (2014), 565–580. According to Sageman, we still don't know the answer to his question.
[3] The idea that the motives and objectives of people like Khan are primarily political rather than theological is made much of by Arun Kundnani in chapter 4 of his book *The Muslims are Coming! Islamophobia, Extremism, and the Domestic War on Terror* (London: Verso, 2014).
[4] Martha Crenshaw, 'The Logic of Terrorism: Terrorist Behavior as a Product of Strategic Choice', in Walter Reich (ed.), *Origins of Terrorism: Psychologies, Ideologies, Theologies, States of Mind* (Washington, D.C.: Woodrow Wilson Center Press, 1990), 7–24.
[5] Crenshaw, 'The Logic of Terrorism', 7.
[6] Richard Jackson, 'The Epistemological Crisis of Counterterrorism', *Critical Studies on Terrorism* **8** (2015), 45. As Jackson notes, the voice of Osama Bin Laden has remained largely unheard among Western audiences despite a vast corpus of open letters, interviews, videos and statements.

but one that focuses on the notion of *radicalisation*.[7] According to the Radicalisation Model (or RAD for short), people turn to political violence because they have been radicalised. It is worth noting that this explanation is most popular in relation to so-called Islam-related terrorism; there was little talk of radicalisation in relation to Irish terrorism in the late 20th century. Nevertheless, it is easy to see why RAD is more attractive to governments than RAM: for although RAD is not strictly incompatible with RAM it doesn't require one to conceive of terrorists as rational agents, it doesn't imply that terrorism might be justifiable, and it has policy implications that governments find congenial. The holy grail of counterterrorism is prediction, and governments and intelligence agencies are attracted by the idea that radicalisation predicts political violence. Moreover, if radicalisation is the problem then the solution with respect to not-yet-radicalised Muslims is to prevent their radicalisation. With respect to the already radicalised the remedy is 'deradicalisation'. Either way, the implication of RAD is that the key to explaining the turn to political violence is to understand 'the radicalisation process'.[8]

I have three aims here. The first is to draw attention to some of the defects of RAM and the conception of rational agency to which it is committed. There are elements of RAM that are of value when it comes to explaining or understanding the turn to political violence but it also has serious limitations. My second aim is to draw attention to the limitations of RAD, which are even more serious than those of RAM. Not only are there serious theoretical objections to RAD, adoption of this model as the basis for policies designed to counter terrorism also causes harms of various kinds, including epistemic harms. As this model has been commonly understood, RAD leads to the stigmatisation of whole communities, gets in the way of a proper understanding of terrorism and increases rather than decreases the likelihood of a turn to political violence.

Some of these difficulties have their source in the failure of RAD and RAM to grasp a metaphysical point: terrorists, like people generally, are complex particulars that, as Gorovitz and MacIntyre put it in

---

[7] It isn't just governments that focus on radicalisation. There is also an extensive scholarly literature that subscribes to this approach. For an overview see Arun Kundnani, 'Radicalisation: The Journey of a Concept,' *Race and Class* **54** (2012), 3–25.

[8] *Contest: The United Kingdom's Strategy for Countering Terrorism* (HM Government, 2011), <https://assets.publishing.service.gov.uk/government/uploads/system/uploads/attachment_data/file/97995/strategy-contest.pdf>, 63.

a rather different context, 'interact continuously with a variety of un-controllable environmental factors'.[9] Our knowledge of complex particulars is necessarily limited and fallible in ways that models like RAD and RAM fail fully to take on board. As will become apparent, there are multiple pathways to terrorism and this means that there is little to be gained by positing a single generic process like 'radicalisation'. Strictly speaking, and contrary to recent pronouncements by the British government, there is really no such thing as *the* radicalisation process. When it comes to understanding the turn to political violence, radicalisation is if anything the effect rather than the cause

My third aim is to develop a different conception (rather than model) of the turn to violence that avoids the pitfalls of RAM and RAD and that is more realistic about complex particulars. My label for this conception is Moderate Epistemic Particularism (MEP). I call it a 'conception' rather than a 'model' because it raises questions about the very idea of modelling radicalisation or the turn to political violence. 'Epistemic particularism' is a view of psychological explanation that has been ascribed to Karl Jaspers.[10] At the core of this view is a distinction between explanation and understanding. According to Jaspers, the former is achieved by 'observation of events, by experiment, and the collection of numerous examples'.[11] In explanation the focus is on the uncovering of general causal laws. In contrast, understanding 'is not achieved by bringing certain facts under general laws established through repeated observation'.[12] In relation to terrorism, MEP focuses on making the turn to violence *intelligible* in specific cases, such as that of Khan, but without any expectation of general laws or the ability to *predict* violence. It works backwards from effects to causes and, instead of positing generic psychological mechanisms to explain why some people carry out acts of terrorism, stresses the extent to which pathways to terrorism tend to be highly individual, idiosyncratic and contingent. As far as MEP is concerned

[9] Samuel Gorovitz and Alasdair MacIntyre, 'Toward a Theory of Medical Fallibility', *The Hastings Center Report* **5** (1975), 16.

[10] See Christoph Hoerl, 'Jaspers on Explaining and Understanding in Psychiatry', in Giovanni Stenghellini and Thomas Fuchs (eds.), *One Century of Karl Jaspers' General Psychopathology* (Oxford: Oxford University Press, 2013), 107–120. 'Epistemic particularism' is Hoerl's label.

[11] Karl Jaspers, *General Psychopathology*, 7th edition, J. Hoenig and M.W. Hamilton (trans.) (Baltimore: Johns Hopkins University Press, 1997), 302.

[12] Hoerl, 'Jaspers on Explaining and Understanding in Psychiatry', 108.

there is no *general* answer to the question: what leads a person to turn to political violence?

In its most extreme form epistemic particularism would deny the existence of *any* interesting generalisations about the turn to political violence. In its more moderate form epistemic particularism allows that there may be such generalisations but insists that they are of limited value when it comes to understanding the actions of specific individuals. It's not that the actions of someone like Khan are wholly unintelligible but neither RAM nor RAD casts much light on them. In many cases it is only in retrospect that an individual's turn to political violence makes sense, and what makes it intelligible is a particular form of empathy or perspective taking. MEP rises to Jackson's challenge and tries to do what RAD doesn't do: to understand terrorist motivations by listening to their own words and messages, and engage with their subjectivity. I'll conclude with some thoughts about the policy implications of MEP and the various ways in which our ability to engage with the subjectivity of people like Khan is limited.

2.

One of the merits of RAM is that it makes space for the idea that terrorism *can* be rational. For RAM 'efficacy is the primary standard by which terrorism is compared with other methods of achieving political goals'.[13] As has often been observed, terrorism is the weapon of the weak and employed by them as the most effective or in some cases only realistic means of achieving their political goals in adverse conditions. When dealing with repressive regimes or dictatorships terrorism may be the only means of bringing about change, given that the ballot box has been ruled out. Another scenario is one in which terrorist groups in democratic societies resort to violence when they fail to mobilise mass support for their cause. As Crenshaw notes, 'generally, small organizations resort to violence to compensate for what they lack in numbers'.[14] Where there is no hope of achieving certain political objectives by democratic means it is not obviously irrational for those committed to these objectives to employ other methods, however objectionable this approach might be on other grounds.

---

[13] Crenshaw, 'The Logic of Terrorism', 8.
[14] Crenshaw, 'The Logic of Terrorism', 11.

One question that RAM doesn't address is how terrorists select their political objectives. Relatedly, there is the question whether their objectives are themselves rational or coherent. Proponents of RAD will see an opening for their position in relation to the first of these questions. For example, if he hadn't been radicalised Khan would not have thought that avenging his Muslim brothers and sisters by killing innocent Londoners was a reasonable objective. He didn't think that his victims were innocent but that is again only a reflection of his radicalised world view. There is more about RAD below but RAM takes terrorists' ends as given and offers no account of their merits or selection. It allows for the possibility that terrorists' objectives might be irrational or incoherent but it does not assume that this is the case. For RAM, it isn't a given that terrorists have irrational or incoherent objectives and many clearly do not. In any event, RAM's focus is on means rather than ends.

If efficacy is the standard by which terrorism is to be compared with other methods of achieving political goals then one question raised by RAM is whether terrorism is, in fact, an efficacious means of achieving such goals. The question, in other words, is: does terrorism work? Even if it generally doesn't work it doesn't follow that terrorism is not the work of rational agents. For there remains the possibility that the *belief* that terrorism is an effective means of achieving political objectives, either in general or in a specific case, is not irrational or unreasonable even if it is a false belief. The problematic cases for RAM are ones in which it is both the case that terrorism doesn't work *and* it is plainly irrational to believe otherwise. In these cases terrorism can't be seen as a rational strategic choice. Accordingly, one might be sceptical about RAM either on the basis that terrorism is by and large inefficacious or on the basis that the belief that terrorism is likely to be efficacious in a given case is irrational given the evidence available to those who have this belief.

These rather abstract points can be brought into sharper focus by considering the work of Richard English and, in particular, his book *Does Terrorism Work?* For English, there is no simple 'Yes' or 'No' answer to his question, though he contrasts 'the profound uncertainty of terrorism achieving its central goals' with the near certainty that 'terrible human suffering will ensue from terrorist violence'.[15] Consider the mass casualty 9/11 attacks on New York and Washington. The human suffering caused by these attacks was

---

[15]   English, *Does Terrorism Work? A History* (Oxford: Oxford University Press, 2016), 265.

enormous but they clearly failed to achieve their primary political objective, which was to persuade the United States to withdraw its forces from the Middle East and, in particular, from Saudi Arabia. The idea that the 9/11 attacks would have such a result could only have been seriously entertained by those with a shaky grasp of political reality. It is true that the U.S withdrew its forces from Lebanon following the lethal truck bombing of its military barracks in Beirut in 1983. However, attacking US forces in the Middle East is one thing but attacking the US homeland and murdering thousands of civilians in the process is a completely different matter. It seems not to have crossed Bin Laden's mind that the 9/11 attacks would be, at least in the short term, a total disaster for Al-Qaeda. The American reaction could and should have been predicted, and Bin Laden's view that the 9/11 attacks would be an effective means of attaining his strategic objectives can only be described as delusional.[16]

The general point has been well made by Thomas Nagel in a review of English's book. Nagel comments on the effectiveness of four specific organisations or movements, Al-Qaeda, the Provisional IRA, Hamas and the Basque separatist group ETA:

> And here the record is dismal. What struck me on reading [English's] book is how delusional these movements are, how little understanding they have of the balance of forces, the motives of their opponents and the political context in which they are operating. In this respect, it is excessively charitable to describe them as rational agents. True, they are employing violent means which they believe will induce their opponents to give up, but that belief is plainly irrational, and in any event false, as shown by the results.[17]

This seems a fair assessment and brings out the limitations of RAM. Clearly, not all terrorist movements have been delusional. For example, it is arguable that the Irgun in Palestine does not fit Nagel's description since, as English notes, 'a good case might be made that the Irgun's violence expedited British withdrawal from Palestine and the establishment of the state of Israel, the primary goal of that terrorist organization'.[18] In this sort of example RAM

---

[16] 'Bin Laden himself certainly underestimated the strength of the United States of America, and his hopes of destroying that superpower were clearly unsuccessful (ludicrously so, in truth)', English, *Does Terrorism Work? A History*, 64.

[17] Nagel, 'By Any Means or None', *London Review of Books* **38** (2016), 19.

[18] English, *Does Terrorism Work? A History*, 221.

has much to offer. However, in the cases that Nagel refers to there is little evidence of anything recognisable as rational agency, as distinct from wishful thinking. This suggests that even if terrorism isn't *necessarily* irrational RAM fails to tell a plausible explanatory story about the strategies of many of the most troublesome and active terrorist organisations in the world today. We can and should try to understand terrorist motivations by listening to their own words and messages but sometimes their words and messages are hard to fathom.

3.

Turning to RAD, the UK government's 2009 *Pursue Prevent Protect Prepare* Strategy for Countering International terrorism defines radicalisation as 'the process by which people come to support violent extremism and, in some cases, join terrorist groups'.[19] The definite article is important in this formulation, and the assumption that there is such a thing as *the* process of radicalisation resurfaces in the *Prevent* strand of the government's 2011 Contest Strategy for Countering Terrorism.[20] Indeed, the idea that there is such a process is one of its key planning assumptions. What, then, is the process of radicalisation? An idea that runs through *Prevent* is that while most people find terrorism repugnant there are a few people who are 'vulnerable to radicalisation'.[21] These people are targeted by 'radicalisers' who disseminate extremist ideologies and exploit 'vulnerabilities in people which make them susceptible to a

[19] *Pursue Prevent Protect Prepare: The United Kingdom's Strategy for Countering International Terrorism* (HM Government, 2009), <https://assets.publishing.service.gov.uk/government/uploads/system/uploads/attachment_data/file/228644/7547.pdf>, 11. *Prevent* first emerged in the 2006 Contest Strategy. Although my focus here is on the UK's *Prevent* strategy, versions of this approach have been implemented across Europe and the EU has created a Radicalisation Awareness Network; see 'Radicalisation Awareness Network', *European Commission,* <https://ec.europa.eu/home-affairs/what-we-do/networks/radicalisation_awareness_network_en>.

[20] The assumption that there is such a thing as *the* radicalisation process also informs counterterrorism strategy elsewhere in Europe. For example, the European Commission describes itself as supporting research and studies 'in order to better understand the radicalisation process' ('Radicalisation', *European Commission,* <https://ec.europa.eu/home-affairs/what-we-do/policies/crisis-and-terrorism/radicalisation_en>). For further discussion see Peter R. Neumann, 'The Trouble with Radicalization', *International Affairs* **89** (2013), 873–93.

[21] *Contest: The United Kingdom's Strategy for Countering Terrorism*, 10.

message of violence'.[22] The hypothesis is that individuals like Mohammad Sidique Khan turn to violence because they have been radicalised, and they were radicalised at least in part because they were vulnerable to radicalisation. Although this vulnerability doesn't have to be conceived of as a personal pre-disposition this is how Contest conceives of it.

The model of radicalisation to which many Western governments are committed is what might be called a 'contagion' model. This re-presents radicalisation as an ideological disease or virus to which some individuals are vulnerable, and they catch the disease by contact with infectious agents, in the form of radicalisers with extremist ideologies. Extremism is defined by *Prevent* as 'vocal or active opposition to fundamental British values, including democracy, the rule of law, individual liberty and mutual respect and tolerance of difference faiths and beliefs'.[23] This leads to the suggestion that vulnerable people can be prevented from catching the extremist virus by being prevented from coming into contact with radicalisers, and being provided with the appropriate prophylaxis in the form of an education in fundamental British values. The pious hope is that people who have absorbed such values will thereby be less susceptible to extremism.

What is wrong with RAD? The first thing to note is that radicalisation can be understood in at least two different ways. One type of radicalisation is cognitive and involves the formation or acquisition of extremist beliefs. Another type is behavioural radicalisation, which involves a turn to violence.[24] A person can be cognitively radicalised without being behaviourally radicalised and, as has often been pointed out, only a very small proportion of cognitively radicalised individuals become behaviourally radicalised.[25] This is one horn of a dilemma for RAD: if the hypothesis is that the turn to violence is explained by cognitive radicalisation then what are we to make of the very limited extent to which the cognitively radicalised actually carry out terrorist acts? Cognitive radicalisation is a notably poor predictor of political violence and the real challenge is to identify the additional factors that lead some but not other cognitively

---

[22] *Contest: The United Kingdom's Strategy for Countering Terrorism*, 60.
[23] *Contest: The United Kingdom's Strategy for Countering Terrorism*, 62, n. 52.
[24] This distinction between cognitive and behavioural radicalisation is due to Marc Sageman. See his *Misunderstanding Terrorism* (Philadelphia: University of Pennsylvania Press), 90.
[25] Sageman notes that 'very few people talking about violence actually go on to use it', *Misunderstanding Terrorism*, 90.

radicalised individuals to turn violent. If, on the other hand, the hypothesis is that *behavioural* radicalisation explains and predicts the turn to violence then RAD is vacuous since behavioural radicalisation *is* the turn to violence. This is the other horn of the dilemma for RAD and brings out the importance of distinguishing between cause and effect. Is radicalisation the cause of the turn to violence or is it the effect that RAD is trying to explain? RAD is not as clear on this issue as one might wish and this is a reflection of a basic lack of clarity about the kind of explanation RAD is putting forward.

There are also questions about the notion of vulnerability to radicalisation. Is this a personal predisposition as *Prevent* implies? If so, what evidence is there that some individuals have this predisposition while others do not? If RAD has serious explanatory ambitions it had better not turn out that the only test for whether a person has this predisposition is that they are in fact radicalised. On reflection, however, perhaps this isn't the proposal. Perhaps the idea is that vulnerability to radicalisation is a contextual rather than a personal matter, and that people are vulnerable to radicalisation insofar as they move in extremist circles or are exposed to radical or extremist messages online. However, mere exposure to extremist ideas does not explain their adoption and many individuals who are exposed to such ideas don't become radicalised. Again, there is a question about cause and effect. Do people become radicalised because they have been exposed to extremist ideas or do they seek out extremist websites because they are already radicalised? The latter hypothesis is at least as plausible as the former.

Underlying these concerns is a deeper concern about RAD's conception of agency, or the lack of it. One of the implications of RAD and the contagion model that underpins it is that radicalisation is something that befalls a person, something that happens to them, somewhat in the way that catching flu is something that happens to a person. Just as people vary in their susceptibility to the flu virus and in their degrees of resistance to it so it might be thought that they vary in their susceptibility to the extremist 'virus' and their resistance to it. But why accept this picture? As Anthony Richards asks:

> [W]hy is it assumed that those who aim to commit terrorist acts are *vulnerable* to violent extremism – that they have succumbed to (violent) extremist ideologies and need guidance so that they can be rescued from manipulation by others (online or otherwise),

and that they would not carry out such acts of their own volition?[26]

In many cases, including that of Mohammad Sidique Khan, the story is not one of individuals being passively radicalised by external agencies. What we see instead is a process of active self-radicalisation in which manipulation by others plays no significant role. To convince oneself, as Khan did, that a given course of action is called for is not to *succumb* to anything in the way that one might succumb to a cold.

Another example that brings out the severe limitations of the notion of vulnerability to radicalisation is that of Anwar al-Awlaki, who was killed by an American drone strike in 2011. Awlaki was born in New Mexico, the son of a U.S. educated pro-American Yemeni technocrat who went on to become president of Sanaa University. The younger Awlaki, who worked as an imam in San Diego after completing a degree at Colorado State University, condemned the 9/11 attacks and was seen by the American media as the voice of moderate Islam. Yet he became virulently anti-American over the next decade, and his role in plotting and inspiring terrorist attacks against U.S. targets led President Obama to instruct the C.I.A. to kill him. Yet there is no interesting sense in which Awlaki was 'vulnerable to radicalisation', and no reason to think that his radicalisation was the responsibility of anyone but himself, or an expression of anything other than his own agency. There is, however, some reason to think that his hatred of America was fuelled by his concern that, quite by chance, the FBI had found out about his use of prostitutes and contemplated using this information against him.[27]

Awlaki's story is of particular interest because, as well as helping to make the point that radicalisation needn't be passive, it brings out the extent to which an individual's radicalisation can be shaped by accidental and extraneous events that may have little to do with politics. This points to perhaps the most serious problem with RAD. Consider this analogy which, for all its apparent frivolity, makes an important philosophical point. In his book on philosophy and sport David Papineau has a nice illustration of what he aptly describes

---

[26]   Anthony Richards, 'The Problem with "Radicalization": The Remit of "Prevent" and the Need to Refocus on Terrorism in the UK', *International Affairs* **84** (2011), 150.
[27]   See the account of all this in chapter 6 of Scott Shane's *Objective Troy: A Terrorist, A President, and the Rise of the Drone* (New York: Tim Duggan Books, 2015).

Quassim Cassam

as the 'contingency of sporting affiliations'.[28] He was once told the following story by a friend, the psychologist Tony Marcel:

> 'My cousin and I were at my mother's bedside when she was in a seemingly terminal coma shortly before her death. We fell to discussing when we had become Arsenal supporters. I remember a photo of me at about three in an Arsenal strip, and wondered if it was a present from a family member. Suddenly, without opening her eyes, my mother said, "No, your uncle's friend Peter gave it to you to spite us. We were all Spurs supporters"'.[29]

What happened to Marcel, one might say, is that he became 'Arsenalised', that is, went from not being an Arsenal supporter to being an Arsenal supporter. Yet his Arsenalisation process was highly idiosyncratic and personal. At the same time that Marcel was being Arsenalised, the same thing was happening but in different ways to many other children and adults in other places. Every Arsenal fan has their own story of their Arsenalisation and if an Arsenalisation scholar were to define 'Arsenalisation' as *the* process by which a person becomes an Arsenal fan then a natural reaction would be to say that there are countless Arsenalisation processes that may have little in common beyond the fact that they are the steps by which a given individual moves from not being an Arsenal supporter to being an Arsenal supporter. Beyond that, there may be some broad generalisations that apply to multiple Arsenal fans - for example, many were Arsenalised by their family or school friends- but not all Arsenal supporters will have been Arsenalised like that and even a story like Marcel's leaves some questions unanswered. For example, how did he come to be Arsenalised by being given an Arsenal strip? One thing that seems clear is that Arsenalisation depends on many factors, and there is no general answer to the question: how do people become Arsenal fans?

As well as the sheer variety of pathways to becoming an Arsenal supporter there is one other point to note. When an individual X is Arsenalised and we ask how they came to be Arsenalised as distinct from say, being Chelseafied, that is, a supporter of Chelsea, there is one thing we don't say: X became Arsenalised because she was vulnerable to Arsenalisation. If someone is raised in a family of passionate Arsenal supporters they might be described as vulnerable to Arsenalisation but that is a comment about their environment

[28] David Papineau, *Knowing the Score: How Sport Teaches Us about Philosophy (and Philosophy about Sport)* (London: Constable, 2017), 117.
[29] Papineau, *Knowing the Score*, 117.

rather than about them. Being vulnerable to Arsenalisation is not a predisposition that some people have and others lack, and the only evidence that someone was vulnerable to Arsenalisation is that they became Arsenal supporters. Saying that they must have been vulnerable to Arsenalisation if they actually became Arsenal fans is not to explain their Arsenalisation.

What goes for Arsenalisation goes for radicalisation. There are multiple highly personal and idiosyncratic pathways to behavioural radicalisation, as illustrated by the cases of Khan and Awlaki, and no such things as *the* radicalisation process. As a member of the tightly knit traditional Pakistani community of Leeds Khan might have been vulnerable to radicalisation in the environmental sense but there is no particular reason to think that Awlaki and many others like him were vulnerable to radicalisation except that they were in fact radicalised. There is, in the words of an Australian government publication on radicalisation, 'no single pathway of radicalisation towards violent extremism, as the process is unique to each person'.[30] As with Arsenalisation there may be some very broad generalisations about radicalisation, that is, some common elements in the experiences of most people who have become radicalised, but these common elements are of limited predictive value. For example, in his ground-breaking work on terrorist networks, Marc Sageman draws attention to the importance of friendship and kinship networks in radicalisation, to the sense in which terrorist groups are often just a 'bunch of guys' who self-radicalise and are bonded to one another by more than politics.[31] But knowing this will not enable one to predict which bunch of guys will self-radicalise and which bunch of guys will not. There is an essential contingency to what Charlotte Heath-Kelly describes as the 'seemingly individualised and disconnected pathways of citizens into armed militancy',[32] and this contingency needs to be acknowledged and managed.

The contingency and unpredictability of behavioural radicalisation is a reflection of the metaphysics of complex particulars. In their seminal work on medical fallibility Gorovitz and MacIntyre argue

[30] 'Understanding the Radicalisation Process', Australian Government, <https://www.livingsafetogether.gov.au/informationadvice/Pages/what-is-radicalisation/understanding-the-radicalisation-process.aspx>.
[31] See Marc Sageman, *Leaderless Jihad: Terror Networks in the Twenty-First Century* (Philadelphia: University of Pennsylvania Press, 2008).
[32] Charlotte Heath-Kelly, 'The Geography of Pre-criminal Space: Epidemiological Imaginations of Radicalisation Risk in the UK Prevent Strategy, 2007-2017', *Critical Studies on Terrorism* **10** (2017), 300.

that in the natural sciences the objects of knowledge are universals, that is, 'properties of objects classified by *kinds*, and the generalizations that link those properties'.[33] On this view, 'to explain the behavior of a particular is nothing else than to subsume its particular properties under the relevant law-like generalizations'.[34] To *predict* the behaviour of a particular is to use the same law-like generalizations about the relevant properties. Gorovitz and MacIntyre argue that there are certain features of particulars that escape notice on this account. There are simple particulars such as ice cubes whose behaviour can be predicted with a high degree of reliability by law-like generalizations because 'each example of the type is, roughly speaking, quite like any other'.[35] But not all particulars are like that. There are more complex particulars such as hurricanes, salt marshes and, above all, people that are such that no one particular of a given type is quite like any other particular of that type. No one hurricane is quite like any other since hurricanes 'interact continuously with a variety of uncontrollable environmental factors' and we can never know 'what historically specific interactions may impact on such historically specific particulars'.[36] However, this is not intended as an *a priori* argument against the possibility of weather forecasting. There are some 'for the most part' generalizations that can be used to predict the behaviour of hurricanes at least to some extent, even if the precise point at which a particular hurricane is going to make landfall is virtually impossible to know in advance.

Predicting and explaining the turn to political violence is even harder. No one terrorist is quite like any other because each one has interacted throughout his or her life with a whole variety of uncontrollable and unknown environmental factors. We cannot know each influence on the individual terrorist and this is what makes it so difficult to predict their actions. So, for example, Jonathan Githens-Mazer and Robert Lambert give the example of the Adam brothers. Based on their exposure to extremist ideas one would have said that Lamine Adam was more likely to become violent but in fact it was his brother Rahman, who 'seemed to embrace western

---

[33] Gorovitz and MacIntyre, 'Toward a Theory of Medical Fallibility', 15.
[34] Gorovitz and MacIntyre, 'Toward a Theory of Medical Fallibility', 15.
[35] Gorovitz and MacIntyre, 'Toward a Theory of Medical Fallibility', 16.
[36] Gorovitz and MacIntyre, 'Toward a Theory of Medical Fallibility', 16.

secular values entirely',[37] who was arrested for conspiracy to cause explosions. Githens-Mazer and Lambert regard the story of the Adam brothers as significant because in their view it indicates the 'inherent unpredictability of who becomes violent and who doesn't'.[38] This lack of predictability is what one would expect in the case of complex particulars. Exposure to certain ideas is one thing, whether those idea will have traction with a particular individual is another.

This way of putting things suggests that there are actually two distinct problems when it comes to explaining and predicting the behaviour of 'extremists'. Not only is it impossible to know all the relevant environmental factors, it is also impossible to know how the same factors affect different individuals. As I have noted, of all the people who become cognitively radicalised only a small number actually turn to violence. Yet the environmental factors that affect people who turn to violence might be hard to distinguish from those that affect people who do not turn to violence, and there may be no further explanation of the difference. Not even the contagion model can eliminate this uncertainty, as G. E. M. Anscombe notes in a famous discussion of causality:

> For example, we have found certain diseases to be contagious. If, then, I have had one and only one contact with someone suffering from such a disease, and I get it myself, we suppose I got it from him. But what if, having had the contact, I ask a doctor whether I will get the disease. He will usually only be able to say, 'I don't know – maybe you will, maybe not'.[39]

In the same way, the contagion model attributes a person's radicalisation to their contact with extremist ideas but if we had been asked to predict whether they would be radicalised the only answer that does justice to our epistemic predicament is 'maybe they will, maybe they won't'. If they are radicalised, and their radicalisation is attributed to their contact with extremist ideas, then we are being wise after the

---

[37]   Jonathan Githens-Mazer and Robert Lambert, 'Why the Conventional Wisdom on Radicalization Fails: The Persistence of a Failed Discourse', *International Affairs* **86** (2010), 892.

[38]   Githens-Mazer and Lambert 'Why the Conventional Wisdom on Radicalization Fails', 893. Rahman Adam changed his name to Anthony Garcia in pursuit of a career as a male model. He was convicted in April 2007 for conspiracy to cause explosions. Lamine Adam, who was subject to a control order, absconded in May 2007.

[39]   G. E. M. Anscombe, 'Causality and Determination', in E. Sosa (ed.) *Causation and Conditionals* (Oxford: Oxford University Press, 1975), 67.

event. To quote Anscombe again, it's easier 'to trace effects back to causes with certainty than to predict effects from causes' and we 'often know a cause without knowing whether there is an exceptionless generalization of the kind envisaged'.[40]

On this account, it would be appropriate to be somewhat sceptical about the project of modelling radicalisation and government programmes to prevent radicalisation. As far as the modelling of radicalisation is concerned, this has become a cottage industry in the intelligence community and university departments of terrorism studies. In order to make sense of terrorism we need to explain how and why people turn to political violence, and what better way could there be of doing that than to construct theoretical models of radicalisation? A 2012 systematic review published by the Youth Justice Board identified no fewer than eight models in the literature, ranging from the NYPD's proposed four stage radicalisation process to McCauley and Maslenko's 12 mechanisms of political radicalisation.[41] No doubt further models have been developed since then. However, even if there are some individuals to whom these models are applicable, they are unlikely to tell the whole story. What these models obscure are the points about contingency and unpredictability that I have been emphasising here. Schematic models of radicalisation can be illuminating, and some are, but their focus on general principles means that they are bound to fail to do justice to the full range of contingent and idiosyncratic factors by which individuals are influenced in transitioning from non-violence to violence. It only requires a cursory acquaintance with the disparate biographies of individual terrorists to grasp the limitations of the project of modelling behavioural radicalisation.

The impact of RAD's limitations on radicalisation prevention programmes is no less obvious. One-size-fits-all prevention or deradicalisation programmes are as improbable as one-size-fits-all models of radicalisation. In order to design effective prevention programmes one would require an intellectually rigorous and evidence-based theory of radicalisation but such theories are thin on the ground. In the absence of a proper understanding of radicalisation it is too easy for governments that are under pressure to be seen to 'do something'

[40] Anscombe, 'Causality and Determination', 66.
[41] Kris Christmann, *Preventing Religious Radicalisation and Violent Extremism: A Systematic Review of the Research Evidence*, <http://www.safe-campuscommunities.ac.uk/uploads/files/2016/08/yjb_preventing_violent_extremism_systematic_review_requires_uploading.pdf>, (Youth Justice Board for England and Wales, 2012).

to substitute supposedly common-sense assumptions about how radicalisation works and devise programmes on this basis. The risk is that these assumptions are mistaken and that they lead to the implementation of radicalisation prevention programmes that worsen the problem they were designed to solve. The U.K. government's prevent programme perfectly illustrates these dangers. Leaving aside the perversity of categorising democracy, rule of law and individual liberty as *British* values, there is no real evidence that the teaching of such values is an effective means of preventing either cognitive or behavioural radicalisation. Indeed, research has shown that the emphasis on British values only serves to alienate Muslim pupils and encourage them to seek alternative identities within the Muslim community.[42] In addition, as Anna Lockley-Scott has noted, the government requires British values to be taught rather than explored, and this 'prevents pupils from growing as open-minded explorers'.[43] This is an example of the epistemic harms that ill-conceived prevention programmes can do. The result is that Muslim pupils feel unable to raise questions about British values for fear of being labelled extremists and there is some anecdotal evidence of Muslim pupils being identified as 'at risk of radicalisation' on the basis of apparently flimsy evidence. The stigmatising of entire communities is not a way to make them less prone to radicalisation. It is a way to make them more prone to radicalisation.

4.

It might seem that the discussion so far is almost entirely negative. I have been critical of RAM and RAD and sceptical about the enterprise of modelling radicalisation and existing efforts to prevent radicalisation. Where does this leave the question: what leads a person to turn to political violence? Is there anything useful that can be said in response to this question, over and above exploring the role of friendship and kinship relations in behavioural radicalisation? What, in practical terms, can be done to tackle such radicalisation? It's easy to be dismissive of programmes like *Prevent* but

---

[42] See Aminul Hoque, *British-Islamic Identity: Third-generation Bangladeshis from East London* (London: Institute of Education Press, 2015).
[43] Anna Lockley-Scott, 'Re-examining the Mission of Education and the Meaning of Learning in an Uncertain World', paper presented at the 2017 Oxford Symposium for Comparative and International Education.

governments that implement such programmes and face demands for a response to political violence are entitled to ask: what is the alternative? Faced with this challenge it's helpful to distinguish two projects, the project of explaining and the project of understanding political violence. With his distinction in place moderate epistemic particularism (MEP) comes into focus as an alternative to RAD and RAM. At least in some cases MEP promises a kind of insight into political violence that can't easily be extracted from RAD or RAM. The next challenge is to identify MEP's distinctive contribution and reflect on its policy implications.

As I've noted, 'epistemic particularism' is a view of psychological explanation that has been ascribed to Karl Jaspers. At the core of this view is a distinction between explanation and understanding, and this distinction is explained as follows by Christoph Hoerl:

> Explaining, Jaspers thinks, requires repeated experience – it is achieved by 'observation of events, by experiment and collection of numerous examples'.... which allow us to formulate general rules and theories. Understanding, by contrast, is achieved (if it is achieved) directly upon confrontation with a particular case.... We might thus say that Jaspers subscribes to a form of *epistemic particularism* regarding understanding. Understanding is not achieved by bringing certain facts under general laws established through repeated observation.[44]

How, then, *is* understanding achieved? The understanding that is at issue here is of how one mental event emerges from another, and the key is *empathy*. Suppose, to borrow one of Jaspers' own examples, one is trying to understand how the long winter nights might have contributed to a particular person's suicide. By empathising with the individual concerned and seeing things from their point of view one might see an intelligible connection in their case between the winter weather and *their* suicide even if, as a matter of statistical fact, there are actually more suicides in the spring. To quote Hoerl once again, 'the specific point Jaspers seems to be making here is that there can be an understandable connection, in a particular case, between one factor, A, and a certain event E, even if, in general, that type of event is less likely to occur in the context of A than in the context of another factor, B'.[45] In other words, a

---

[44] Hoerl, 'Jaspers on Explaining and Understanding in Psychiatry', 108.

[45] Hoerl, 'Jaspers on Explaining and Understanding in Psychiatry', 108.

particular individual's suicide might be made intelligible by the weather or some other even more idiosyncratic factor even if there is no general law connecting that factor with that outcome. Finding something intelligible is one thing, explaining it by reference to law-like generalisations is another.

What more is there to say about the nature of empathy and the kind of intelligibility it delivers? In her contribution to this volume Olivia Bailey helpfully characterises empathy as 'the activity of emotionally charged perspective-taking'.[46] It involves 'using one's imagination to "transport" oneself' and 'considering the other's situation as though one were occupying the other's position'.[47] As Bailey understands it, empathising is not a purely intellectual exercise and draws upon the emotional resources of the empathizer. Take the case of Awlaki. Starting from where he started in New Mexico how did he end up as America's international public enemy number two, second only to Bin Laden? Instead of looking for general causal laws or models of radicalisation that might explain his transformation one might engage in a bit of perspective-taking and see how things look when one considers his situation as if it were one's own. This means trying to identify with his sense of being hounded by the FBI and his increasing anxiety about being outed for his misdemeanours. Then there was the increasing and perhaps, from his point of view, totally unexpected success of his recorded sermons and addresses. One can imagine a young man like Awlaki being tempted by his growing fame and reputation as a sage and scholar of Islam to develop more radical themes and ideas on account of their popularity with his online audiences. Viewed from this perspective his gradual transformation becomes at least somewhat intelligible. On the one hand he felt cornered in the country of his birth. On the other hand, there was his growing celebrity abroad. It is not hard to imagine how these two factors might have contributed to Awlaki's transformation but it makes little sense to generalise from Awlaki's experience or attempt to construct a general theory of radicalisation on the basis of his experience. It is the particularity of his circumstances that does the explanatory work and there may be little to be learned about radicalisation 'in general' from that experience.

This is not to say, however, that radicalisation is only a response to contingent *personal* factors. It has a political as well as a personal

---

[46]   Olivia Bailey, 'Empathy and Testimonial Trust', *Royal Institute of Philosophy Supplement* **84**, 139.
[47]   Bailey, 'Empathy and Testimonial Trust', 143.

dimension but an adequate understanding of its political dimension also requires empathy. A point that has often been made about radical Islam is that it is to some extent a response to feelings of humiliation: the humiliation of political marginalisation, of repeated military defeat and of occupation. It is one thing to understand this at an intellectual level and another to *feel* it by empathy. If one can feel another's political pain and resentment one might then be in a positon to understand behaviours that would otherwise be unfathomable as well as unpredictable. Engaging in political perspective-taking is an effective way of rising to Jackson's challenge to engage with the terrorist's subjectivity in order to understand their motivations. The point is that listening to their own words and messages is insufficient for understanding without a serious emotional engagement with their humiliation and resentment.

What practical purpose could such perspective-taking possibly serve? What good does it do have the kind of understanding of terrorist motivations that perspective-taking supposedly delivers? One might argue that understanding is valuable for its own sake, or at any rate, that it satisfies a deep psychological need to make sense of the world we inhabit. When one hears of the latest terrorist outrage it is natural to ask how such things can happen and why they happen. Answering the latter question requires an understanding of the political and other motivations of those who carry out such acts and perspective-taking can provide us with some insight into these motivations. Understanding also has policy implications. If, in 2003, those who planned the American invasion and occupation of Iraq had engaged in some serious perspective-taking and considered how the invasion would look and feel from the Arab standpoint they might have been less surprised by the sheer scale and violence of the insurgency that greeted American troops. More generally, trying to understand terrorist motivations by listening to their own words and messages and engaging with their subjectivity should be an essential element of any realistic and worthwhile counterterrorism policy. How can one even begin to develop such a policy if one has no real understanding of why terrorists believe what they believe and do what they do?

One reason why the attempt to empathise with terrorist motivations is often viewed with suspicion that this exercise implies or even requires a degree of sympathy with those motivations, and this is regarded by many as morally and politically unacceptable.

There is the view that, as Bailey puts it, 'there is a deep connection between empathy and approval' and that when we empathize with the passions of another 'it is extremely difficult to dismiss them as wholly inappropriate'.[48] If this is right, and the idea of approving of the actions of someone like Khan or Awlaki strikes us as utterly repugnant, then doesn't it follow that perspective-taking of the kind that I have been describing is something that most of us can't and won't do? One reaction to this might be to question the strength of the connection between empathy and approval. A simpler strategy is to insist on distinguishing sharply between a person's motivations and their actions. Even if there is a genuine sense in which empathising with Awlaki's resentment and feelings of humiliation requires one to regard these emotions as appropriate this doesn't require one to view Awlaki's *actions* as appropriate. There is, for example, no question of empathising with his plot to destroy a transatlantic airliner on Christmas Day 2009.

Even at the level of motivations there is a limit to how much genuine perspective-taking is possible for counterterrorism officials whose culture, values and political assumptions are utterly different from those of the people they are trying to understand. For example, Elisabeth Kendall has written compellingly about the significance and functions of poetry in winning hearts and minds for the jihadist cause. It is difficult to empathise with the words and deeds of individuals like Bin Laden and Awlaki without any knowledge of the literary background. For example, Bin Laden's 1996 'Declaration of War Against the United States' contained something like fifteen poetry excerpts. As Kendall comments, by failing to take account of the key ways in which 'poetry refines and targets messages' Western intelligence agencies 'are approaching jihadist ideology through a skewed prism that is out of synch with that of its primary Arab audience'.[49] Other limitations to perspective-taking are not so much a reflection of cultural differences as of the incomprehensibility of the target actions and emotions. However hard one tries it is extraordinarily difficult to empathise with, say, the actions and emotions

[48]   'Empathy and Testimonial Trust', 148.
[49]   Elisabeth Kendall, 'Jihadist Propaganda and its Exploitation of the Arab Poetic Tradition', in Elisabeth Kendall and Ahmad Khan (eds.), *Reclaiming Islamic Tradition: Modern Interpretations of the Classical Heritage* (Edinburgh: Edinburgh University Press, 2016), 224–5.

of Mohammad Atta as he piloted American Airlines flight 11 into the north tower of the World Trade Center on 9/11.

What are the practical implications of the particularist turn in terrorism studies that I've been recommending? The implication is not that there is nothing one can usefully say in general terms about the turn to political violence. It is one thing to shift the focus from explanation to understanding and another to reject all attempts at explanation. MEP is more than happy to take on board the insights of terrorism researchers like Sageman, and accept that there are some things of a general nature that can be said about the processes or mechanisms of radicalisation. The formulation of general rules and theories which is at the heart of explanation is not ruled out by MEP but what this type of particularist is keen to emphasise are the inherent limitations of the explanatory project. When it comes to terrorism there is very little prospect of researchers being able to employ the experimental method or run randomised controlled trials. In this case, as in the case of much human conduct, a different perspective is required.

For those tasked with developing counterterrorism strategies, taking on board the lessons of MEP means giving up on the idea that the turn to violence in individual cases can be predicted by explanatory models of radicalisation. It means giving up on prevention and deradicalisation programmes that overlook the individuality and contingency of pathways to radicalisation and end up alienating the communities at which they are directed. It means hiring intelligence analysts who not only have the necessary linguistic skills and cultural knowledge but also a willingness to engage with the subjectivity of terrorists in order to develop a deep empathetic understanding of their motives and actions. Engaging with their subjectivity will help one to see that, in many cases, terrorists are authors of their own beliefs and actions rather than passive victims of radicalisation by others. There is the practical challenge of preventing terrorist attacks but models of radicalisations are of little help when it comes to doing that. There is really no substitute here for knowledge acquired by employing traditional methods of intelligence gathering rather than by the application of generic, simplistic and largely untested theories of behavioural radicalisation. Some terrorist attacks can be and have been predicted but on the basis of concrete intelligence rather than the application of abstract theoretical models. The hardest thing is to learn to live with the large element of chance and contingency in terrorism and the inherent limits to our knowledge in this domain. In this field, as in others, epistemic humility is an underrated virtue.[50]

The University of Warwick
q.cassam@warwick.ac.uk

[50]   I thank the editors, an anonymous referee, Olivia Bailey, Charlotte Heath-Kelly, Anna Lockley-Scott and Daniel Thornton for helpful comments. I am grateful to John Campbell for the initial suggestion that Jaspers' work might be helpful for an understanding of terrorism. Earlier drafts of this paper were presented in 2017 at a workshop at the University of Warwick on the Epistemology of Counterterrorism, a conference at Sheffield University on Harms and Wrongs in Epistemic Practice and the Oriel Colloquium on Education, Security and Intelligence Studies. Work on this paper was supported by an Arts and Humanities Research Council Leadership Fellowship. I thank the AHRC for its generous support.

Healthcare Practice, Epistemic Injustice, and Naturalism

IAN JAMES KIDD AND HAVI CAREL

Abstract

Ill persons suffer from a variety of epistemically-inflected harms and wrongs. Many of these are interpretable as specific forms of what we dub *pathocentric epistemic injustices*, these being ones that target and track ill persons. We sketch the general forms of pathocentric testimonial and hermeneutical injustice, each of which are pervasive within the experiences of ill persons during their encounters in healthcare contexts and the social world. What's epistemically unjust might not be only agents, communities and institutions, but the theoretical conceptions of health that structure our responses to illness. Thus, we suggest that although such pathocentric epistemic injustices have a variety of interpersonal and structural causes, they are also sustained by a deeper naturalistic conception of the nature of illness.

1. Epistemic Injustice and Illness

Experiences of chronic somatic illness, in their many forms, impose a variety of harms, including physical pain, cognitive disorientation, loss of bodily capacities, and emotional and psychological distress, but also a diverse range of wrongs, ranging from social marginalization to professional discrimination. Such negative experiences are abundantly documented in illness pathography, healthcare psychology, medical anthropology, and other sources for the everyday realities of 'onerous citizenship' in what Susan Sontag called 'the night side of life'.[1]

The shared features of such experiences have been described in the philosophical literature by S.K. Toombs, who writes about illness as a series of losses, by Fredrik Svenaeus, who characterises experiences of illness as 'unhomelike being in the world', by Matthew Ratcliffe's analysis of altered 'existential feelings', and by Havi Carel, who characterises illness as a fundamental disruption

---

[1] Susan Sontag, *Illness as Metaphor* (Toronto: McGraw-Hill Ryerson, 1978), 3.

doi:10.1017/S1358246118000620

of the body's transparency and to the familiar habits and routines of everyday life.[2]

Perhaps less obvious, but no less important, are a complex range of epistemically-toned harms and wrongs, defined broadly as disadvantages that occur due to interference with the capacities needed to pursue epistemic interests in the context of ill health. Such negative epistemic experiences manifest, within healthcare discourse and pathographies, in miscommunications between patients and health professionals, complaints by patients of their concerns and interests being ignored, overlooked, or dismissed, in rhetorics of 'silencing', and continued feelings of dissatisfaction, as well as, in some cases, flawed clinical care. These have for a long time been responded to with policy proposals for inclusion of 'patient perspectives' and the instigation of 'patient-centred care', and castigation by patient activists of the communicative failures endemic to healthcare encounters.

The epistemic harms and wrongs suffered by ill persons have several related negative effects. First, they impact upon patients' clinical care, psychological and physical health, social confidence, and lived experience; they are no longer 'at home' within the world, to use a term from phenomenology of illness. Second, experiences of being ignored, dismissed or even silenced, and other wrongs that occur within healthcare contexts, typically compromise the epistemic relationships between ill persons and health professionals. The sense that they are somehow at odds with one another or that their interests and perspectives conflict should be a source of serious concern to healthcare providers.

Third, the injustices experienced by ill persons typically intersect with other axes of oppression, such as gendered, racist, and ageist discrimination.[3] Finally, judging by their sheer scale and persistence, the epistemic harms and wrongs experienced by ill persons reflect entrenched, systematic features of our healthcare and social environments. Although these features may appear primarily sociological

---

[2]   See, *inter alia*, S.K. Toombs, *The Meaning of Illness: A Phenomenological Account of the Different Perspectives of Physician and Patient* (Amsterdam: Kluwer, 1993); Fredrik Svenaeus, *The Hermeneutics of Medicine and the Phenomenology of Health: Steps towards a Philosophy of Medical Practice* (Dordrecht: Kluwer, 2000); Matthew Ratcliffe, *Feelings of Being: Phenomenology, Psychiatry, and the Sense of Reality* (Oxford: Oxford University Press, 2008); Havi Carel, *Phenomenology of Illness* (Oxford: Oxford University Press, 2016).

[3]   The intersectional character of health inequities is the theme of Amy J. Schulz and Leith Mullings (eds.), *Gender, Race, Class and Health: Intersectional Approaches* (Oxford: Wiley, 2005).

or pragmatic in nature, we suggest that they go deeper, because radical epistemic incapacitation is an ineradicable dimension of illness, conceived – following Maurice Merleau-Ponty – as a 'complete way of being'.[4]

Different conceptual frameworks exist for investigating the variety of epistemic harms and wrongs intrinsic to sustained experiences of illness. Within contemporary philosophy, particular use is made of Miranda Fricker's concept of epistemic injustice – 'a wrong done to someone specifically in their capacity as a knower'.[5] Subsequent work has identified new forms and sources of epistemic injustice and further documented their prevalence throughout the social world. A growing literature now exists devoted to epistemic injustice and a variety of somatic and psychiatric illness, alongside wider themes in medical and healthcare practice.[6]

In this paper, we develop this work by arguing that many of the epistemic harms and wrongs experienced by persons with chronic somatic illness reflect specific forms of *pathocentric epistemic injustice*: ones that target and track people who are, or are perceived as, chronically somatically ill. We use this term to refer to a distinct and relatively stable social group, although are aware of the shortcomings of this definition and its overlap with other categories, such as progressive disease, acute illness with lasting effects, and disability.[7] We bracket these issues here as we wish to focus on the group of people who are significantly and chronically ill, such that they have continued and necessary interactions with health professionals, as well as being exposed to stereotype and stigma of the sort that do not usually affect someone with an acute illness, such as a fractured bone.

---

[4]   Maurice Merleau-Ponty, *Phenomenology of Perception* (New York: Routledge, 2012), 110.

[5]   Miranda Fricker, *Epistemic Injustice: Power and the Ethics of Knowing* (Oxford: Oxford University Press, 2007), 1.

[6]   An up-to-date account of current work on epistemic injustice is Ian James Kidd, José Medina, and Gaile Pohlhaus, Jr. (eds.), *The Routledge Handbook to Epistemic Injustice* (New York: Routledge, 2017). A bibliography of work on epistemic injustice, illness, healthcare, and disability is available at <www.ianjameskidd.weebly.com>.

[7]   On epistemic injustice and disability, see Anita Ho, 'Trusting Experts and Epistemic Humility in Disability', *International Journal of Feminist Approaches to Bioethics* **4**.2 (2011), 102–123 and Jackie Leach Scully, 'From "She Would Say That, Wouldn't She?" to "Does She Take Sugar?": Epistemic Injustice and Disability', *International Journal of Feminist Approaches to Bioethics* **11**.1 (2018), 106–124.

Ian James Kidd and Havi Carel

Pathocentric epistemic injustice intersects with other, more generic forms of epistemic injustice. Our claim is that many of the epistemic harms and wrongs to which ill persons are subjected take the form of specifically pathocentric forms of testimonial and hermeneutical injustice. Such pathocentric injustices are produced and sustained by economies of credibility and intelligibility, themselves sustained by deeper theoretical conceptions of the nature of health – which are often labelled 'naturalistic' conceptions – that epistemically privilege the concepts and methods of biomedical science. Our aim is to show that the privileging of these naturalistic conceptions is an important, fundamental source of these pathocentric epistemic injustices. If that is right, then achieving epistemic justice for ill persons requires more than social and healthcare reform – a complex enough task in its own right – but, at its most ambitious, deep epistemic reform of our most fundamental ways of conceptualising human health, flourishing and wellbeing in ways that transcend and transgress the implicit and commonly accepted idea that health is the *sine qua non* of the good life.

2. Testimonial Injustice and Pathographic Testimony

The core epistemic activities of giving testimony to, and making sense of, one's experiences assume a special complexity in cases of chronic illness. Amid the turmoil of diagnosis, concerns about treatment choices, anxiety about prognosis, and the often-profound changes to previous life, a new urgency inflects our epistemic needs – to speak, be listened to, understood, and to attain a degree of cognitive command over our practical and existential situation.

Diagnosis of a serious illness has been described as biographical disruption and a life changing event, amplified by the intersubjective character of our narrative practices and the essential involvement of other agents whose collaboration cannot be taken for granted.[8] Such disruption gives rise to a deep need to make sense of these profound events and incorporate them into the ill person's life. This process is comprised of narrative and testimony and involves talking about events, decisions, feelings, and practical changes, as well as private narration in the form of writing, video diaries, and

---

[8]   Michael Bury, 'Chronic Illness as Biological Disruption', *Sociology of Health and Ilness* **4**.2 (1982), 167–182; Kate C. McLean, *The Co-authored Self: Family Stories and the Construction of Personal Identity* (Oxford: Oxford University Press, 2015); Havi Carel, *Illness: The Cry of the Flesh* (Stocksfield: Acumen, 2007).

other forms of sense-making. Ill persons often seek support in the form of conversation as well as being required to provide ongoing information to health professionals, information which is often intimate, upsetting, and painful.

Important aspects of this process are the need to be understood and empathised with, help with decision making, and finding solutions for practical concerns. Such discussions may involve family, carers, health professionals, friends, a wider support network as well as social care and other professionals. For all of these, clear communication, and the ability to make oneself heard, understood, and taken seriously, are paramount.

Another significant issue is a sense of isolation, borne of practical constraints, like being house-bound, stigma, the sense of unfairness often experienced when one falls ill, or isolation, an important factor in wellbeing and patient outcomes. Other problems characterising being ill include alienation, bodily estrangement, objectification, and a sense of 'unhomelikeness', which undermine effective and authentic communication while also exacerbating the need for such communication.

Such testimonial and hermeneutical needs can only be recognised and fulfilled through social conditions that sustain appropriately diverse and inclusive economies of credibility and intelligibility. Unfortunately, as we know from work in feminist epistemology and critical race theory, this is rarely what obtains in our social cultures. Injustice is, as Judith Shklar observed, quite the norm, including the specifically epistemic injustices described by Fricker.[9] In Fricker's account, there are two main types of epistemic injustice – *testimonial* and *hermeneutical*, pertaining to a discriminatory affordance of credibility and intelligibility, respectively. In what follows, we summarise accounts we have provided elsewhere of what we now call pathocentric epistemic injustices, before moving on to discuss naturalism.[10]

Testimonial injustice occurs when negative stereotyping leads a hearer to prejudicially deflate the credibility assigned to a speaker. The effects include reduced testimonial authority, frustration of practical and social agency, and erosion of the epistemic confidence of the

[9] Judith Shklar, *The Faces of Injustice* (New Haven and London: Yale University Press, 1990), 15.

[10] Havi Carel and Ian James Kidd, 'Epistemic Injustice in Healthcare: a Philosophical Analysis', *Medicine, Healthcare, and Philosophy* **17**.4 (2014), 529–540; Ian James Kidd and Havi Carel, 'Epistemic Injustice and Illness', *Journal of Applied Philosophy* **33**.2 (2017), 172–190.

Ian James Kidd and Havi Carel

speaker, which can ultimately lead them to cease trying to communicate altogether. Though originally analysed in its agential forms, subsequent work has recognised structural forms of testimonial injustice, since acts of credibility deflation can be embedded in social structures, alongside the corrupted perceptions and judgments of agents. A variety of negative prejudices and stereotypes can inform testimonial injustice, including the gendered and racialized cases discussed in Fricker's original account. Moreover, further forms of intersectional epistemic injustices are now recognised, many articulated using the conceptual resources of a variety of social justice movements.[11]

We propose that ill persons, *qua* ill persons, are especially vulnerable to testimonial injustice because appraisals of their credibility can be corrupted by *pathophobic* prejudices and stereotypes. These arise from tendencies to operate with negative attitudes towards illness or ill persons. Such attitudes include what earlier generations of sociologists described as 'stigma', but a distinctive advantage of the concept of epistemic injustice is its obvious sensitivity to the characteristically *epistemic* dimensions of the injustices experienced by ill persons.

Such epistemic injustices assume particular force within healthcare contexts, for instance because they rely heavily on certain forms of knowledge and information when plotting the course of treatment of an individual patient. And being that patient means that the decision will impact you in the most direct and intimate manner, by influencing how your body will be treated, what will be done to it, and the length and forms of life available to oneself.

To criticise pathophobia isn't to deny the various negative aspects and effects of illness, nor to acquiesce in what Barbara Ehrenreich calls 'bright-siding' – a wilfully myopic insistence on the positive effects, real or imagined, of adversity and suffering.[12] Instead, it marks an attempt to achieve a more complex understanding of the diversity of forms of experiences of illness. Between resolute pathophobic pessimism and dogmatically optimistic 'bright-siding', one can achieve a subtler perception of chronic illness as what Carel describes as a 'life-transforming process', containing 'plenty of bad, but also, surprisingly, some good'.[13]

---

[11] See the essays in Parts II and III of Kidd, Medina, and Pohlhaus, Jr. (eds.), *The Routledge Handbook to Epistemic Injustice*.

[12] Barbara Ehrenreich, *Smile or Die: How Positive Thinking Fooled America and the World* (London: Granta, 2009).

[13] Carel, *Illness*, 12. The corrupting effects of 'bright-siding' on narratives of adversity is discussed in Ian James Kidd, 'Adversity, Wisdom, and Exemplarism', *Journal of Value Inquiry* (forthcoming).

Since achieving this understanding requires careful, critical attention to ill persons' testimonies and narratives, ensuring fair appraisal of their credibility is crucial. But credibility judgments are not made in a vacuum: they are shaped by some sense or conception of what counts as credibility within a given domain, relative to a certain set of epistemic and practical interests and concerns – a theoretical conception of health and illness, say, of the sort described later in the paper.

The credibility of ill persons can be eroded in one or more of at least two ways. First, there is pre-emptive derogation of the epistemic credibility and capacities of ill persons owing to pathophobic stereotyping – a prior view, for instance, of ill persons as being confused, incapable, or incompetent, that distorts an evaluation of their actual epistemic performance. Second, hearers can presuppose that an ill person will be dominated by their illness, unable to reflect on other issues, such that they cannot be perceived as impartial or objective. Since they are preconditions of epistemic credibility and of good decision-making, a presumption that ill persons are dominated by their illness leads to credibility-deflation. As a consequence, ill persons often report the downgrading of their testimonies, including ones which would ordinarily elicit testimonial credibility. Careful, articulate reportage of one's bodily experiences often fails to secure affordances of credibility, as they ordinarily would in epistemic life. Experiencing an inability to persuade others by performing acts of epistemic competence gives rise to 'shock', according to the titular subjects of Robert Klitzman's book, *When Doctors Become Patients*.[14]

Here are two illustrative examples of testimonial injustice within a healthcare context. The first comes from a woman with a severe respiratory disease, reporting a worrying symptom that is laughed off by a physician:

> I asked a professor whether being exposed to reduced oxygen levels long-term, the way I am, would have any detrimental effects on cognitive function e.g. would that explain why my memory had rapidly become much worse? He just laughed off my genuine and serious concern by saying he had the same problem and sometimes couldn't even remember his wife's name. I never did get a proper reply to that question.[15]

[14]   Robert Klitzman, *When Doctors Become Patients* (Oxford: Oxford University Press, 2008).
[15]   This testimony was elicited from a LAM (lymphangioleiomyomatosis) patient mailing list. We are grateful to the patients who responded to our query.

The second example involves a female patient whose symptoms are explained as psychological; intersectionality may be at play here, as her female identity makes it more likely that a psychological explanation for her pain will be accepted, rather than continuing to search for a somatic one. It also illustrates the dismissive attitudes still evident in some healthcare cultures towards pain:

> I had acute epigastric pain going through to the back during the night but got no relief. It was implied that it was anxiety, and diazepam was prescribed with no effect. It seemed to me that in view of the massive and rapid changes in my body, a physical cause was quite likely. I felt the interest in me had waned and there was less understanding. No one took the pain seriously.[16]

Since these testimonial injustices are generated by pathophobic prejudices and stereotypes, they target and track ill persons through the social world. The evident tenacity of these prejudices ensures their effects reach far beyond the clinical setting to affect education, housing and employment opportunities, due to biases that are still rife in many cultures. They are abundantly documented by patient activists, researchers, and pathographers who feel compelled to adopt a 'stance of silence', when their 'actual stories' are denied the credibility needed for uptake.[17] This stance describes the thwarted epistemic situation of those ill persons who are consistent victims of testimonial injustice.

3. Hermeneutical Injustice and Experiences of Illness

Experiences of illness involve radical transformation in a person's sense of time, space, embodiment, and intersubjective possibility, manifesting in an altered 'sense of reality' or 'form of existence'.[18] Understanding these changes is the task of a phenomenology of illness informed by careful attention to illness narratives and pathographies. What such attention reveals, we argue, is that a pervasive

---

[16] 'Gwendolyn Austen', quoted in H.N. Mandell and H.M. Spiro (eds.), *When Doctors Get Sick* (Dordrecht: Springer, 2013), 376.

[17] Stephen P. Hinshaw, *Breaking the Silence: Mental Health Professionals Disclose their Personal and Family Experiences of Mental Illness* (Oxford: Oxford University Press, 2008), 8–9.

[18] The latter two terms belong to the phenomenologies of psychiatric and somatic illness developed by Ratcliffe, *Feelings of Being*, and Carel, *Phenomenology of Illness*, respectively.

feature of the lived experience of ill persons is subjection to specific-ally pathocentric forms of hermeneutical injustice.

In their general forms, hermeneutical injustices occur when the capacity of a person or group to make intelligible certain of their bodily, existential, and social experiences to themselves or to others is unjustly constrained or undermined. The effort to make sense of our social experiences requires an array of hermeneutical practices and resources – appropriate language, metaphors, and images, shared and recognised within a community, through which we can make sense of the structure, significance, and complexities of the lived experience of ourselves and others. Often, creating and actively updating this understanding comes naturally, especially to the members of hermeneutically privileged groups – members of racial majorities, say, whose characteristic social experiences are complexly supported by a rich supporting structure that typically, if not auto-matically, renders them intelligible. But this is not the case for the hermeneutically marginalised, those who cannot create or share sense of their social experiences in comparably involuntary, lucid ways.[19]

Although such failures to achieve mutual intelligibility affect both hearers and speakers, they are differentially disadvantaged: the more privileged group tends to suffer less, epistemically and practically, and often has an interest in *not* understanding the experiences of the underprivileged. The injustice lies in the harmfulness, unfair-ness, and discrimination constitutive of these hermeneutical situa-tions in which certain illness experiences have no socially accepted way of being expressed and understood.

Unsurprisingly, therefore, forms of hermeneutical injustice can be 'wildly heterogeneous', depending, for instance, on whether they arise from an absence of appropriate hermeneutical resources or from prejudices against certain communicative or expressive styles. The injustice may be that people are prevented from *making sense* of their experiences, or of *sharing* that sense with others. Moreover, forms of hermeneutical injustice may be sustained by structural or interpersonal dynamics, which, if sufficiently oppressive, can pre-cipitate the total destruction of hermeneutical agency.[20]

We propose that ill persons are especially vulnerable to a variety of forms of complexly-related hermeneutical injustices. Although these

---

[19]   Fricker, *Epistemic Injustice*, ch. 7.
[20]   José Medina, 'Varieties of Hermeneutical Injustice', in Ian James Kidd, José Medina, and Gaile Pohlhaus, Jr. (eds.), *The Routledge Handbook to Epistemic Injustice* (New York: Routledge, 2017), 41–52.

share the general features of unfair and harmful constraints on hermeneutical agency, they are specific to certain features of the experience of illness—for instance, the difficulty of talking about one's illness, the traumatic nature of many illnesses, the deep fear and anxiety that accompany illness, and the common tendency to shy away from discussing illness and death can all hamper expressive attempts. Illness itself intrinsically constrains hermeneutical agency, imposing difficult new demands, while disrupting or ruining one's capacities to make and share intelligible understanding of one's experiences.

Even among health professionals, there continues to be an unwillingness to discuss, *inter alia*, death, existential suffering, and subjective symptoms, such as pain, mental distress, and 'contested illnesses', such as chronic fatigue syndrome (CFS/ME). Such active silences are evident in documented cases of epistemic injustice in the case of CFS/ME, increased vulnerability to stigma in the case of mental disorder, and refusals to discuss assisted dying.[21]

But there can also be situations where healthcare practitioners may want to discuss such issues when patients do not, perhaps due to social stigma, or a fear of facing the medical and existential reality in cases of end-of-life care. What ought to be shared hermeneutical agency becomes unidirectional, as either practitioners or patients are unable to reciprocally respond to the other. Indeed, although most analyses of failed communication in end-of-life contexts focus exclusively on healthcare providers, recent research indicates that patients, their families, and healthcare practitioners often 'collude to avoid mentioning death or dying, even when the patient's suffering is severe and prognosis is poor'.[22]

Given the heterogeneity of those injustices and the diversity of lived experiences of illness, our aim here is simply to sketch some of the general features of pathocentric hermeneutical injustice.

[21] Charlotte Blease, Havi Carel, Keith Geraghty, 'Epistemic Injustice in Healthcare Encounters: Evidence from Chronic Fatigue Syndrome', *Journal of Medical Ethics* **43** (2017), 549–557; Paul Crichton, Havi Carel, and Ian James Kidd, 'Epistemic Injustice in Psychiatry', *British Journal of Psychiatry Bulletin* **41** (2017), 65–70; and doctoral research by Paul Teed (personal communication).

[22] Timothy E. Quill, 'Initiating End-of-Life Discussions with Seriously Ill Patients: Addressing the "Elephant in the Room"', *Journal of the American Medical Association* **284**.19 (2000), 2502–2507. See, further, Dale G. Larson and Daniel R. Tobin, 'End-of-Life Conversations: Evolving Practice and Theory', *Journal of the American Medical Association* **284**.12 (2000), 1573–1578.

Unintelligibility, confusion, and other forms of hermeneutical frustration are abiding themes of pathography in two related ways. First, as components of an agent's efforts at self-understanding, and second, as features of their social interactions and experiences. As formerly stable structures of meaning destabilise, the world ceases to be 'a space of salient possibilities', reliably reflective of one's goals and purposes. It is no longer 'a safe context that offers opportunities for activity but [becomes] something one is at the mercy of'.[23] Understood outside the strictures of clinical medicine, illness is experienced as a 'breakdown of meaning', a harsh disclosure of the truth that 'meaning and intelligibility depend on consistent patterns of embodiment' that no longer – and, poignantly and painfully, may never again – obtain.[24]

Identifying genuinely pathocentric hermeneutical injustices is a delicate task, given the variety of difficulties or obstacles encountered by ill persons during efforts to make and share meaningful accounts of their experiences. Although some of these are harmful, not all are due to wrongful or discriminatory attitudes, actions, or structures. Many of these difficulties and obstacles reflect two phenomenologically distinctive features of chronic illness – *inarticulacy* and *ineffability*.

The inarticulacy arises, typically, from the difficulties of communicating alterations in the structures of one's lived experience, of 'finding the right words'. Since one's sense of the ordinary meanings of things becomes disrupted, as one's relationship to previous habits and lived environment are affected by illness, one's existing hermeneutical resources and competences cease to be effortlessly effective, while developing new ones appears, often, as another set of demands imposed by illness. Toombs explains:

> [T]he bookcase outside my bedroom was once intended by my body as a 'repository for books'; then as 'that which is to be grasped for support on the way to the bathroom', and is now intended as 'an obstacle to get around with my wheelchair'.[25]

In the same way that the meaning of the word 'bookcase' has changed with her increasing limitations, other words and concepts may no longer be part of the shared meaning that underpins the intelligibility of everyday human life. That may form part of a process of

---

[23] Ratcliffe, *Feelings of Being*, 113, 115.

[24] Carel, *Phenomenology of Illness*, 14, 15.

[25] S.K. Toombs, 'The Lived Experience of Disability', *Human Studies* **18** (1995), 9–23, at 16.

hermeneutical marginalisation, where meanings become increasingly specific and unshared and may even be experienced as entirely idio-syncratic. Such idiosyncrasy is a powerful hermeneutical obstacle, and if coupled with others' culpable failures to attend to or accept those idiosyncratic meanings, may mark some types of hermeneutical injustice.

Moreover, even for those with robust hermeneutical support, a further difficulty may remain: the *ineffability* of certain dimensions of the experience of illness, their resistance to any articulable under-standing, of a sort shareable with others. Sometimes, one can't find the words, but, at other times, there really are no words – none ad-equate to the project of cogently conveying to others, in mutually sat-isfying ways, the dynamics and character of one's new, altered 'way of being'. It may be that certain life experiences are so unique, dramatic, or traumatic, that they are accompanied by a sense of ineffability. Typical examples include giving birth, losing a loved one, or experi-encing trauma. Undergoing a major medical procedure, such as an organ transplant or open heart surgery are also such examples. The radically and irreducibly subjective character of such experiences ar-guably generates fundamental obstacles to the possibility of collective hermeneutical agency – an inability to comprehend and enter into and then imaginatively explore the epistemic and phenomenological standpoint of those undergoing those experiences.

4. Exclusionary Practices and Expressive Restrictions

Although inarticulacy and ineffability are intrinsic to chronic illness, they can be amplified by obstacles or difficulties imposed by the agents, practices, and structures of the social world. Only in these cases would an ill person be experiencing pathocentric hermeneutical injustice. Unfortunately, this appears to be a common occurrence: our social and healthcare cultures have features that impede the her-meneutical agency of ill persons. Since there are many such features – including those discussed in the following section – our aim is, again, only to sketch some of the general features of pathocentric hermen-eutical injustice. Specifically, we examine two of the ways that they are generated.

First, there is a range of *exclusionary practices*, inherent in social and healthcare systems, that act to exclude ill persons from the au-thoritative sites and practices in which social meanings are created, le-gitimated, and enacted. The exclusion may be physical, epistemic, social, or some combination of these, simultaneously or in succession.

Whatever the order, such exclusion prevents ill persons from participating in shared hermeneutical practices. An example would be the exclusion of patients from certain socially authoritative places of deliberation and decision, such as hospital committees or policy writing.

Second, attempts by ill persons at participation in hermeneutical practice may be thwarted by *expressive restrictions*. Corresponding to what Medina calls the 'performative' forms of hermeneutical injustice, these take the form of restrictions on the types of expressive styles affirmed to be epistemically legitimate. Typically, in the case of illness, legitimacy is confined to the norms, language, and terminology of biomedicine which may promote an impersonal, 'objective' expressive style. Such a style is stripped of the existential particularity, affective depth, and contextual richness of lived experience. It also reduces the amount of discomfort health professionals experience when exposed to highly personal and emotive expressive styles. Most healthcare interactions are between people who are strangers to each other, and whose considerations, interests and perspectives are vastly different. This creates a fertile ground for shutting down expressive attempts that diverge from the standards accepted in healthcare discourse.

The expressive styles judged by ill persons to be adequate for the task of conveying their existential and social experiences are quite different – anecdotal, episodic, autobiographical, rich in affective and existentially complex description and full of difficult emotions such as anger and grief. Within modern healthcare systems these styles and the content they are especially apt to convey are typically excluded or derogated as irrelevant to or ineffective for the epistemic needs of clinical practice. Thus, a physician may wait until the patient stops crying in order to proceed with the epistemic act of asking about a symptom. This is particularly significant when breaking bad news or discussing a poor prognosis. This tendency to derogate certain expressive styles when describing illness is often reinforced by philosophers who advocate a tacit set of 'objective' communicative norms.[26]

Pathocentric hermeneutical injustices occur when ill persons suffer limitations to their capacity to participate in collective hermeneutical

---

[26] For criticisms of the derogation of typical pathographic expressive styles, see Mikel Burley, 'Emotion and Anecdote in Philosophical Argument: The Case of Havi Carel's *Illness*', *Metaphilosophy* **42** (2011), 33–48; Ian James Kidd, 'Exemplars, Ethics, and Illness Narratives', *Theoretical Medicine and Bioethics* **38**.4 (2017), 323–334.

agency due to practices of exclusion or expressive restrictions. Such injustices map on to and exacerbate the hermeneutical difficulties of inarticulacy and ineffability, which are intrinsic to chronic illness. Despite progress one may make in addressing those, a further set of limitations is generated by unjust hermeneutical practices and cultures. The typical situation is that communities of ill persons have effective hermeneutical resources but these are deprived of the socially sanctioned legitimacy that would enable them to feature in authoritative practices of social meaning-making, specifically, in healthcare practice and policy.

Such unjust hermeneutical situations can obviously be challenged, in various ways; these include patient activism, academic research, and better uptake of the perspectives of health professionals who come to occupy the social role of 'ill person' themselves. Reflecting on the testimonies of doctors who become patients, Klitzman says that, very often, 'only the experience of becoming seriously ill finally compels them to change their thinking, and see themselves and their work more broadly, and from a different vantage point'.[27] Much current scholarship on epistemic injustice and illness is devoted to finding effective ways to enhance the receptivity of those who currently inhabit what Sontag called 'the kingdom of the well' to the very different lived experiences of those in 'the kingdom of the sick'.[28]

We are hopeful about the prospects for such work. A study of epistemic injustice should always be motivated by a desire to promote epistemic justice. But this requires a sufficiently deep understanding of the sources of the problem. In the case of pathocentric epistemic injustice, these extend beyond negative stereotypes, invidious communicative norms, and cultures that impose 'stances of silence'. There is, we suggest, a more fundamental source, one that helps sustain and license the pathocentric epistemic injustices which underlies norms, practices, and cultures. This is the entrenchment of a certain theoretical conception of illness. If so, analyses of pathocentric epistemic injustices must extend beyond individual and collective agents and institutions, right down to the theoretical conceptions that structure our thinking about illness, to which we now turn.

5. Naturalism, Disease, and Epistemic Injustice

Within modern healthcare systems, the dominant conception of the nature of disease is largely tacit, but is variously described as

[27] Klitzman, *When Doctors Become Patients*, 12.
[28] Sontag, *Illness as Metaphor*, 3.

naturalistic or biomedical. Most famously articulated within philosophy by Christopher Boorse, this family of theories conceives of health in terms of biological function, defined as statistical norms within a relevant reference class.[29] Integral to such naturalistic conceptions is, we suggest, an epistemic privileging of the values, concepts, and terminologies of biomedical science. It reflects the conceptualisation of health as being, in Lennart Nordenfelt's words, a set of 'internal processes' relevant to 'reproduction and survival', that excludes consideration of 'extra-biological' factors – 'intentional actions', 'goals', and other integral aspects of human life.[30]

In response to this naturalistic conception, a group of alternative accounts emerged, variously described as normativist, humanistic, or 'holistic'. Some phenomenological approaches are explicitly characterised as anti-naturalist and hence offer an alternative to the naturalistic model, while others suggest that a phenomenological approach should augment, rather than replace, those naturalist frameworks.[31] Indeed, the phenomenologists' talk of augmenting and enriching our available ways of conceptualising illness means their criticism is confined to claims that naturalism alone contains the necessary resources to provide an exhaustive description and understanding of illness.[32] A vocabulary of *enrichment* and *augmentation* is intended to underscore the critics' target, which is the distinctively *philosophical* confidence that, for the project of understanding and responding to human experiences of health and illness, what naturalism can offer is 'exclusively sufficient'.[33]

Most of the approaches that are critical of naturalism about the definition of disease aim to restore attention to what their advocates urge are integral dimensions – axiological, existential, conceptual – of

[29] See, for instance, Christopher Boorse, 'Health as a Theoretical Concept', *Philosophy of Science* **44**.4 (1977), 542–573. An important critical response is Rachel Cooper, 'Disease', *Studies in History and Philosophy of Biological and Biomedical Sciences* **33**.2 (2002), 263–282.
[30] Lennart Nordenfelt, 'The Opposition Between Naturalistic and Holistic Theories of Health and Disease', Havi Carel and Rachel Cooper (eds.), *Health, Illness, and Disease: Philosophical Essays* (New York: Routledge, 2014), 23–36, at 25.
[31] For an anti-naturalist stance, see Fredrik Svenaeus, *Phenomenological Bioethics: Medical Technologies, Human Suffering, and the Meaning of Being Alive* (London: Routledge, 2017). For the augmentative stance, see Carel, *Phenomenology of Illness*.
[32] See, for instance, Carel, *Illness*, 10.
[33] Bas van Fraassen, *The Empirical Stance* (New Haven: Yale University Press, 2002), 155.

illness. The dimensions nominated, along with the concepts and vocabularies deployed, are diverse – health as, for instance, 'homelike being-in-the-world', a stable 'rhythm of life', that sustains 'a sense of order and meaningfulness' or, like Rachel Cooper, the unluckiness and badness of being ill, relative to structures of social resources and expectations.[34] Such conceptions point to and legitimate a set of epistemic resources distinct from the biomedical sciences, though without denying their usefulness to healthcare.

Given the language of augmentation and enrichment, phenomenologists of illness face three related tasks. First, to identify the aspects of illness (and, derivatively, of health) occluded or excluded by naturalistic conceptions. Second, to demonstrate the epistemic and practical significance of those aspects, for instance to clinical practice or for what Carel calls 'reflective coping' with one's illness.[35] Such demonstrations can cooperate as a two-part strategy, addressing both the advantages of inclusion and the costs of exclusion.

The third task is to identify effective practices for the inclusion or restoration of the occluded aspects, while also giving conceptual tools, like those provided by the concept of epistemic injustice, to expose and interdict entrenched exclusionary practices. This is a complex set of intellectual and practical objectives, pointing to a larger agenda for a humanistic philosophy of illness and healthcare.[36] In the present context, our interest is in the relationship of these tasks to the amelioration of pathocentric epistemic injustice. Our question is: does the entrenchment and privileging of naturalistic conceptions of health tend to generate or exacerbate pathocentric epistemic injustice? Pending a fuller analysis, which will be carried out in future work, we confine ourselves in what follows to sketching an affirmative answer.

We claim that naturalistic conceptions of health are epistemically unjust insofar as they promote and require the exercise of epistemically unjust behaviours. This has two advantages for the study of epistemic injustice in healthcare. The first is that it allows us to identify the ultimate source of those pathocentric injustices. Rather than attacking health professionals, charges of epistemic injustice should

---

[34] Svenaeus, *The Hermeneutics of Medicine and the Phenomenology of Health*, §§2.7–2.8, *passim*; Cooper, 'Disease', 276f.

[35] Carel, *Phenomenology of Illness*, 214.

[36] The scope and agenda for such a project in the philosophy of illness is sketched by Ian James Kidd, 'Phenomenology of Illness, Philosophy, and Life', *Studies in History and Philosophy of Biological and Biomedical Sciences* **62** (2017), 56–60.

attend to the operative background conceptions of health and disease. The second advantage is ameliorative. Assuming our analysis is correct, then reform of all agents perpetrating pathocentric injustices would not be enough. The deep source of those injustices – the theoretical conception – must be changed, otherwise it will continue to generate those injustices. Ultimately, the background system must be changed, since merely interdicting specific components (e.g. individual actors, such as health professionals) is unlikely to permanently resolve the problem. More specifically, analysis and amelioration must go 'all the way down', to the deep theoretical structure generating those epistemic harms and wrongs.

We propose that naturalistic conceptions of health can be described as epistemically unjust in one of two ways. First, *promotion*: a conception will be epistemically unjust if it promotes epistemically unjust attitudes, actions, and assumptions. There are many ways to promote epistemically unjust behaviours – for instance, they could be valorised as the clinically proper or professionally correct thing to do. Thus, for example, clinicians often point to a need to remain 'objective' as a rationale for unempathic cold behaviour towards patients. When curare was widely used as an anaesthetic, many patients complained of their being entirely conscious during surgery: their reports were ignored by surgeons, until finally one brave doctor volunteered for a test. His testimonies confirming the patients' reports were believed. In this case, testimonial authority was entirely confined to the doctor, as a professionally accredited trained expert, enabling him to 'confirm' the reports of the patients, whose avowals were ignored until 'confirmed'. Such maldistributions of testimonial authority are consequences of a naturalistic conception of health, where a capacity for first-person avowals are rendered nugatory, unless and until they are confirmed by those whose professional credentials owe to that conception.[37]

Second, *exercise*: a conception will be epistemically unjust if its employment or enactment requires exercise or performance of epistemically unjust dispositions or acts. If putting that way of thinking about illness into practice requires people to exercise injustice, then that way of thinking is unjust. Consider the privileging of testimonial styles that are cool, 'objective', and impersonal: in practice, this leads health professionals to systematically downgrade the credibility of testimonies given in a more anecdotal, emotional, personal style. Internalising the conception's testimonial norms translates, in

---

[37]   Quoted and discussed in Daniel Dennett, *Brainstorms: Philosophical Essays on Mind and Psychology* (Cambridge, Mass.: MIT Press, 1981), 209.

practice, to an active deflation of the credibility of anything said in alternative styles. Both the promotion and exercise of epistemic injustice can be seen in epistemic relations within a healthcare context.

These two modes of epistemic injustice differ in their strength. A conception that promotes epistemically unjust actions increases the risk of epistemic injustice, while one that requires or necessitates the exercise of unjust actions increases the incidence of epistemic injustice. Although both should invite concern, there will be a greater degree of urgency with the latter, since it is actively inscribing epistemic injustice into the practices and structures of the communities it governs.

6. Credibility, Relevance, and Intelligibility

We further analyse these two ways of causing epistemic injustice by examining how testimonial and hermeneutical injustice operate within naturalistic conceptions of health and the healthcare practices that emerge from it. Starting with testimonial injustice, naturalistic conceptions of health can entrench discriminative economies of credibility, ones that define *relevance*, *salience*, and similar norms to a delimited range of knowledge, experiences, and methods. Credibility becomes confined to, because defined in terms of, the methods and deliverances of biomedical science, to the exclusion of, for example, detailed first-person accounts of changes to one's embodiment. The significance of the body to health and illness is not exhausted by its physiological functions and pathologies, an object among others for scientific investigation.

Bodies are, more fundamentally, the abiding condition for all experience, agency, and understanding, a fact disclosable only through phenomenological analysis of subjective embodiment.[38] But insofar as a conception of health confines credibility to the third-person stances of scientific enquiry, it deprives subjective accounts of altered embodied experience of the weight and attention they need to achieve uptake into healthcare systems. The significance of ill bodies being 'obtrusive', 'intrusive', and 'obstinate', for example, or the ways in which the lost transparency of health creates a state of occluded attention, cannot gain purchase within an exclusively naturalistic conception of health: those terms track

---

[38]   See, *inter alia*, Edmund Husserl, *Ideas Pertaining to a Pure Phenomenology and to a Phenomenological Philosophy, Second Book*, F. Kersten (trans.) (Dordrecht: Springer, 1982); Merleau-Ponty, *Phenomenology of Perception*, Part I; Carel, *Phenomenology of Illness*, chs. 2–4.

phenomenological rather than physiological dimensions of the process of illness. The distinction between *disease* and *illness* as biological dysfunction and as the lived experience of those dysfunctions is intended to honour that difference.[39]

The concerns about testimonial injustice arise because altered bodily experience is central to the lived experience of illness, but judged irrelevant to medical science. Our claim here is not that health professionals do not care or do not notice subjective symptoms and limitations; of course, they do. But if these are not placed within an interpretative framework that allows them to be understood as part of a general embodied experience that has gone awry in significant ways, and hence modifies the entire lifeworld of the ill person, understanding remains limited.

Arguably, the problem is not that testimonies to altered embodiment are deprived of *credibility*, but of *relevance*. Doctors might regard such testimonies as perfectly credible, yet irrelevant to clinical practice. This attitude is at the very least strongly linked to a naturalistic conception of disease and the forms of professional education and training it informs.

The attempt to move beyond this attitude underpins much work in qualitative health research, patient-centred care, and other humanist and phenomenological approaches which aim to improve and humanise patients' experience of illness and of receiving healthcare within a naturalistically based healthcare system. Such amelioration depends, however, on a robust rethinking of the economies of intelligibility, relevance, and credibility assigned to the variety of experiences and testimonies that emerge within the context of human health. In her classic book, *Heartsounds* – an account of her husband's heart condition – Martha Weinman Lear describes how reports of the subjective dimensions of illness tend to be reduced to epistemically uncertain 'things':

> The thing fits no clinical profile. It yields no diagnosis. It submits to none of their tests, invites no techniques, and so what are they to do? [...] Whatever cannot be diagnosed or treated by technique is suspect, vaguely inauthentic, and quite possibly does not exist.[40]

---

[39] Havi Carel, 'Conspicuous, Obtrusive, and Obstinate: A Phenomenology of the Ill Body', Darian Meacham (ed.), *Medicine and Society: New Perspectives in Continental Philosophy* (Dordrecht: Springer, 2015), 105–123, informed by Jean-Paul Sartre, *Being and Nothingness* (London: Routledge, 2003).

[40] Martha Weinman Lear, *Heartsounds: The Story of a Love and Loss* (New York: Simon and Schuster, 1980), 187.

Ian James Kidd and Havi Carel

Here, a naturalistic conception of health renders certain experiences and testimonies as 'suspect', obscure items of epistemic ephemera, deprived of salience. It is for this reason that the entrenchment of naturalistic conceptions generates and exacerbates pathocentric hermeneutical injustices.

Specifically, those conceptions can give a socially authoritative theoretical rationale for a variety of exclusionary practices, while also licensing expressive restrictions. Illness is primarily construed as a biomedical and clinical problem, and only secondarily, if at all, as one of existence, meaning, and suffering. Issues such as addiction, treatment compliance, mental disorder and chronic pain are not easily understood under such a problem-based scientifically-oriented perspective (which is often aligned with naturalism about disease) and such diseases as well as existential dimensions of other conditions are most often excluded from the medical purview.

A conception of disease is hermeneutically influential in two related ways: it affects which experiences can be candidates for discussion and interpretation and, secondly, shapes the forms of intelligibility applicable to them. Experiences of feeling 'estranged' from one's body might not register as intelligible, such that they ought to be dismissed, or they may be judged intelligible, but as inchoate expressions of anxiety or distress. If so, the active exclusion of those experiences and the expressive styles appropriate to them will seem to be epistemically and pragmatically sensible, for no sense could obtain that anything of value was being excluded.

Moreover, such conceptions are not only institutionally entrenched within healthcare and the social world, but can also be internalised by ill persons. Many pathographies include a form of self-censoring, such as one patient who opted not to 'mention [certain] problems because though they are real for me, they're minor in the grand scheme of things' – an instance of what Kristie Dotson calls *testimonial smothering*, whereby speakers limit or shape their testimony to make it conform to the expectations of a socially dominant type of audience. In this case, the patient omitted to mention problems they judged irrelevant to scientifically informed clinical practice.[41]

One may respond that exclusion from medical discourse is justified because these kinds of experiences lie outside the domain of clinical practice and therefore are, and should remain, external to it. Exclusion of such expressions, the response may go, thus supports the focus and clarity needed in order to provide good clinical care;

---

[41] Kristie Dotson, 'Tracking Epistemic Violence, Tracking Practices of Silencing', *Hypatia: A Journal of Feminist Philosophy* **26**.2 (2011), 236–257.

exclusion is not in itself objectionable, since there can be good pragmatic, moral, or other reasons for the legitimate exclusion of certain
claims or perspectives.

We reply that this swings both ways: the exclusion of existential experiences of ill persons from healthcare theory and practice must be
justified, not least in the face of the ample and articulate accounts,
by patients, activists, and researchers, of the importance of inclusion
of sensitivity to the lived experience of illness.[42] Often, these accounts
make clear the many ways that existential and phenomenological
issues are integral to clinical practice and medical theory.[43] Many decisions made on putatively 'pure' clinical grounds necessarily interact, and often conflict, with ill persons' goals, values and desires,
for instance, while any actual or perceived neglect of these by
health professionals will tend to erode their relationship with
patients.

Such relationships are constituted and sustained by moral and epistemic trust, testimonial credibility, and active efforts to achieve and
sustain mutual intelligibility – all marks of epistemic justice. Insofar
as naturalistic conceptions of disease tend to erode or diminish the
possibility of these dynamics of trust, credibility, and intelligibility,
they are sources and amplifiers of pathocentric epistemic injustice.

7. Conclusion

Although our criticisms of the entrenchment of exclusivist attitudes
towards naturalistic conceptions of disease are intended correctively,
several clarifications are in order. First, we are not arguing that there
is anything necessarily or intrinsically epistemically unjust about naturalistic conceptions – much turns on the contingent ways those conceptions come to be institutionally realised and culturally reinforced.
We suggest that the real source of the problems is *exclusive privileging*
of those conceptions, the conviction that these alone do or could

[42]   Aside from the literature cited throughout this paper, influential ex-
amples include Rita Charon, *Narrative Medicine: Honouring the Stories of
Illness* (Oxford: Oxford University Press, 2006), Anne Hunsaker
Hawkins, *Reconstructing Illness: Studies in Pathography*, 2nd ed. (West
Layayette: Purdue University Press, 1999), and the rich resource that is
<www.patientvoices.org.uk>.

[43]   See for example Alison Tresidder's study of experiences of diagnosis
with lymphangioleiomyomatosis (unpublished PhD dissertation,
Northampton University, 2018). The delays in diagnosis, misdiagnosis, and
poor professional practice are a central theme in the interviews she conducted.

provide the relevant sorts of conceptual and epistemic resources, something now entrenched in much of contemporary clinical and biomedical science and throughout healthcare systems.[44]

A second clarification is that the pathocentric epistemic injustices generated by those conceptions and systems, although widespread, are not at all totalising or all-pervasive. There are many critics internal to biomedical science and healthcare systems who call for enriched estimations of the sorts of epistemic resources pertinent to the understanding and amelioration of illness. Such expansions of the imagination are obvious in the rise of 'humanistic', 'person-centred', 'values-based', and 'participatory' healthcare.[45] Finally, our criticism of exclusive privileging of naturalism about disease does not entail any denial of the epistemic and practical results that this approach has yielded. Our claim is that additional methods offering different results are possible, many of which, moreover, are only accessible through inclusion of a wider conception of illness that draws on resources outside the sciences.

There are many obstacles to the exploration and development of these sorts of enriched epistemic resources, including many of a practical and economic sort. An essential strategy for overcoming those obstacles will be to secure acceptance of the fundamental claim that there are essential roles for inclusion of the lived experience of illness in their variety of forms. Such acceptance is itself apt to be blocked by a set of further obstacles, many of which are either generated or amplified by the set of pathocentric epistemic injustices that prevent recognition and uptake of the insights and understanding of ill persons. As long as ill persons are deprived of credibility and intelligibility by epistemically unjust agents, structures, concepts, and environments, they will continue to face epistemic harms and wrongs, including those pathocentric epistemic injustices that obstruct possibilities for epistemic enrichment and activity while also contributing to their epistemic oppression.

---

[44] James Marcum refers to this attitude of problematic and exclusive privileging of naturalistic models of health as 'medical scientism'. *The Bloomsbury Companion to Contemporary Philosophy of Medicine* (London: Bloomsbury, 2017), 22–23.

[45] Influential examples include Atul Gawande, *Being Mortal: Illness, Medicine, and What Matters in the End* (London: Profile, 2014); K.W.M. Fulford, Ed Peile, and Heidi Carroll, *Essential Values-Based Practice: Clinical Stories Linking Science with People* (Cambridge: Cambridge University Press, 2012); James A. Marcum, *An Introductory Philosophy of Medicine: Humanizing Modern Medicine* (Dordrecht: Springer, 2008).

Healthcare Practice, Epistemic Injustice, and Naturalism

We explored some of the assumptions, stereotypes and conceptions that underpin what we have termed *pathocentric epistemic injustices* – ones that target and track those who are ill. These particular types of injustice occur when the testimonies, narratives, interpretations, and self-understanding of ill persons are unfairly excluded from and marginalised within medical discourse.

After sketching the general forms of pathocentric testimonial and hermeneutical injustice, we argued that both are pervasive within the experiences of ill persons during their encounters in healthcare contexts and the social world. Although they have a variety of interpersonal and structural causes, they are also generated and amplified by a deeper naturalistic conception of the nature of disease. If this is right, then studying pathocentric epistemic injustice requires scrutiny of the more fundamental ways of conceptualising disease that inform our medical science and healthcare systems. Although those injustices have many social and psychological causes, they are also amplified, disguised and legitimated by the ways of conceptualising disease that we have contingently inherited – ones that come to inscribe a set of pathophobic prejudices, stereotypes, and preconceptions.

Identifying these requires us to go 'all the way down', into the deep socio-epistemic structures of our biomedical and healthcare systems, and 'all the way back' through the contingent histories that shaped them. Such genealogical projects, familiar from other critical discourses, are often directed toward the achievement of epistemic justice.[46] There is therefore good reason to hope for progress in the amelioration of the epistemic harms and wrongs suffered by ill persons, including those classifiable as pathocentric epistemic injustices.[47]

University of Nottingham
ian.kidd@nottingham.ac.uk
University of Bristol
havi.carel@bristol.ac.uk

[46] Amy Allen, 'Power/Knowledge/Resistance: Foucault and Epistemic Injustice', in *The Routledge Handbook to Epistemic Injustice*, Kidd, Medina, and Pohlhaus, Jr. (eds.), 187–194. Alongside Foucault, an important role should be made for Georges Canguilhem, *On the Normal and the Pathological* (London: Dordrecht, 1978).

[47] We are grateful to the audience at the *Harms and Wrongs in Epistemic Practice* conference for helpful discussion and to the editors of this volume and an anonymous referee for generous comments. Havi Carel gratefully acknowledges the support of the Wellcome Trust provided through the grant 'Life of Breath: breathing in cultural, clinical and lived experience' (grant ref. number 103340); for more information, visit <www.lifeofbreath.org>.

What's Epistemically Wrong with Conspiracy Theorising?

KEITH HARRIS

Abstract

Belief in conspiracy theories is often taken to be a paradigm of epistemic irrationality. Yet, as I argue in the first half of this paper, standard criticisms of conspiracy theorising fail to demonstrate that the practice is invariably irrational. Perhaps for this reason, many scholars have taken a relatively charitable attitude toward conspiracy theorists and conspiracy theorising in recent years. Still, it would be a mistake to conclude from the defence of conspiracy theorising offered here that belief in conspiracy theories is on an epistemic par with belief in other theories. I argue that a range of epistemic errors are pervasive among conspiracy theorists. First, the refusal of conspiracy theorists to accept the official account of some target event often seems to be due to the exercise of a probabilistic, and fallacious, extension of *modus tollens*. Additionally, conspiracy theorists tend to be inconsistent in their intellectual attention insofar as the effort they expend on uncovering the truth excludes attention to their own capacities for biased or otherwise erroneous reasoning. Finally, the scepticism with which conspiracy theorists tend to view common sources of information leaves little room for conspiracy theorists to attain positive warrant for their preferred explanations of target events.

Introduction

Conspiracy theorising is often regarded as a paradigm of epistemically irrational behaviour. Yet it is strikingly difficult to identify the epistemic errors, if any, characteristic of conspiracy theorising. In fact, many of the supposed faults associated with conspiracy theorising are not faults at all, and some are common in well-respected theoretical domains. Hence, as I argue in the first half of this paper, the faults standardly associated with conspiracy theorising do not warrant the sort of criticism to which the practice is often subjected. It is perhaps due to the resilience of conspiracy theorising to standard criticisms that many scholars have taken a relatively charitable attitude toward the practice in recent years.

It would be a mistake to conclude from the defence of conspiracy theorising offered in the first part of this paper that the practice is above criticism. Given the pernicious effects of widespread

doi:10.1017/S1358246118000619   © The Royal Institute of Philosophy and the contributors 2018

Royal Institute of Philosophy Supplement **84** 2018

conspiracy theorising on society,[1] there is reason to be wary of the conclusion that conspiracy theorising is epistemically innocent. Of course, any adverse social or political effects of widespread belief in conspiracy theories are irrelevant to the *epistemic* merits of conspiracy theorising. However, I argue in the latter half of this paper that there are epistemic defects characteristic of conspiracy theorising. Belief in conspiracy theories often involves a probabilistic, and fallacious, extension of *modus tollens*. Moreover, conspiracy theorists often exhibit a degree of intellectual attention that is inconsistent insofar as this effort does not extend to the subject's own potential for biased or otherwise erroneous reasoning. Finally, the suspicion conspiracy theorists exhibit toward official accounts of target events deprives conspiracy theorists of a basis on which to justify their preferred explanations. There is reason to think these errors are more prevalent among conspiracy theorists than their counterparts. The upshot is that criticism of conspiracy theorising is typically – though not invariably – warranted.

1. Conspiracy Theories and Conspiracy Theorising

It will be essential, for what follows, to establish some terminology. First, we require an adequate definition of 'conspiracy theory'. There is a great deal of ambiguity surrounding the term, within the philosophical literature and without. Hence, it will be useful to stipulate a definition for the sake of clarity. As I will use the term, a conspiracy theory:[2]

(1)   Posits an explanation for a target event or set of target events that is alternative to the official account of the event(s).

(2)   Claims that the event(s) was/were brought about by one or more conspirators.

---

[1]   These effects, including distrust of scientific authorities and the stoking of racial resentments, are emphasized by Cass R. Sunstein and Adrian Vermeule in 'Conspiracy Theories: Causes and Cures', *Journal of Political Philosophy* **17**.2 (2009), 202–227.

[2]   The stipulated definition owes much to Brian Keeley's definition of 'unwarranted conspiracy theories' in Brian Keeley, 'Of Conspiracy Theories', in *Conspiracy Theories: The Philosophical Debate*, (ed.) David Coady (Farnham: Ashgate, 2006), 45–60, as well as Susan Feldman's definition of 'explanatory conspiracy theories' in Susan Feldman, 'Counterfact Conspiracy Theories', *The International Journal of Applied Philosophy* **25**.1 (2011), 19.

(3)   Posits that the architects of the event(s) are involved in promoting the official account.

(4)   Has greater explanatory power than the official account.

To take a prominent example, one conspiracy theory surrounding the events of September 11, 2001 posits that the World Trade Center buildings were brought down by agents within the United States government, rather than members of Al-Qaeda, and that the latter narrative was devised and disseminated by the true conspirators.

This definition calls for several comments. First, the definition offered here is narrower than the one preferred by some philosophers interested in conspiracy theories. As (1) makes clear, only those theories that run counter to the official account of some target event will be counted as conspiracy theories on this definition. Matthew R.X. Dentith, seemingly concerned that the condition that conspiracy theories always run counter to official theories stacks the deck against the rationality of belief in conspiracy theories, proposes to eschew any condition of this sort from the definition.[3] Indeed, Dentith suggests that the proper definition of 'conspiracy theory' would extend to all theories that explain events by reference to conspiracies.

I find Dentith's case for broadening the definition of 'conspiracy theory' unconvincing. While one of Dentith's aims is to show that conspiracy theories may or may not be official, his evidence for this claim helps to establish only that the officialness of a given theory need not indicate that it is well-supported by evidence. Moreover, as Dentith acknowledges, admitting official theories as conspiracy theories is a departure from common usage of the term.[4] For instance, on Dentith's proposal, the claim that Al-Qaeda conspired to bring down the World Trade Center buildings would be considered a conspiracy theory. Finally, even some philosophers that adopt a highly charitable attitude toward conspiracy theories and conspiracy theorists acknowledge that official accounts of events are not regarded as conspiracy theories, even when those official accounts explain events through reference to conspiracies[5]. So, insofar as our project is to evaluate those theories typically considered to be conspiracy theories, and belief therein, we ought to focus on those theories that run counter to official explanations of events.

---

[3]   Matthew R. X. Dentith, *The Philosophy of Conspiracy Theories* (Basingstoke: Palgrave Macmillan, 2014), 123.

[4]   Dentith, *The Philosophy of Conspiracy Theories*, 123.

[5]   David Coady, *What to Believe Now: Applying Epistemology to Contemporary Issues* (Oxford: Wiley-Blackwell, 2012).

Even if one accepts that conspiracy theories are invariably contrary to official theories, one might maintain that the definition offered here is excessively narrow. On the present account, conspiracy theories always centre on explanations of events. Certain theories labelled as conspiracy theories – the claim that the Earth is flat, for instance – are not centred on the explanation of events.[6] My own view is that the assimilation of such theories under the label 'conspiracy theories' involves a loose use of the term, but the issue need not divert us here. At the least, the definition above picks out a broad and important subclass of conspiracy theories. Those that prefer a broader definition may proceed with the caveat that the remarks to come are primarily directed at this subclass of conspiracy theories. Even if one prefers the broader definition, some of the remarks to follow will apply to theories excluded from the narrower definition.

The inclusion of (1) in the definition above has interesting consequences with respect to what counts as a conspiracy theory. The officially-accepted explanation of some target event may vary over time. Thus, through mainstream acceptance, a theory that was once a conspiracy theory may achieve official status and thereby cease to be a conspiracy theory. What theories are official, and thus what theories count as conspiracy theories, may differ across geographical regions as well as over time.[7] The official account of some event in the United States may differ from the account officially accepted in Russia, for instance. Consequently, a theory that counts as a conspiracy theory in the United States may not count as a conspiracy theory in Russia, and vice-versa. Additionally, (1) makes it likely that the processes whereby one comes to believe a conspiracy theory will differ from the processes whereby one comes to believe the official accounts of some event. One will generally not believe a conspiracy theory, for instance, based on official testimony. This is crucial for present purposes, as our ultimate focus will be on evaluating the intellectual traits and reasoning processes that lead individuals to believe conspiracy theories, rather than evaluating the theories themselves.

[6]   Although the theory that the Earth is flat is not itself a claim about the correct explanation of some event, endorsement of the flat Earth theory will typically be attended by a host of conspiracy theories intended to explain recalcitrant data.

[7]   The suggestion that what counts as a conspiracy theory may vary across countries is explicitly criticized by Charles Pidgen, 'Conspiracy Theories and the Conventional Wisdom', *Episteme* **4.2** (2007), 229. However, the absurd consequences that Pidgen associates with this view arise only on the supposition that belief in conspiracy theories is invariably irrational and so such criticism need not concern us here.

What's Epistemically Wrong with Conspiracy Theorising?

It is worth explaining why (3) and (4) are included in the definition above. From the perspective of the conspiracy theorist, it is natural to expect that the true conspirators behind the event to be explained will have a strong incentive to disguise their involvement. One means of doing so is to disseminate or at least allow the dissemination of a false explanation of that event – this being the official account. Hence, part of the explanatory power of a conspiracy theory consists in its ability to explain the prominence of the official account. Official accounts, in contrast, tend not to explain attendant conspiracy theories. Moreover, as we will see, much of the supposed justification for accepting conspiracy theories is derived from the seeming ability of such theories to explain data left mysterious by the official account.

With a definition of conspiracy theory in place, we may now define 'conspiracy theorising'. As I will use the term, conspiracy theorising simply consists in the belief-forming practices or reasoning processes whereby individuals come to believe conspiracy theories.

2. The Evaluation of Conspiracy Theorising

I wish to emphasize here that the aim of the definition provided above is not to pick out a class of theories that, by their nature, one cannot rationally believe. As others have noted,[8] some previous work on conspiracy theories has attempted to find a blanket argument that, analogously to David Hume's attack on the rationality of belief in miracles,[9] shows belief in conspiracy theories to be invariably irrational. For reasons I discuss below, I believe that any such attempt is doomed to failure.

Even if no argument shows that belief in conspiracy theories is invariably irrational, there might be reason to think that conspiracy theorising typically involves errors of reasoning. Here it may be useful to make some clarificatory remarks about the strength of the conclusion I intend to support here. It may be useful to invoke a distinction sometimes made by discussants of conspiracy theories in the philosophical literature. Joel Buenting and Jason Taylor distinguish between two approaches to the evaluation of conspiracy theories.[10] According to the *generalist* view, conspiracy theories may be

---

[8]   Keeley, 'Of Conspiracy Theories', 47.

[9]   David Hume, *An Enquiry Concerning Human Understanding: 2nd Edition*, Eric Steinberg (ed.) (Cambridge: Hackett, 1993).

[10]   Joel Buenting and Jason Taylor, 'Conspiracy Theories and Fortuitous Data', *Philosophy of the Social Sciences* **40**.4 (2010), 567–578.

evaluated as a class, without regard to the details of any particular conspiracy theory. In contrast, *particularists* hold that the merits and demerits of individual conspiracy theories must be considered independently. We may construct a corresponding distinction between generalist and particularist evaluations of the rationality of conspiracy theorising.

Neither view aligns well with the position taken here nor, I suspect, with the best existing critiques of conspiracy theorising. A generalist view, according to which conspiracy theorising is invariably irrational, is plainly unfounded. Some conspiracy theories are true. That some such theories are true does not, by itself, ensure that it is sometimes rational to believe conspiracy theories or to engage in conspiracy theorising, as the truth of a theory is in general logically independent of whether any individual rationally believes that theory. However, there are plainly instances of rational belief in conspiracy theories and rational conspiracy theorising. Parties to a conspiracy, for instance, are rational to believe at least one conspiracy theory. Similarly, dedicated investigators may amass sufficient evidence to rationally believe certain conspiracy theories.

Yet the alternative position, according to which whether conspiracy theorising is irrational must strictly be evaluated on a case-by-case basis, fails to recognize the extent to which conspiracy theorising may involve problematic reasoning patterns. If there are problematic traits or reasoning strategies characteristic of conspiracy theorising, there may be *prima facie* grounds for scepticism about the epistemic merits of conspiracy theorising even if certain instances of conspiracy theorising are epistemically unimpeachable. There is good reason to think that there are traits or reasoning strategies characteristic of conspiracy theorising. Belief in a given conspiracy theory strongly predicts belief in other conspiracy theories,[11] even in cases where the conspiracy theories are incompatible.[12]

The central task of the remainder of this paper is thus to consider whether there are *negative* epistemic traits and processes characteristic of conspiracy theorising. My focus is on whether popular and academic criticism of conspiracy theorists and conspiracy theorising is warranted, and thus I focus on those traits and processes for which conspiracy theorists could reasonably be considered blameworthy.

[11]   Ted Goertzel, 'Belief in Conspiracy Theories,' *Political Psychology* **15**.4 (1994), 731–742.
[12]   Michael J. Wood, Karen M. Douglas and Robbie M. Sutton, 'Dead and Alive: Beliefs in Contradictory Conspiracy Theories.' *Social Psychology and Personality Science* **3**.6 (2012), 767–773.

3. Conspiracy Theorising and Epistemic Vice

One possibility is that conspiracy theorising is a manifestation of epistemic vice.[13] Broadly speaking, there are two branches of virtue epistemology. Virtue reliabilism, the branch of virtue epistemology endorsed by, for instance Ernest Sosa and John Greco, understands epistemic virtues as well-functioning faculties along the lines of perception, memory, and so on.[14] In contrast, virtue responsibilism, as endorsed by Linda Zagzebski and Jason Baehr, among others, understands epistemic virtues as character traits like open-mindedness, diligence, and so on.[15]

While virtue reliabilists and responsibilists offer radically different accounts of epistemic virtue, both traditions typically allow that certain traits of character constitute epistemic vices. That virtue responsibilists regard certain traits of character as epistemically vicious is hardly surprising, given that the responsibilist ontology of epistemic virtues is populated by character traits. It is more surprising that virtue reliabilists likewise tend to understand certain character traits as intellectual vices.[16] Ernest Sosa, for instance, cites haste and inattentiveness as obstacles to attaining knowledge.[17] Baehr points out that such obstacles are best understood as either character traits or manifestations of character traits, rather than faculties.[18]

Hence it seems that for virtue reliabilists and responsibilists alike certain traits of character are epistemically vicious. Importantly for present purposes, an agent can be blameworthy for exhibiting epistemically vicious traits of character.[19] This is in contrast to agents that

---

[13]   This possibility is suggested by Quassim Cassam, 'Vice Epistemology', *The Monist* **99**.2 (2016), 159–180 and briefly suggested by Feldman, 'Counterfact Conspiracy Theories', 22.

[14]   Ernest Sosa, *A Virtue Epistemology: Apt Belief and Reflective Knowledge* (Oxford University Press, 2007); John Greco, *Achieving Knowledge: A Virtue-Theoretic Account of Epistemic Normativity* (Cambridge: Cambridge University Press, 2010).

[15]   Linda Zagzebski, *Virtues of the Mind: An Inquiry into the Nature of Virtue and the Ethical Foundations of Knowledge* (Cambridge: Cambridge University Press, 1996); Jason Baehr, *The Inquiring Mind: On Intellectual Virtues and Virtue Epistemology* (Oxford: Oxford University Press, 2011).

[16]   Baehr, *The Inquiring Mind*, 55.

[17]   Ernest Sosa, *Knowledge in Perspective* (Cambridge: Cambridge University Press, 1991), 229.

[18]   Baehr, *The Inquiring Mind*, 55.

[19]   Guy Axtell, 'Epistemic Luck in Light of the Virtues', in Abrol Fairweather and Linda Zagzebski (eds.), *Virtue Epistemology: Essays on*

Keith Harris

have difficulty forming true beliefs due to deficiencies in their faculties, rather than character traits. It seems *prima facie* plausible that conspiracy theorising typically involves the manifestation of epistemic vice, understood thusly. Hence, it is worth considering in greater detail whether conspiracy theorists exhibit intellectual vices in such a way as to be worthy of epistemic criticism that does not apply equally to their counterparts.

To some extent, any answer to this question must await empirical study, and so the answer given here will be speculative. Nonetheless, strong considerations militate against the idea that conspiracy theorists exhibit familiar epistemically vicious character traits to a greater degree than their counterparts. To see this, consider the paradigmatic conspiracy theorist, who goes to great lengths to investigate the target event and amasses evidence that they take to undermine the official account of that event. Such an individual devotes a great deal of time – considerably more than non-conspiracy theorists – to uncovering the truth.[20] Indeed, conspiracy theorists are often more knowledgeable about the circumstances surrounding target events than their counterparts, and this is plausibly a result of greater devotion to uncovering the truth, a hallmark of intellectual virtue in the responsibilist tradition.[21] Far short of exhibiting epistemically vicious traits of character, the paradigm conspiracy theorist exhibits a great deal of epistemically virtuous traits of character. If conspiracy theorists are worthier of epistemic criticism than their counterparts, it is not clear that it is because they exhibit epistemic vice in a way their counterparts do not.

It may be argued here that this defence of conspiracy theorists is too quick. Even if conspiracy theorists exhibit some intellectual virtue, they may also exhibit intellectual vice. It seems plausible, for instance, that conspiracy theorists often exhibit a sort of closed-mindedness – an unwillingness to earnestly engage with other perspectives. I consider this suggestion in greater detail in section five. For now, it suffices to note that it is far from clear that conspiracy theorists exhibit intellectual closed-mindedness to a degree their counterparts do not. It is probably true that conspiracy theorists exhibit closed-

---

Epistemic Virtue and Responsibility (Oxford: Oxford University Press, 2001), 162.

[20] Steve Clarke, 'Conspiracy Theories and Conspiracy Theorizing' in David Coady (ed.), *Conspiracy Theories: The Philosophical Debate*, (Farnham: Ashgate, 2006), 77–92.

[21] Zagzebski, *Virtues of the Mind*.

mindedness with respect to the testimony of proponents of the official account. But adherents to the official account are likewise not likely to take conspiracy theorists seriously. Hence, this criticism is not, on its own, sufficient to show that conspiracy theorising is subject to a sort of epistemic criticism to which endorsement of official accounts of events is not.

The defence of conspiracy theorising provided here rests on a sort of parity between conspiracy theorists and their counterparts vis-à-vis closed-mindedness. Quassim Cassam rejects this supposed parity, noting that while both conspiracy theorists and their counterparts dismiss evidence from certain sources, only the conspiracy theorist fails to give proper weight to the sources they dismiss.[22] The suggestion here seems to be that the sources favoured by conspiracy theorists are epistemically dubious, while the sources favoured by their counterparts are not. I concur with this claim, as far as it concerns the objective epistemic merit of each category of source. However, from the perspective of each agent, it is not immediately clear that the non-conspiracy theorist has more grounds to dismiss conspiracist sources than the conspiracy theorist has to dismiss non-conspiracist sources. The quality of the sources that each epistemic agent dismisses is external to their epistemic agency is such a way that differences on this score cannot ground differences in the epistemic rationality of conspiracy theorising and acceptance of the official account.

4. Conspiracy Theories and the Evidence

A striking feature of beliefs in conspiracy theories is that such beliefs are difficult to shake. Indeed, such beliefs are arguably *too* difficult to shake. A criticism of conspiracy theorising can be developed on this basis along the following lines. Conspiracy theories are empirical theories. Hence there ought to be, in principle, some observations that would be inconsistent with any given conspiracy theory. But conspiracy theories, unlike other empirical theories, can accommodate any observation. In short, conspiracy theories are unfalsifiable. It is irrational to believe unfalsifiable theories. Therefore, belief in conspiracy theories is irrational. This line of argument has been criticized elsewhere.[23] Nonetheless, it will be useful for what follows to

---

[22]   Cassam, 'Vice Epistemology'.
[23]   Keeley, 'Of Conspiracy Theories', 55–56. Keeley's central response to the present objection to belief in conspiracy theories is that conspiracy

Keith Harris

develop a response to this criticism of belief in conspiracy theories in detail.

First, it is crucial to understand why one might take conspiracy theories to be unfalsifiable. We may illustrate with the following simple example. Suppose that Sam, like many in his community, suspects that his mayor and the mayor's associates staged an assassination attempt to garner political support. The local police department concludes that the assassination attempt was genuine. Most members of Sam's community are convinced by the police department's testimony, but not Sam. Sam instead concludes that the police department is in cahoots with the mayor. A journalistic investigation further corroborates the mayor's story. Sam is still not satisfied. He comes to believe that the mayor, the police, and the local paper are in league together.

It seems clear that there is something wrong with Sam's reasoning. However, it is worth first pointing out a few ways in which Sam's reasoning is plainly *not* irrational. First, at each point in the sequence, Sam's beliefs form a coherent set. This would not be the case if, for instance, Sam accepted the conclusion reached by the police while retaining his belief in the mayor's guilt. Sam maintains the coherence of his beliefs though a process of updating. He first updates his attitudes toward the police, then toward the local paper. In short, he adjusts his belief to accommodate new evidence. Sam's behavior is therefore consistent with another requirement of rationality. Sam's mistake, if he makes one, is that he updates his beliefs in an inappropriate way. Rather than abandoning his conspiracy theory, he instead alters his other beliefs to make that theory fit his observations.

The problem with Sam's theory, one might think, is that no conceivable evidence could conflict with it. Indeed, pieces of evidence that seemingly point toward opposite conclusions support Sam's theory equally. The fact that the police uncovered no hint of wrongdoing suggests to him that there is a conspiracy, albeit a wider conspiracy than Sam originally thought. But if the police *had* found something, we might imagine that Sam would still have taken his

---

theorists have good grounds for thinking that those individuals responsible for a given target event will attempt to cover it up by generating data that appears to conflict with the conspiracy theory. Keeley thus suggests that, while falsifiability is a reasonable criterion of goodness in the case of hypotheses in the natural sciences, the fact that conspiracy theories are unfalsifiable is not a strike against them. I concur with Keeley that the unfalsifiability of conspiracy theories is not enough to dismiss them. In what follows I argue that the sort of straightforward falsifiability at work in this objection is too much to expect of any theory, not just of conspiracy theories.

initial theory to be vindicated. All conceivable evidence points toward the same conclusion.

Sam's case, contrived though it is, illustrates epistemic behavior characteristic of conspiracy theorising. Some collection of individuals – the conspirators – are taken to have an interest in obscuring the truth. As a result, evidence that appears to conflict with a conspiracy theory poses no threat to the theory. Indeed, such evidence, insofar as it is what one would expect to encounter, given the existence of a conspiracy, goes some way toward confirming the theory. Brian Keeley[24] puts the point as follows: 'conspiracy theories are the only theories for which evidence *against* them is actually construed as evidence in favor of them.' I would put the point differently. The apparent problem with many conspiracy theories is that there can be no evidence against them and, indeed, conspiracy theories seem to illicitly derive support from what appear to be conflicting observations.

On the face of it, the unfalsifiability of many conspiracy theories seems to constitute a strike against such theories and, derivatively, those that accept them. However, resilience to falsification is hardly unique to conspiracy theories. Scientific theories in general are resistant to falsification. This point is emphasized by Imre Lakatos, among others.[25] As Lakatos emphasizes, the reason for the resilience of scientific theories to falsification is that scientific theories are not tested in isolation. A scientific theory on its own makes few, if any, substantive claims about the world. For this reason, as Lakatos writes, the research programme – not the theory – is the 'typical descriptive unit of great scientific achievements'.[26] Research programmes include a 'hard core' of theories, as well as a more dispensable set of auxiliary hypotheses. Lakatos writes, for example, that a Newtonian astronomer's predictions would rely not only on some central theories to which he was deeply committed, but also on some more peripheral hypotheses about, for instance, atmospheric refraction of light.[27] More generally, auxiliary hypotheses play a vital role in research programmes, conjoining with theories to derive testable predictions.

The need to conjoin theories to auxiliary hypotheses to derive testable predictions ensures that scientific theories are not straightforwardly falsifiable. To borrow Lakatos's illuminating metaphor, auxiliary hypotheses form a 'protective belt' around scientific

---

[24] Keeley, 'Of Conspiracy Theories', 54.
[25] Imre Lakatos, *The Methodology of Scientific Research Programmes*, (Cambridge: Cambridge University Press, 1989).
[26] Lakatos, *The Methodology of Scientific Research Programmes*, 4.
[27] Lakatos, *The Methodology of Scientific Research Programmes*, 4.

theories.[28] When a given prediction is not borne out, this may indicate a mistaken auxiliary hypothesis, rather than a mistaken theory. Auxiliary hypotheses therefore enable testing of scientific theories, but the need for auxiliary hypotheses renders the strict falsification of scientific theories by empirical test impossible – at least on the assumption that auxiliary hypotheses cannot be independently verified.

The upshot for present purposes is this. If there is an epistemic problem with conspiracy theories, and belief in them, it is not that such theories are unfalsifiable. Scientific theories are similarly resistant to falsification, and it is hardly plausible that scientific theorising is generally irrational.

Perhaps there is a related problem with conspiracy theories – or at least a subset of them. Scientific theories are generally not subject to straightforward falsification, but there nonetheless comes a time at which adherence to a scientific theory becomes unreasonable. This occurs when a scientific theory is embedded in a research program in a persistent state of degeneration. Perhaps some conspiracy theorists are, as Steve Clarke[29] suggests, comparable to scientists who cling too long to degenerating research programmes. To assess this criticism, it is necessary to answer two questions. First, what distinguishes a healthy research programme from one in a state of degeneration? Second, do conspiracy theories, in conjunction with the worldviews surrounding them, exhibit the features of degenerating research programmes?

A central criterion for the health of a research programme is, according to Lakatos, the ability to predict novel observations.[30] A degenerating research programme, in contrast, can accommodate novel observations through manipulation of auxiliary hypotheses, but generally fails to predict observations before they occur. Plausibly, there comes a point at which adherence to a degenerating research programme becomes unreasonable – even though such a point is bound to be vague.

Clarke concurs with the worry about vagueness, but contends that 'there clearly are cases where a research programme has degenerated beyond the point where it is reasonable to hold on to it'.[31] Perhaps conspiracy theories tend to reach a similar state of degeneration, and perhaps this is what accounts for the irrationality of belief in

---

28 Lakatos, *The Methodology of Scientific Research Programmes*, 48.
29 Clarke, 'Conspiracy Theories and Conspiracy Theorizing', 81.
30 Lakatos, *The Methodology of Scientific Research Programmes*, 49.
31 Clarke, 'Conspiracy Theories and Conspiracy Theorizing', 82.

many such theories. On the face of it, this seems to be precisely what is wrong with Sam's epistemic attitudes. However, there are difficulties with comparing conspiracy theorists to scientists that cling to degenerating research programmes.

First, it seems that belief in conspiracy theories may allow one to predict novel facts. Consider a simple variation on Sam's case. Suppose Sam began with the suspicion that many prominent members of his town were in cahoots with the mayor. Then, he would have predicted that neither the police nor local journalists would uncover any incriminating evidence. More generally, the truth of a given conspiracy theory would ordinarily suggest that there are individuals actively working to shield the conspiracy from discovery. Hence, conspiracy theorists may predict that evidence apparently conflicting with the conspiracy theory will be presented, and such predictions will ordinarily be borne out. Hence, it would be inaccurate to claim that conspiracy theories are not capable of predicting novel observations.

Even if one denies that conspiracy theories can predict novel facts, it is not clear that this would be a strike against such theories. As Keeley points out, the objects whose behavior is described by conspiracy theories are unlike the objects of ordinary empirical sciences insofar as the objects of conspiracy theories can be expected to actively resist investigation.[32] Thus, even if one does not interpret the absence of evidence of a conspiracy as evidence of that conspiracy, one may maintain that the absence is consistent with the truth of the conspiracy theory.

The criticism that conspiracy theorising is analogous to clinging to a degenerating research programme struggles on two scores. First, it is not clear that conspiracy theories, like degenerating research programmes, are incapable of predicting novel facts. Second, it is not clear that the ability to predict novel facts is a reasonable criterion of goodness for a conspiracy theory. If there is a reason to criticize conspiracy theorising on epistemic grounds, it must be located elsewhere.

5. What's Epistemically Wrong with Conspiracy Theorising?

Standard criticisms of conspiracy theorising are misguided. It is perhaps in virtue of the failure of such criticisms that many scholars have taken a relatively charitable attitude toward conspiracy

---

[32] Keeley, 'Of Conspiracy Theories', 55.

theorising in recent years[33]. This turn is, I now argue, premature. An implication of my account of conspiracy theories is that belief in a conspiracy theory involves two distinct theoretical stances. First, adherence to a conspiracy theory involves the rejection of some official account of an event. Second, adherence to a conspiracy theory involves acceptance of an alternative explanation. I now argue that both theoretical stances involved in conspiracy theorising typically involve epistemic errors.

5.1. Probabilistic Modus Tollens

Keeley suggests that conspiracy theorising typically involves placing significant evidential weight on what he calls *errant data*.[34] This suggestion, common in academic discussions of conspiracy theories, is reinforced by recent psychological findings suggesting that conspiracy theorising is strongly correlated with illusory pattern perception.[35] A plausible explanatory hypothesis to account for these experimental findings is that conspiracy theorising involves the perception of illusory patterns in sets of errant data.

Errant data comes in two forms, according to Keeley. *Unaccounted-for data* is data that the official account simply fails to explain. As an example of an unaccounted-for datum, Keeley cites the fact that no Bureau of Alcohol, Tobacco and Firearms employees were in the targeted building at the time of the Oklahoma City bombing. *Contradictory data*, in contrast, is data that 'if true, would contradict the received account'.[36] That Timothy McVeigh fled the scene of the bombing in a car without license plates is, according to Keeley, an example of a contradictory datum.

An initial concern for Keeley's discussion of errant data is that it is unclear that data ever contradict official accounts. Official accounts of events, like scientific theories, assert little about the state of the world

---

[33]   David Coady, 'Are Conspiracy Theorists Epistemically Irrational?', *Episteme*, **4**.2 (2007), 193–204; Dentith, *The Philosophy of Conspiracy Theories*; Charles Pidgen, 'Complots of Mischief', in David Coady (ed.), *Conspiracy Theories: The Philosophical Debate* (Farnham: Ashgate, 2006), 139–166.

[34]   Keeley, 'Of Conspiracy Theories', 52.

[35]   Jan-Willem van Prooijen, Karen M. Douglas and Clara de Inocencio, 'Connecting the Dots: Illusory Pattern Perception Predicts Belief in Conspiracies and the Supernatural', *European Journal of Social Psychology* **48**.3 (2018), 320–335.

[36]   Keeley, 'Of Conspiracy Theories', 53.

in the absence of background hypotheses. Thus, it is difficult to conceive of data that literally contradict an official account. That McVeigh fled in a car without license plates certainly does not do so. More generally, it is implausible that conspiracy theorists typically rely on contradictory data, as there may well be no such data even when the official account is false. Thus, to the extent that conspiracy theorists rely on errant data, they must rely on unaccounted-for data.

Keeley's definition of unaccounted-for data requires revision. Every theory fails to account for a great deal of data, especially data concerning systems unrelated to the theory. For instance, even the best biological theories fail to account for astronomical facts. It would be uncharitable to conspiracy theorists to suppose that these individuals take the inability of the official story to account for data concerning unrelated systems to be a strike against the official account. We therefore require a revised definition of unaccounted-for data.

Fortunately, such a revision is easy enough to perform. Conspiracy theorists do not merely maintain that there is a body of data for which the official story fails to account. Conspiracy theorists maintain that their own theories better account for some such data. We may thus understand unaccounted-for data as data for which the official story, but purportedly not the conspiracy theory, fail to account. We may make this definition more precise by appeal to conditional probability. Unaccounted-for errant data is data that has a low probability conditional on the truth of the official account, but purportedly has a high probability conditional on the truth of the conspiracy account. Because data rarely if ever outright contradicts a theory, I focus in what follows on unaccounted-for data as defined here. Subsequent references to errant data should be understood as references to unaccounted-for data.

Keeley suggests that there is something wrong with the role errant data plays in conspiracy theorising. He writes that '[o]ne's theory should not fit all the available data because not all the available data are, in fact, true'[37]. I concur with Keeley's assessment that conspiracy theorists are often wrong to think that errant data undermines the official account, but not simply because such data may be false. Even if there is genuine data that is errant with respect to the official account, as I am understanding such data here, this need not indicate that one ought to abandon the official account or even to assign it a low

---

[37]   Keeley, 'Of Conspiracy Theories', 55.

probability. In fact, to suggest otherwise would be to rely on a deeply problematic form of inference, *probabilistic modus tollens*.

Some valid inference rules have legitimate probabilistic counterparts. Consider *modus ponens*. *Modus ponens* allows one to infer q from the propositions p, and $p \rightarrow q$. *Modus ponens* has a legitimate probabilistic counterpart. If it is true that if p, then q is probable then, if p is true, q is indeed probable. But *modus tollens* does not have a parallel legitimate probabilistic counterpart.[38] Suppose that if p is true, it is enormously improbable that q. Now suppose that one observes that q. Does it follow that p is improbable? No. A simple example brings out the point. If any given lottery with many participants is fair, it is improbable that any particular entrant will win. However, it would be absurd to conclude, once a winner is named, that the lottery was probably unfair. This remains the case even if the lottery was not guaranteed to have a winner and even if one compares the hypothesis that the lottery was fair against the hypothesis that the lottery was rigged in favour of the individual that won.

The observation of errant data is, I suggest, analogous to the observation that some lottery entrant has won. The observation of errant data is improbable – perhaps extremely improbable – given the official account, but this alone does not provide reason to abandon the official account. To see this, consider the following real-world errant datum:

> At 4:54 Eastern Time on the afternoon of September 11, 2001, a BBC correspondent in New York City, with the distant, smoking ruins of the Twin Towers in shot behind her, reported that a third skyscraper had just collapsed – World Trade Center Building 7. The only problem with the report was that Building 7 hadn't collapsed. In fact, it could be seen in the background of the shot, over the reporter's shoulder, still very much standing. If that had been the end of the report, the mistaken report would have probably been long forgotten. But twenty-six minutes later, at 5:20 – and just five minutes after the reporter's satellite feed to the BBC's London studio had mysteriously cut out – the building came down.[39]

Given that the official account of the September 11 attacks is true, it is highly improbable that the mistaken report would occur. On the face of it at least, the mistaken report would be considerably more

[38] Elliott Sober, 'Intelligent Design and Probability Reasoning', *International Journal for Philosophy of Religion* **52**.2 (2002), 65–80.
[39] Rob Brotherton, *Suspicious Minds: Why we Believe Conspiracy Theories* (London: Bloomsbury Publishing, 2015).

probable if, for instance, the conspiracy theory positing that the September 11 attacks were carried out by American operatives and aided by various media outlets were true. The mistaken report hence constitutes an errant datum with respect to the official account. This errant datum cannot be dismissed as false – the report did indeed occur. Nonetheless, the report does not demonstrate that the official account is probably false. It was highly improbable, given the official account, that the reporter would assert that the tower had already collapsed, rather than that it would collapse. But only an application of probabilistic *modus tollens* would lead one, on this basis alone, to conclude that the official account is probably false.

One may object that I have misrepresented the sort of reasoning involved in conspiracy theorising. The conspiracy theorist does not notice a single errant datum and conclude, on this basis, that the official account is probably false. Rather, the conspiracy theorist notices a pattern of errant data, which jointly undermine the official account. But this objection is not enough to block the present criticism of conspiracy theorising. A set of errant data does not tell against the official account in a fundamentally different way than a single errant datum does. The observation of any single errant datum is improbable if the official account is true, while the observation of a set of errant data is even more improbable. Nonetheless, to reject the official account because it would make one's observations improbable would be a mistake in either case.

Here it is worth considering a related objection. In discounting the ability of errant data to undermine the official account, have I not advocated an absurd sort of epistemic conservatism? After all, recalcitrant data plays a vital role in the progress of science. However, it is not clear that errant data can play, for conspiracy theories, a role equivalent to the one recalcitrant data performs in the context of science. When a given datum supports one theory over another, it is because the former theory would, if true, make the datum more probable than the latter would. But it is typically not clear what conspiracy theories predict[40]. One interpretation of a given conspiracy theory may predict certain observations that are errant with respect to the official account, while another interpretation may predict that the conspirators will be sufficiently competent to disguise any potential errant data. For instance, the mistaken BBC report may or

---

[40]   For more on the inability of many conspiracy theories to generate specific predictions, see Steve Clarke, 'Conspiracy Theories and the Internet: Controlled Demolition and Arrested Development', *Episteme* **4**.2 (2007), 167–180.

may not have been probable conditional on the conspiracy theory that the attacks were carried out by American operatives aided by members of the media, depending on whether or not one expects members of the BBC to flawlessly enact the plan. More generally, because the likelihood ratio between an official account and its conspiracy theory counterpart(s) with respect to errant data is typically indeterminate, errant data generally cannot support a conspiracy theory over the official account.

It is worth emphasizing here that the import of errant data for an official account depends on relative likelihoods, and therefore on a comparison with the conspiracy theory, only because the implications of the official account will typically be probabilistic. If, by contrast, the official account entailed some deductive consequence, p, but $\sim p$ were observed, one could determine the falsity of the official account, even absent knowledge of the conspiracy account's predictions vis-à-vis p.[41] However, given that the official account will typically only imply what is likely to happen, rather than what will happen, errant data could motivate abandonment of the official account only through a fallacious application of probabilistic modus tollens or through an appeal to relative likelihoods – which will typically be undefined. Hence, errant data ordinarily does not provide a reason to reject the official account.

5.2. The Risks and Rewards of Conspiracy Theorising

If the argument developed in the previous section is correct, then conspiracy theorising is often irrational insofar as it involves a misuse of errant data. But belief in a conspiracy theory does not consist merely in the rejection of the official account, conspiracy theories also assert the truth of some alternative explanation of the target event. I now argue that this second theoretical stance is likewise fraught.

In section three, I noted that conspiracy theorists are not so epistemically vicious as one might ordinarily suppose. Conspiracy theorists exhibit a sort of intellectual diligence, a motivation to uncover the truth, that seems downright praiseworthy. But the fact that conspiracy theorists exhibit some epistemically virtuous behaviour is consistent with conspiracy theorists likewise exhibiting some epistemic vices. Plausibly, conspiracy theorists are typically guilty of a sort of closed-mindedness – especially an unwillingness to take proponents of the official account seriously. Relatedly, and in perhaps more

---

[41] Sober, 'Intelligent Design and Probability Reasoning', 70–71.

familiar terms, it seems plausible that conspiracy theorists tend to be susceptible to confirmation bias. They exhibit intellectual diligence, but this diligence is specifically directed toward evidence that supports their theory. They are not likely to pursue evidence that might tell against their preferred theory and, even if they encounter such evidence, are likely to either assimilate the evidence under their theory or discount its importance.

But the susceptibility of the conspiracy theorists to these intellectual shortcomings is not, I would suggest, a dimension in which conspiracy theorists are clearly distinguished from their counterparts. The ubiquity of confirmation bias is well-documented and is manifested in a range of behaviours that tend to exaggerate the significance of confirming evidence while downplaying the significance of recalcitrant evidence.[42] More to the point, while conspiracy theorists are unlikely to seek out evidence against their own theories or to place much weight on testimony proffered by proponents of the official account, adherents to the official account are likely to exhibit comparably dismissive attitudes toward conspiracy theorists and the sources they endorse. Crucially, critics of conspiracy theorising do not simply wish to show that the practice is irrational, they wish to show that the practice is irrational in a way that endorsement of the official account is not. Thus, to the extent that proponents of conspiracy theories and official accounts alike are both prone to confirmation bias and closed-mindedness, appeals to such things cannot fully ground the relevant sort of criticism of conspiracy theorising.

Although vulnerability to confirmation bias and intellectual closed-mindedness are apparently not sufficient to ground epistemic criticisms of conspiracy theorists that do not apply equally to non-conspiracy theorists, such traits may figure into a more nuanced criticism that applies primarily to conspiracy theorists. The reason for this disparity, in my view, is precisely the fact that conspiracy theorising typically involves a greater degree of intellectual activity than that involved in acceptance of an official account. Conspiracy theorists put considerable effort into developing and motivating their theories, while downplaying the possibility that their conclusions are due in large part to the exhibition of intellectual vice and reliance on unreliable sources of information. In short, the fact that conspiracy theorists' enthusiasm for the pursuit of truth is not matched by a correspondingly heightened sensitivity to their own cognitive

---

[42] For a thorough survey of experimental evidence of confirmation bias, see Raymond Nickerson, 'Confirmation Bias: A Ubiquitous Phenomenon in Many Guises', *Review of General Psychology* **2**.2 (1998), 175–220.

biases and potential for error exposes conspiracy theorists to unique epistemic criticism.

It may be objected that this criticism places an unfair burden on the shoulders of the conspiracy theorist. Why should the level of intellectual effort exhibited by the conspiracy theorist saddle her with greater epistemic responsibilities than her non-conspiracy theorist counterpart? In short, greater intellectual effort in general has the potential to go awry if it is not matched by greater intellectual caution. The collection of additional evidence may leave one worse off, epistemically, when that evidence is drawn from a biased pool. The epistemic results of active but biased inquiry are particularly negative in the case of conspiracy theories. The official account, promoted by mainstream sources, is subjected to at least some degree of truth-oriented filtering. The mere fact that mainstream sources enjoy more attention ensures that, at least when it comes to simple questions of fact, errors are comparatively likely to be noticed and corrected. Moreover, mainstream purveyors of information have a powerful incentive to avoid errors and to correct erroneous reporting, as uncorrected errors are likely to lead consumers to defect to alternative sources in the media marketplace.[43] Because sources outside of the mainstream depend on consumers to seek them out – an act that requires some degree of commitment on the part of consumers – it is unclear that such sources are subject to comparable competition. Thus, when one pursues evidence of a conspiracy from outside of mainstream sources, one encounters a significant risk of drawing evidence from a biased pool that is subject to minimal scrutiny.

The point here is not that the conspiracy theorist deserves epistemic criticism simply for relying on sources of information outside of the mainstream. As I noted in section three, the relative unreliability of conspiracist sources is external to the epistemic agency of conspiracy theorists in such a way as to preclude conspiracy theorists from being blameworthy simply for their reliance on such sources. However, the conspiracist's comparatively greater devotion to inquiry – manifested in their pursuit of inquiry beyond mainstream sources of information – is incongruous with her lack of attention toward her own biases and potential for error. Significantly, the comparatively intellectually passive non-conspiracy theorist displays no such incongruity in his failure to consider his own potential for error.

---

[43]   Nicola Mößner, 'Trusting the Media? TV News as a Source of Knowledge', *International Journal of Philosophical Studies* **26**.2 (2018), 205–220.

What's Epistemically Wrong with Conspiracy Theorising?

One way to put the present point is that conspiracy theorists exhibit a sort of higher-order epistemic vice – a cocktail of intellectual traits that jointly impede successful inquiry. Some of these traits – e.g. closed-mindedness – are themselves vicious. But these traits might well be had in common with non-conspiracy theorists. Other traits in the cocktail – e.g. devotion to inquiry – may be virtuous in themselves but produce negative results in conjunction with the attendant vices. Cassam makes a similar point regarding the intellectual traits of conspiracy theorists, noting that 'intellectual curiosity and a proclivity for new ideas would normally be regarded as intellectual virtues, but they become vices when unconstrained by good judgement and a healthy dose of skepticism'.[44] Plausibly, it is in part some such combination of traits – rather than any standard intellectual vice or cognitive bias – that may render her susceptible to criticism that does not apply equally to her counterpart.[45]

5.3. Acceptance of a Conspiracy Account

There is a final criticism of conspiracy theorising worth making here. As I have emphasized, the behaviour constitutive of conspiracy theorising does not simply consist in rejection of the official account. It also involves acceptance of some alternative account. It is difficult to understand, however, how the conspiracy theorist might motivate this latter theoretical stance.

First, just as evidence for the official account is primarily filtered through the testimony of media and public figures, evidence for the conspiracy account will typically be filtered through the testimony of various sources. But, given the level of scepticism that conspiracy theorists must adopt toward certain sources of information, it is unclear how a conspiracy theorist can maintain trust in the alternative sources needed to derive warrant for their preferred conspiratorial explanation. We may illustrate the present point with an historical analogy. Consider René Descartes' epistemic position at two points

---

[44]   Cassam, 'Vice Epistemology', 172.

[45]   Note that it is consistent with conspiracy theorists exhibiting epistemic vice in a way that their counterparts do not that there might be other vices more prevalent among non-conspiracy theorists, as suggested by Charles Pidgen in 'Are Conspiracy Theorists Epistemically Vicious?', in Kasper Lippert-Rasmussen, Kimberly Brownlee, and David Coady (eds.), *A Companion to Applied Philosophy* (Oxford: Wiley-Blackwell, 2017), 120–132.

in the *Meditations*.[46] At the close of the first meditation, Descartes has apparently adopted an extreme form of scepticism. We may regard this theoretical stance as impractical, but not inconsistent. Many commentators believe the project goes awry only when Descartes seemingly conjoins his skepticism to a reliance on the accuracy of clear and distinct perception. Similarly, bracketing the criticisms I have developed earlier in this section, it is often not the conspiracy theorist's skepticism that appears epistemically objectionable. Rather, what is objectionable about conspiracy theorising is that such skepticism is often attended by, and even motivated in part by, a dogmatic acceptance of certain sources of information as reliable.

Moreover, even setting aside this concern, a second problem for deriving positive warrant for conspiracy explanations has to do with the way in which conspiracy explanations account for the evidence. The conspiracy theorist posits that some group of conspirators is responsible for the occurrence of some event, the official account of some event, as well as data that is errant with respect to the official account. But if one seeks to provide explanations of this sort, any number of conspiratorial explanations will fit the data, and hence will be equally supported. Thus, the conspiracy theorist has no basis for determining that some particular group of conspirators, as opposed to some other group, is responsible for the event in question.[47] Any data that appears to favor one explanation over its competitors can of course be understood as a red herring planted by the true conspirators. Thus, even if one grants that the conspiracy theorist is rational to reject the official account, there often remains no motivation for the conspiracy theorist to adopt the second theoretical stance constitutive of conspiracy theorising. Because any number of conspiratorial explanations can be constructed, all of which account for the data equally well, the conspiracy theorist often lacks sufficient warrant for belief in any particular conspiratorial explanation.

6. Concluding Remarks

Conspiracy theorists have often been subjected to a rather dismissive attitude on the part of academics and those in the public realm. This

---

[46] René Descartes, *Meditations on First Philosophy: with Selections from the Objections and Replies*, John Cottingham (ed.) (Cambridge: Cambridge University Press, 2015).

[47] Feldman raises a similar objection to what she calls 'counterfact conspiracy theories' in her 'Counterfact Conspiracy Theories', 20.

attitude might be justified if conspiracy theorists were generally delusional, or otherwise guilty of extraordinary epistemic fault. We have seen that the errors typically made by conspiracy theorists are subtler than one might expect. But, contra recent trends toward a more charitable attitude toward conspiracy theorising, there are epistemic errors heavily implicated in conspiracy theorising. I do not mean to suggest that *all* conspiracy theorists commit the sort of errors described in the preceding sections. However, there are epistemic grounds on which to criticize those that do.[48]

University of Missouri
krh396@mail.missouri.edu

[48] I am deeply indebted to the participants of the 2017 Harms and Wrongs in Epistemic Practice conference for their invaluable feedback on an early version of this paper. I owe additional thanks to the conference organizers and an anonymous referee for their thoughtful comments on later versions.